SOUTH AFRICA'S
SUSPENDED
REVOL
UTION
HOPES AND PROSPECTS

SOUTH AFRICA'S SUSPENDED REVOLUTION

HOPES AND PROSPECTS

ADAM HABIB

Ohio University Press

Athens

Ohio University Press
Athens, Ohio 45701
ohioswallow.com
All rights reserved

First published in South Africa by
Wits University Press
1 Jan Smuts Avenue
Johannesburg 2001
www.witspress.co.za

Published in North America by
Ohio University Press
Athens, Ohio 45701

To obtain permission to quote, reprint, or otherwise reproduce or
distribute material from Ohio University Press publications, please
contact our rights and permissions department at (740) 593-1154 or
(740) 593-4536 (fax).

Printed in the United States of America
Ohio University Press books are printed on acid-free paper ⊗ ™

20 19 18 17 16 15 14 13   5 4 3 2 1

Hardcover edition ISBN   978-0-8214-2076-8
Paperback edition ISBN   978-0-8214-2072-0
Electronic edition ISBN   978-0-8214-4477-1

Library of Congress Cataloging-in-Publication Data available

To Irfan and Zidaan,

for living a life that I can only write about, and

to Fatima,

for partnering me in creating our most important legacy –
our children.

Contents

Preface

This book has long been in the making. I have been meaning to write it for over a decade but work pressures, new jobs, alternative research projects, and deferred sabbaticals all conspired against it. So, when the opportunity for a sabbatical emerged at the end of my first term as deputy vice-chancellor at the University of Johannesburg, I had no doubt as to how I should spend the time. For many years, I have been immersed in academic and public discourse about South Africa and its future. The book is, therefore, a culmination of at least two decades of debates, reflections and thoughts about resistance in South Africa, its political and socio-economic evolution, and the conundrums and dilemmas related to the making of this society. In many ways the book is about how we got to where we are, why our present is not what we had hoped it would be, and what we need to do about it.

I see myself as both an academic and an activist. Although some may view these as separate endeavours, I have always seen them as mutually compatible. Indeed, my decision to take political science as a subject in my undergraduate years was motivated by a belief that this would enable me to better address the challenges that my compatriots and I confronted as activists. Of course, this didn't work out in the way I had imagined it might, but the academic grounding provided by my undergraduate and especially my postgraduate studies, were essential in developing my understanding of my country and world.

This book therefore reflects both of these facets of my life – academic and activist. The debates I engage with in the book occur both within the academy and in the broader public sphere. In my view, newspapers and magazines, as well as academic journals, are of intellectual relevance, and I therefore challenge, support and reference political leaders and activists as well as academics in this text. But the book is unashamedly scholarly. Although some suggested that I strip the book of its academic debates and theories, with a view to broadening its readership, it seemed to me that this would undermine one of the central purposes of writing it; namely, to bridge academic and public discourse in order to enrich each with the reflections and debates of the other. I have, however, tried to write as plainly as I can, and to avoid academic jargon, so that the book has the potential to appeal to anyone who is interested in South Africa's problems, and in how these can be resolved. In this vein, I conclude with two chapters aimed at different audiences. Chapter Seven is directed mainly at activists and political leaders, and in it I consider what needs to be done to overcome our challenges. Chapter Eight is aimed particularly at academics, and includes an analysis of how the South African experience speaks to the debates within the national and global academies.

Progressive academics and scholars often cite Edward Said's famous maxim, 'speak truth to power' as the aim of their work. I hope this book does so frankly and plainly. However, I do not aim to speak only to state power, as Said intended. I aim to engage societal power as well. That is, I aim to speak with those at the apex of business corporations; with leaders and activists in the trade union movement; with members of the ruling and opposition political parties; with those who are part of social movements and other civil society expressions; and even with intellectual brokers within the academy. Progressive scholars all too often ignore the power wielded by individuals in these groups. This book, therefore, is directed at our country's president and those around him, but it is also for the CEOs of corporations, the general secretaries of trade unions and civic organisations, and the leading mainstream and radical lights within the academy as well. I aim to speak plainly to all manifestations of power, to challenge ideological, political and strategic orthodoxies, and to urge everyone to interrogate conventional wisdoms in an effort to fashion strategic solutions that enable us to collectively transcend the challenges of our historical moment.

As mentioned, the book is the culmination of my reflections about South Africa over two decades. Most of it is new, but parts of Chapters Four, Five and Six are drawn from earlier work that was published in *Social Research* 72 (2005), the Institute for Justice and Reconciliation's 2009 Transformation Audit, and the *South African Journal of International Affairs* 16 (2009) respectively. However, all the material has been extensively reworked to consider new developments, debates and challenges. In addition, 'opinion pieces' published in various South African newspapers have been revised and incorporated into some of the chapters.

I have of course accumulated many intellectual debts, and it would take too much space to acknowledge them all. Some, however, contributed directly to this text: Imraan Valodia, Fiona Tregenna, Elke Zuern, and the South Africa reading group at the Centre for African Studies, in St Antony College at Oxford University – William Beinart, Colin Bundy, Jonny Steinberg and Noor Nieftagodien – read and commented on at least parts of the manuscript. I am grateful to them all. Ashley Coates was a truly fantastic and efficient research assistant, and was central to finalising the manuscript. Mary Ralphs was a gem of an editor – efficient, always pleasant, and with an incredible ability to transform my academic writing into text that is more readable and accessible. Veronica Klipp and Roshan Cader from Wits University Press were phenomenal publishing professionals, always dealing courteously with my multiple requests and demands. Karen Bruns, a close friend from our days at the Human Sciences Research Council, played a crucial role in brokering the conversation and negotiating with publishers once a draft of the manuscript was completed. I must also record my appreciation to the University of Johannesburg and the Oppenheimer Foundation for underwriting some of the costs of the sabbatical. Most of all, I owe much to Fatima, Irfan and Zidaan, who uprooted themselves for six months, and accompanied me on my sabbatical to Oxford, so that I could finish this book. It is dedicated to them.

The pages that follow, and the thoughts contained within them, are offered as a small contribution to all those committed to making South Africa, and our world, a better place to live.

1

Introduction

South Africa is in the midst of a high-stakes leadership drama that has been underway for some years. The stage is the South African state, including its national departments and ministries, provincial governments and local municipalities. It is a drama that has pitted comrade against comrade, and the ensuing battle has led to friends becoming enemies, and erstwhile enemies becoming friends. The ultimate prize is the presidency and the political power and spoils of patronage that go with it.

The drama's multiple acts have so far each been marked by a symbolic high point. The opening act was the firing of then deputy president, Jacob Zuma, by then president, Thabo Mbeki, in 2005. This was followed by the fightback by Zuma and his allies, which culminated in December 2007, when Zuma was elected president of the African National Congress (ANC) at the party's national electoral conference in Polokwane. Nine months later, in September 2008, Mbeki was unceremoniously ejected from his position as president of South Africa, and after a short caretaker presidency by then deputy president, Kgalema Motlanthe, Zuma ascended to the presidential throne in April 2009. Significant sections of the senior hierarchy in the political establishment and state bureaucracy were soon replaced as cadre deployment within the ruling party morphed into factional deployment.

Soon after this, however, the battle lines were redrawn and a new act in the drama began. This time Zuma, as presidential incumbent, was the focus of the attempted ejection. His nemeses were his one-time allies, Julius Malema, Fikile Mbalula, Mathews Phosa, Tokyo Sexwale, and even Kgalema Motlanthe. Malema was effectively fired as president of the Youth League through the mechanism of the ANC's disciplinary committee. In December 2012, Motlanthe, who was deputy president of both the ruling party and the country at the time, stood against Zuma for the presidency of the ANC at the party's national conference in Mangaung. He lost, and having withdrawn from the candidature for the party's deputy-presidency in favour of Tokyo Sexwale and Mathews Phosa, Motlanthe was effectively cast into the political wilderness. His role in the ANC has been confined to heading up political education within the party. Cyril Ramaphosa, billionaire, the second-richest black businessman in the country, and architect of South Africa's much admired Constitution, was elected at Mangaung as the party's new deputy president. However, despite the party's overwhelmingly large endorsement of Zuma at the Mangaung conference – he received 75 per cent of the vote for the position as president – the party's members left the conference as divided as when they had arrived.

Even though he won so many votes, Zuma cannot afford to be sanguine about his situation. The reason for this is that his opposition, although small, is mainly located in Gauteng province – the economic heartland of the country. As fourth largest contributor to Africa's GDP, this economic hub has to be central to any economic revitalisation and transformation agenda. Its inclusion in the alliance of the 'forces for change' must be of concern to him. Moreover, his internal opposition involve people of means. Tokyo Sexwale and Mathews Phosa have enormous financial resources at their disposal. Paul Mashatile, chair of the ANC in Gauteng, and Fikile Mbalula (once an ardent Zuma supporter) have enormous organisational abilities. All have liberation pedigrees within the ANC. But perhaps the biggest indication of a divided organisation is the slate system, whereby delegates vote, not on the merits of the individual candidates, but rather according to which faction's slate they appear on. The ANC, its Youth League, its allies in the Tripartite Alliance – the Congress of South African Trade Unions

(COSATU) and the South African Communist Party (SACP) – as well as various key state departments, including intelligence and safety and security, as well as provincial governments, all remain arenas in which the leadership battle will continue to play itself out.

Throughout this period the drama has been broadcast live. The South African media has insisted on providing the nation with front-row seats to the unfolding spectacle. In the process, the ANC, the political home of Nobel laureates Albert Luthuli and Nelson Mandela, has been seen for what it is increasingly becoming: a grubby instrument of enrichment that speaks the language of empowerment and democracy, while its leadership and cadres plunder the nation's resources and undermine both the judiciary and the media – the former because it may be used to hold various actors to account, and the latter for having the temerity to broadcast the drama.

Elsewhere I have described representations of this political drama as revealing a public contest 'between different sets of heroes and villains, themselves personified in the individual personalities of Thabo Mbeki and Jacob Zuma'. The distinguishing feature of this contest, I argued, is that its heroes and villains change depending on who is telling the story (Habib, 2008a: 46). Thus reports of the story are deeply politicised and divisive,[1] and all contending parties imagine political advance and success to be the point at which their particular hero ascends to the highest political office in the land and becomes the country's first citizen. In other words, most accounts of the drama are deeply voluntarist; that is, leaders and other actors are treated as unfettered agents whose choices and behaviour are merely the result of their own abilities or follies. South Africa's potential future is therefore imagined through the prism of the character of its leaders. Seen in this way, the country's future looks fairly bleak.

In this book I aim to provide an antidote to these imaginings. I explain how South Africa has developed since the advent of democracy by locating its actors in context. I try to analyse the institutional constraints within which they operate, how these have conditioned their choices, and what the consequences of those choices have been. I also explore the failures of political, economic, civic and other leaders, and consider what other policy options and behavioural choices may have been available to them as well as why these alternatives were forsaken. My aim is to offer a deeply historical view, in the sense of revealing why certain possibilities may have existed in one moment, but not in another. Societies evolve and the potential for political and socio-economic advances change too. I thus analyse the dynamic interplay between actors and context, how the latter can constrain and condition the former, but also how individuals and institutions can, with imagination, act against the grain of their location and historical moment, thereby transforming the range of possibilities open to them and, in the process, transforming society itself.

The leadership and succession dramas have played themselves out against the backdrop of South Africa's changing social landscape. An understanding of this landscape is necessary for developing an analytical grasp of how the country has come to be where it is, and what needs to be done to take it to where it wants to be. It is therefore prudent to begin this intellectual exploration with a brief review of the state of the nation at this historical moment.

The state of the nation

Thabo Mbeki gave his two greatest speeches prior to and at the end of his presidential tenure. The first, known as his 'I am an African' speech, was delivered to the Constituent Assembly in 1996 in his capacity as deputy president of the Republic. It was a speech that defined the South African nation as a product of its multiple roots – black and white, chief and layman, citizen and migrant, Afrikaner and English, worker and peasant, and rich and poor. It was also a speech that celebrated the Afrikaner rebellion against English imperialism (the Anglo-Boer War) as much as it did tribal resistance to settler encroachment, and the more recent resistance to apartheid (Mbeki, 1996). The speech imagined a cosmopolitan, non-racial and prosperous democracy, confident of its place in the world. It spoke to the aspirations of South Africans from all walks of life, and galvanised the country's newly ascendant black professionals in particular.

The second great speech was Mbeki's address to the nation after he had resigned his presidency in 2008 under pressure from the ANC. It was a noble and dignified exit for a president who had lost the confidence of his party. Mbeki stressed his loyalty to the ANC and his commitment to remaining within the organisation. He spoke of the ruling party's commitment to a prosperous non-racial nation, and underscored his administration's great success in having achieved economic growth rates for the longest period in South Africa's history. Yet, he also acknowledged that the dividends of this economic growth had not been equally shared, and that too many still lived in poverty and squalor. Finally, Mbeki reiterated his respect for the Constitution and the rule of law, and categorically denied having influenced the decisions of the National Prosecuting Authority, in its case against Jacob Zuma or any other individual that had appeared before the courts. He concluded his speech by reminding South Africans that the true measure of a people is how they respond to adversity, and he wished the incoming administration well in their governance of South Africa's affairs (Mbeki, 2008).

How did this situation come to be? Mbeki was correct to note in his resignation speech that South Africa in 2008 was a fundamentally different place from what it had been in 1994. Its public institutions had largely been deracialised, and the post-apartheid government had passed multiple laws, including the

Labour Relations Act of 1995 and the Employment Equity Act of 1998, to address the inequities of the country's past. The country's Constitution codified the socio-economic and political rights of all citizens, and despite being qualified by 'practicality' clauses, its Bill of Rights nevertheless provides citizens with enormous leverage if they want to better their circumstances. The state had also done much to improve living conditions for the majority. The government's review of its performance on the tenth anniversary of the democracy (PCAS, 2003) indicated that 1 985 545 housing subsidies had been approved to a value of R24.22 billion; new water connections benefitted 9 million people; 70 per cent of households had electricity connections by 2001; 1.8 million hectares of land had been redistributed since 1994; and 1 600 633 new jobs had been created. The review maintained that if these social provisions were taken into account, poverty rates could be considered to have declined significantly in South African society (PCAS, 2003: 17–18, 24–26, 36).

Unfortunately this is only one side of the story. As demonstrated in Chapter Three, there is a darker side to South Africa's economic successes. The post-apartheid regime, particularly after 1996, coupled a conservative macro-economic programme – the Growth, Employment and Redistribution strategy (GEAR) – with a narrow black-empowerment agenda. The net effect was the consolidation and reinforcement of the bifurcated social structure bequeathed by apartheid, albeit with some deracialisation among its upper echelons. Thus, while water, electricity and communications infrastructure was being expanded, the introduction of a new cost-recovery model meant that millions of people were denied access to water and power because of their inability to pay for these services (McDonald and Pape, 2002). In addition, although GEAR may have facilitated economic growth and allowed some to benefit enormously, it left millions unemployed. The middle classes expanded dramatically, with the rise of black professionals and the appointment of black civil servants. A small politically connected black business elite also emerged, largely from politically brokered and state-financed transfers of corporate ownership. The net effect was that while poverty first increased and then decreased, levels of inequality have risen consistently throughout the post-apartheid era. In my view, this particular feature of the transition contributed to Mbeki's downfall at Polokwane.

Of course, there were other contributing factors. As Mark Gevisser (2007) convincingly argues, Mbeki's support base was always among the intelligentsia, and the urban middle and upper-middle classes, mainly within the black community and to some extent among the white population. This grouping, especially its black component, constituted a significant proportion of the activist and leadership base of the ANC, and for years they constituted Mbeki's primary support base. Even when they disagreed with one or other of Mbeki's policies, he remained their philosopher president. They were proud of the fact that he could hold his own with politicians in London and New York. He represented African modernity: proud of his roots, but cosmopolitan in orientation, a national politician and a global statesman, pursuing a liberal economic agenda, with a socially responsive progressive political rhetoric. He represented an African version of the global middle-class dream.

Yet in the later years of his presidency, this stratum largely abandoned Mbeki, believing that he had betrayed their hopes and vision. For them, South Africa was meant to be a caring, modern, cosmopolitan social democracy. Of course this vision was a shallow one, and the only people who could afford to harbour it were the middle and upper-middle classes. For the vast majority, there was nothing caring or social about South Africa's democracy. Nevertheless, despite the shallowness of this dream, it did galvanise the imagination of the privileged, or at least the relatively privileged, classes that were the mainstay of Mbeki's support base.

Three developments shattered their vision. First, in the later years of his presidency there was a growing perception that Mbeki was incapable of empathising with ordinary citizens. For example, the reputation of the president and his minister of health, Manto Tshabalala-Msimang, fell to pieces as a result of their AIDS denialism. When subsequent scandals broke about the quality of care and the death of new-born babies at Mount Frere hospital in the Eastern Cape (*Daily Dispatch*, 12/07/2007), the Mbeki administration's response was to cover things up.[2] Witch-hunts became the order of the day, and the political leadership led by the president and the health minister went into denial. Those who broke the story, and leaders who attempted to address the problem, were reprimanded and harassed. Thus, when then deputy minister of health, Nozizwe Madlala-Routledge, paid an unscheduled visit to the hospital and confirmed that conditions were dire, she was first reprimanded and subsequently fired, forcing the respected medical journal, *The Lancet* (18/08/2007), to condemn the decision. Instead of empathising with the victims of the service delivery failure, and the mothers who had lost their children, Mbeki and Tshabalala-Msimang buried their heads in the sand, and continued to deny that there was anything wrong with the public health system.

Similarly, when confronted with a question about crime in an interview on national television in January 2007, Mbeki remarked that the problem was being seriously overplayed. Indeed, in the same interview, he argued that one could walk freely in the Johannesburg suburb of Auckland Park, where the interview was being filmed, without fear of being mugged and attacked (*Mail & Guardian*, 2/02/2007). Not only did this betray ignorance about levels of crime in Johannesburg, and in much of the rest of the country, it also downplayed the seriousness of the problem of violent crime. Instead of sympathising with victims of murder, rape and robbery, Mbeki refused to engage with the fears of his citizens, accusing them instead of being active or unwitting agents of racial bigotry.

Again, Mbeki showed no empathy for victims, and his immediate response was to deny the social reality. This behaviour seemed to signal a leader incapable of empathy and seriously out of touch with his country's citizens.

Second, there was a growing perception that state institutions were being manipulated for personal and political gain. Of course, Zuma levelled this charge against Mbeki. COSATU and the SACP supported Zuma, arguing that the National Prosecuting Authority and other state institutions were being deployed against Mbeki's political opponents. Initially, this was treated, at least publicly, with a degree of scepticism. But Mbeki's behaviour, and that of those around him, increasingly suggested that the charge may not be completely unfounded. The processes involved in appointments to the board of the state-owned South African Broadcasting Corporation, for instance, violated legitimate democratic protocols when MPs were instructed to appoint a set of individuals decided on by the ANC's leadership (*The Sunday Independent*, 16/09/2007). Similarly, Mbeki's suspension of Vusi Pikoli as head of South Africa's National Prosecuting Authority in 2008 created political waves and was seen as indirectly protecting then police commissioner Jackie Selebi from prosecution. Selebi has subsequently been imprisoned for corruption (*Mail & Guardian*, 5/10/2007). Both cases were seen as examples of Mbeki manipulating decision making within state institutions to serve his own political ends.

Third, and this is clearly related to both of the preceding points, there was a widespread perception that Mbeki's Machiavellian behaviour – that is, his defence of those close to him, while dealing severely with opponents – contravened democratic norms. Again dramatic evidence of this emerged in the last few years of Mbeki's reign. Mbeki dismissed Jacob Zuma but refused to fire Jackie Selebi, even though the allegations against both men were equally serious. Similarly, Mbeki went out of his way to defend an incompetent health minister who brought the ANC and the nation into disrepute,

9

but fired a popular deputy minister who supported the interests of the poor and the marginalised, including people living with HIV and AIDS. These incidents gave credence to the view held by many in COSATU, the SACP, and even in the ANC, that Mbeki was inconsistent in his application of the rules, and was using his position to undermine the political contestation that should have been the stuff of everyday democratic practice.

Ultimately these and similar developments exposed as a fallacy the vision of 'the caring and socially responsive democratic society' harboured by the middle and upper-middle classes during South Africa's early transition. Feeling betrayed, they turned against Mbeki. He began to be seen as an autocrat, not the democrat they had supported; as a manipulator, not the politically astute entrepreneur they had endorsed; one who turned against those closest to him, not the resolute politician who stood up against the forces of populism. Indeed, the popular image of Mbeki at the end of 2007 was one of a vindictive politician who had caused his own misfortunes. As these social strata turned against him, they left him vulnerable to the growing list of political enemies that he had accumulated in his rise to power.

What took place at the ANC's national electoral conference in Polokwane in 2007 has become the stuff of legend.[3] The conference was preceded by a divisive election campaign led by Zuma, in which he criss-crossed the country, lobbying various ANC branches to support him. Eventually, the Mbeki and Zuma camps went to Polokwane having each secured about 40 per cent of delegates' votes. The remaining 20 per cent of the delegates remained neutral, and were in search of an alternative candidate. It was this independent group that turned the tide in favour of Zuma. Confronted with a choice between Mbeki and Zuma, they went for the latter in the hope of bringing about change. The elections were a rout of Mbeki's camp. Not only did Zuma win 60 per cent of the votes, he got his entire slate of candidates elected by a similar margin (Fikeni, 2009).

It is important to note that the political alliance that brought Zuma to power at Polokwane was never ideologically coherent. Zuma simply galvanised a wide range of disaffected ANC members and leaders. These included social democrats marginalised by Mbeki (including COSATU and the SACP), traditionalists alarmed by Mbeki's modernist and internationalist desires, disaffected black business leaders looking for an opportunity at the feeding trough, and rogue intelligence officials. It is therefore not surprising that the Zuma administration represents an odd mix of contested economic radicalism and social conservatism.

As discussed in more detail in Chapter Three, the South African government's shift to the left in terms of economic policy has been heavily contested. On the one hand, the Zuma administration has formally launched some new economic policies such as the New Growth Path (Department of Economic Development, 2010) and revitalised some older ones such as the Industrial Policy Action Plan (Department of Trade and Industry, 2010), which have the reindustrialisation of South Africa as their agenda. Both programmes focus on growing industrial and economic sectors in ways that can absorb semi-skilled and unskilled labour, broaden black economic empowerment and reduce economic inequality. At the same time rumblings about the impracticality of the New Growth Path and the need for fiscal conservatism are growing louder within the ruling party and in various state departments, including the finance ministry. Intra-party rebellions led by certain members of the ANC's national executive committee, supported particularly by black business moguls, have criticised the extent to which COSATU and the SACP influence the Zuma administration's economic direction (see Chapter Three for more on this).

The ANC hoped to resolve these tensions at its national elective conference held in Mangaung in December 2012, the first one to be held after the dramatic events at Polokwane. Instead, it compounded the confusion by adopting resolutions on the economy that provide little detail or clarity, and by overturning earlier decisions, such as the one on banning labour brokers, that had been made at Polokwane five years earlier. In addition, although Zuma's address to the Mangaung Conference expressly indicated a commitment to socio-economic equality, the conference then proceeded to appoint billionaire businessman, Cyril Ramaphosa, as deputy president. All of this suggests that the ANC is a deeply divided party still seeking its collective economic raison d'être.

The social conservatism of the Zuma administration similarly divides the ruling party. Evident in the militarist strategy that has been evoked to deal with the scourge of violent crime, this social conservatism is equally visible in incursions into civil liberties. For example, the justice system has been weakened through the appointment of dubious civil servants and conservative judges,[4] and the passing of controversial legislation such as the Protection of State Information Bill and the Traditional Courts Bill. The former undermines public transparency and effectively enables the intelligence services to cloak their activities behind a veil of national security, while the latter empowers traditional leaders vis-à-vis rural residents and establishes what Mahmood Mamdani has referred to as a bifurcated state and mode of political rule (Mamdani, 1996).

These developments have provoked opposition from civil society while dividing the ruling party and its alliance partners. The passage of the Protection of State Information Bill, for instance, has been opposed by COSATU, which is a founding member of the Right2Know campaign, a civil society alliance, which challenged the Bill in the Constitutional Court. These developments, together with COSATU's continuous criticism of corruption in the upper echelons of the government and the ANC, paint a picture of a ruling party riddled with divisions and rivalries. The expulsion of Julius Malema and the increasingly strained relations between the ANC Youth League and its parent body have further consolidated the image of a ruling party paralysed by internal fissures.

Similar divisions have imprinted themselves on the nation as a whole. Although the Zuma administration has deepened the economic shift to the left, this has not yet translated into real gains for the poor on the ground. As shown in Chapter Three, South Africa's economy has continued to grow, but at a slower rate than that of its competitors and neighbours. Unemployment, poverty and inequality continue to plague the nation. In Chapter Four, I review the ways in which corruption, enrichment and crass consumption distinguish the conduct of many in the political and economic elite. Strikes and service-delivery protests – numbering 12 654 and 11 033 in 2010 and 2011 respectively – continue to multiply, earning South Africa the title of 'protest capital of the world' (Alexander, 2012). Whereas public institutions have deracialised, public discourse regularly degenerates into racial rhetoric, often led by ruling party politicians themselves.[5] Thus, in many ways, South Africa has hardly moved since the end of Mbeki's presidential tenure, and the country is no closer to the prosperous cosmopolitan vision Mbeki projected in his speech to the constituent assembly in 1996.

Many attempts have been made to explain this state of affairs. Most, as indicated earlier, focus on actors, and on Thabo Mbeki in particular. See for example, Xolela Mangcu's *To the Brink* (2008), his subsequent *The Democratic Moment* (2009), and Mark Gevisser's biography of Mbeki, *The Dream Deferred* (2007). Mangcu (2008) explains the heightened racial discourse and South Africa's foreign policy (particularly in relation to Zimbabwe) as flowing from Mbeki's insecurities and fears about his own political future. Mangcu's hopes for the Zuma presidency (2009) are similarly predicated on the individual character traits of the president. Gevisser (2007) provides a more sophisticated explanation, accounting for the centralisation of power in South Africa's political system and its neo-liberal economics through an analysis of Mbeki's personality which, he argues, was defined by the fact that the president grew up in a space between worlds – between rural and urban, between modernism and traditionalism, between father and comrade, and between the international and the national. Gevisser argues that this profoundly affected Mbeki, generated the aloof personality that the world has come to know, and defined both his technocratic orientation manifested in GEAR and his centralised style of management.

However, although these views illuminate aspects of South Africa's transition, they do not offer a comprehensive understanding of the country's democratisation and evolution. That is, they fail to recognise that individuals, however powerful they may be, are constrained by the institutional constraints of the positions they occupy and the pressures they face. In the celebrated words of Karl Marx (1852/1972: 437), people 'make their own history, but they do not make it just as they please; they do not make it under circumstances chosen by themselves, but under circumstances directly found, given and transmitted from the past'.

In a similar vein, and influenced by the methodological premise encapsulated in these words, Henrique Fernando Cardoso, one of the former presidents of Brazil, and his co-author, the late Chilean academic Enzo Faletto, explained Latin American development in the 1960s by emphasising what they called 'the structural conditioning of social life', and 'the historical transformation of structures by conflict, social movements and class struggles' (1979: x). Such historical-structuralist explanations dissect the dynamic interplay between actors and context, between historical conditions and present circumstances. This methodological premise facilitates a deeper and clearer understanding of the current state of affairs in South Africa.

Three influential scholarly works grounded within this methodological perspective have been published on the South African transition, each offering a distinctive explanation of how South Africa got to where it is now. Two of these, *Why Race Matters in South Africa* (MacDonald, 2006), and *Class Race and Inequality in South Africa* (Seekings and Nattrass, 2006), were published soon after South Africa's new democracy celebrated its tenth anniversary, while the third, *Pushed to the Limit* (Marais, 2011) came out after Jacob Zuma ascended to the presidency. All three offer macro-studies of South Africa, and attempt to explain the overall dynamics and outcomes of the transition. All three critique the transition's current trajectory and recommend or imply alternative policies and agendas.

Michael MacDonald began his study by explaining that citizenship under apartheid was defined by a group identity, which was primarily determined by the state's actions, behaviours and policies (2006: 3–4). The apartheid state also fashioned a partnership with capital, which made special allowances for white citizens in exchange for cheap black labour. This led to an overlap between racial and class categories, with white being equated with prosperity, and black with poverty. Moreover, unlike in other societies where prosperity is arguably the product of the endowments in the private sphere – such as intelligence, skills and inheritance – in South Africa it is readily apparent to all that wealth is a direct product of political processes (2006: 49–63).

MacDonald identified this as the central conundrum confronting both capital and the ANC at the dawn of the transition. He argued that, by the 1980s, apartheid had become too expensive for capital. Apartheid not only jeopardised the entire system, it failed to create the stability required for its effective functioning. As a result, important elements within the business community recognised the necessity of arriving at a political accommodation and establishing a democracy since, as MacDonald maintains, this was perceived to be a more legitimate political host for capitalism (2006: 71–74; 88). It is important to note that those who eventually broke ranks with the apartheid regime included representatives of both English and Afrikaans sections of capital.[6]

Like the apartheid state, the ANC was confronted with two options: transform the socio-economic system or find a way of accommodating the interests of capital. MacDonald argues that, given the power of the corporate sector, the ANC chose the latter. But, he maintained, the ANC was then confronted with the problem of how to legitimise the system? Its answer, he argues, was to deracialise the apex of corporate power by creating a black bourgeoisie and upper-middle class (2006: 124–160). This, however, would only work if the interests of black elites could pass as being identical to those of the black population as a whole. The only way this could be done, MacDonald argues, was by advancing a culturalist conception of politics, one more typical of representatives of apartheid South Africa, where nation was conceived of as originating in culture defined, of course, in terms of race. In MacDonald's view, this capitulation to a culturalist conception undermined the concept of nationhood that the liberation struggle was based on, especially during the 1970s and 1980s. In this intellectual tradition, he argues, both the ANC and the Black Consciousness Movement gravitated towards a politicist definition of nation; that is, nationhood was conceived as originating in a common experience of oppression. The practical consequences of the ANC's shift away from this tradition 'is the reifying of racial identities, its repudiation of the principles of non-racialism, and its abandonment of the construction of a non-racial people' (2006: 174).

Jeremy Seekings and Nicoli Nattrass's (2006) *Class Race and Inequality in South Africa* is an altogether different book, focused more on the political economy, more engaged with the development of policy, and far more quantitatively grounded. It is one of the more important academic contributions to an understanding of South Africa's political economy and its transition. Marshalling a wealth of evidence, Seekings and Nattrass demonstrate a strong continuity in public policy between the late-apartheid and post-apartheid periods, effectively making the case that the overall increase in inequalities in South Africa was not simply a matter of inheritance, but also the product of policy choices made by the political elites under the new democratic dispensation. Their argument is essentially that the post-apartheid 'distributional regime' – their term for the mix of economic growth path and public policies on education, the labour market, and social welfare which together structure income patterns in South Africa – incorporates significant features of its late-apartheid predecessor, with similar results and consequences. The most dramatic example of this is the capital-intensive, high-wage growth strategy that typified both the late apartheid and post-apartheid periods (2006: 165–187; 340–375). The only difference being that the deracialisation of public policy has meant that the beneficiary community has broadened from capital and white workers only, to include black industrial workers. The costs of this growth strategy have been borne by the large pool of unskilled labour: the primary victims of apartheid's distributional regime have now become the underclasses of post-apartheid South Africa (2006: 300–339).

Since Seekings and Nattrass view the post-apartheid distributional regime as representing a deal between business and organised workers, the solution they propose, and which they label as a social democratic, pro-poor outcome, involves a labour-intensive, low-wage, and less-regulated growth strategy that has the capacity to soak up the millions of unemployed. This, they argue, should be coupled with greater education opportunities for children of the unemployed, a redistribution of assets through land reform and worker ownership of firms, as well as welfare distribution targeted primarily at the unemployed. It was precisely the latter that drove them to support the recommendation for a basic-income grant, which they suggested should be funded not through a rise in income tax, but rather by indirect taxes on expenditure, the most important of which is value-added tax. It is worth noting that in their recommendations on how the state could generate the resources required to sustain a basic-income grant, Seekings and Nattrass ensured that only the unemployed underclasses would benefit, and that the costs of the intervention would be borne not only by the rich, but also by the middle and the employed working classes (2006: 376–399).

It may be useful to indicate the fundamental difference between these two powerful narratives of the South African transition. Seekings and Nattrass see the beneficiaries of this transition – the 'insiders', to use their term – as capital, both black and white, and the organised working class. The victims in their view are the marginalised, defined mainly as the unemployed, who constitute the real underclass in contemporary South African society. MacDonald, by contrast, tends to construct beneficiaries and victims in more aggregated terms. He views the beneficiaries as capital and the black bourgeoisie, whereas the victims are seen as being a wider section of the black population. Although not explicitly stated, it does seem that MacDonald counted organised workers, the lower middle class and the unemployed underclasses as among the losers in this transition.

The two narratives need not be irreconcilable, however. After all, it can be argued that beneficiaries and victims need not experience gains and incur costs in equal measure. It is possible to conceive of organised workers and the lower middle class as having experienced some socio-economic benefits from the transition, while recognising that these have been far fewer than those enjoyed by the white and black bourgeoisie and the upper classes. Similarly, it can be held that while this layer is relatively more advantaged than the unemployed underclasses, they can still be conceived as being among the losers of this transition. It is certainly true that the principal institutional instruments of the organised working class, the union federations, see themselves as having been relatively disadvantaged in the post-apartheid era (COSATU, 2006: 24).

There is, however, a weakness common to both analyses, which relates to their inadequate readings of the political dynamics within the ANC-led Tripartite Alliance and the opportunities available for constructing an alternative development trajectory. Of course, this manifests in very different ways in the two books.

MacDonald's work presents the shift away from non-racialism and a cosmopolitan view of citizenship in too absolute a way. Although this is indeed one side (if not the dominant interpretation) of the story, competing developments point to the fact that alternative understandings, that imply more progressive futures, are also possible. And these are not reflected only in the values enshrined in the Constitution, as MacDonald rightly recognised (2006: 179–181), or in the policy options articulated by and the behaviour of the ANC alliance partners. They are also reflected in the behaviour and agendas of the state elites themselves. For example, a cosmopolitan value system permeates the commitment to the African renaissance and the particular brand of African nationalism that Mbeki espoused.[7] Similarly, Mbeki's commitment to non-racialism was reflected not only in the language of the redress and other legislation,[8] but also in the make-up of his Cabinet, his inner circle and his general behaviour (Habib et al., 2003: 2–5).

This is not to suggest that my reading of state elite behaviour is necessarily more accurate than that presented by MacDonald. Rather, I am pointing to the tensions between, and conflicting elements within, the agendas of state elites. This means that given a different configuration of power, state agendas could be directed in a more non-racial and cosmopolitan direction.

My criticism of Seekings and Nattrass's work is of a different nature. It is addressed at two levels. First, they assumed that South Africa's corporatist traditions and institutions (such as the National Economic Development and Labour Council (NEDLAC) and the willingness of various players to consult around at least some policies) had sufficient strength to implement the low-wage, labour-intensive, less-regulated economic strategy that they proposed (2006: 388–392). But were South Africa's corporatist institutions and traditions as strong as they assumed when Seekings and Nattrass put forward their proposals? As discussed in Chapter Four, a careful assessment of the outcomes of these institutions, and a reading of the broader literature, suggests that this was really not the case. After all, other than the Labour Relations Act (1995), all other significant legislation and documents, including the state's economic policy as encapsulated in GEAR, bypassed the deliberations of corporatist institutions (see Adam et al., 1997; Alexander, 2002; Bond, 2000; Marais, 2001). Moreover, at the time, COSATU and other labour federations tended to view institutions such as NEDLAC as relatively toothless, and saw themselves as having, on balance, lost out in the transition (COSATU: 2006: 8–9; 24).

It is true that the labour federation consistently supported the continuation and strengthening of NEDLAC and other corporatist institutions. Care must be taken, however, not to read more into this than is necessary. Despite its formal commitment to these institutions, COSATU had learnt in the course of the transition to bypass them when they failed to serve its interests. Moreover, as I argue in Chapter Four, while the structural conditions have become more facilitative of a social pact in the post-Polokwane period, this is unlikely to be realised on the one-sided terms proposed by Seekings and Nattrass. It is likely to be realised only if elite expectations – read the aspirations of politicians and corporate mandarins – are as circumscribed as those of organised workers. The essential problem with Seekings and Nattrass's analysis is that the only way they conceptualised policy impact was through formal institutional processes. However, as is well known, extra-institutional action and mobilisation can prompt elites to undertake policy reform and behave more appropriately, if not more effectively, than institutional negotiations and corporatist pacts (Ballard et al., 2006).[9]

This raises the second and more serious criticism that can be levelled against Seekings and Nattrass. Their book, as does much of their earlier work (Nattrass and Seekings, 1997; Seekings and Nattrass, 2002), makes the case for how a high-wage, capital-intensive strategy hurts the unskilled unemployed underclasses and ensures that employed workers are relatively privileged (2006: 340–375). Indeed, they go so far as to describe employed workers as a privileged group and as among the winners in the transition (2006: 46, 374). But as Franco Barchiesi (2011: 206) demonstrates, the precariousness of their jobs, the 'uneven and fragile' nature of the benefits that they have gained, and the fact that 'democratisation and racial redress have largely not reversed the injuries of unilateral corporate power', means that unionised black workers cannot be 'conceived among the winners of the post-apartheid transition' or as being 'on the way to become a prosperous middle class'.

But even if one disputes Barchiesi's conclusion, and views the beneficiaries as both employed workers and capital, why, given that the latter is more privileged than the former, should the lower middle and working classes help to pay the cost of raising the underclasses out of poverty? As COSATU argues (COSATU and NEHAWU, 2003), why should the rich not be financially responsible for the achievement of this collective social good? After all, they were one of the primary beneficiaries of apartheid.

Given their explicit commitment to social democracy (2006: 380), how do we explain Seekings and Nattrass's moral position in this regard? The only answer that makes sense is that they believe that in the global system business is too powerful and therefore will not be persuaded to carry the costs of this initiative. If this is their position, is it a fair assumption to make? There are a number of cases across the world, such as the Scandinavian countries or western Europe more generally, and even the Asian Tigers – Japan, South Korea and Taiwan – in which economic and political elites have been prompted to choose a human-oriented development trajectory. Does it not make sense, then, to establish a research agenda on the politics of policy making, with the express aim of trying to understand under what conditions elites can be made to behave in systemically beneficial ways?

Such a moral charge cannot be laid against Hein Marais's *Pushed to the Limit* (2011), which has a very different philosophical tenor. The essential thesis of this sequel to his earlier work, *Limits to Change* (2001), is that South Africa's democratic transition is merely an attempt by the ruling class to establish a new growth path after its previous attempts in the late-apartheid period failed to address the economic crisis that overcame the country from the 1970s. His view is that the ruling class gave the ANC a mandate to deliver stable and sustainable economic growth in exchange for a limited redress project that involved the creation of a black capitalist class (2011: 389). While the ruling party hoped that this would create a level of political and social stability, thereby creating a momentum for a slow but steady project of empowerment and transformation, the economic policies of the post-apartheid era instead aggravated the social inheritance bequeathed by apartheid, provoking intense resistance from the poor.

Marais argues that the Mbeki administration responded to this with a dual agenda of pacification and fear. The former resulted in the expansion of social support grants, and the latter culminated in the centralisation of power, the marginalisation of critics, and the isolation and sometimes public humiliation of political competitors. Despite this, the resistance and protests grew louder and, in Marais' view, Zuma's ascendancy to the leadership was an attempt by the party to re-establish its hold over the citizenry (2011: 403). Marais is convinced that this is unlikely to work given the level of policy continuity between Zuma's administration and that of his predecessor. Indeed, Marais notes that the ANC's rule is less stable than it was a decade ago and anticipates the continuation of social struggles (2011: 400–403). Marais suggests, however, that these do not constitute as coherent a rebellion as many activists imagine, but remain sporadic and isolated. He concludes by arguing that progressives have to prepare for a long and arduous road of 'experimenting, building and adapting' (2011: 460).

Without doubt, Marais's book is a useful one, that combines very detailed descriptions with an understanding of how political and policy choices are conditioned by the balance of power within South Africa. His analysis contains three significant weaknesses, however. First, he explicitly suggests that capital is trying to reconstruct its hegemonic project and that the ANC is a junior partner in this regard. This projects a level of coherence onto the corporate sector that is just not evident. Even a cursory engagement with the business community reveals that it is seriously divided and unlikely to reach consensus on the terms of any newly reconfigured hegemonic project.[10] Moreover, the ANC is not a junior partner in the initiative. Indeed, it is the pre-eminent actor, even though it is constrained by the balance of power, and sometimes overestimates its abilities while underestimating the consequences of its choices. It therefore seems more appropriate to conceive of the ANC as the flawed and constrained but leading player in the drama of South Africa's transition.

Second, Marais does not sufficiently recognise the subtle shifts in the balance of power that resulted from developments at the Polokwane conference. This may be because he seems to be seeking substantive ruptures rather than subtle shifts. Although dramatic for the key actors in the drama, Polokwane led to a relatively subtle shift in the balance of power, manifested in the enhancement in the leverage capacity of organised labour and in increased levels of uncertainty within the business community. These shifts create the potential for different outcomes, even if these may not be revolutionary in nature. In addition, Marais is not sufficiently cognisant of the differences between the Mbeki and Zuma administrations. Yet, as I indicate in Chapter Three, there are important economic programmes that the Zuma administration is either pioneering or deepening, and while some of these may have emerged since the publication of his book, Marais's analysis clearly did not anticipate the left-leaning agenda implicit in these initiatives. Of course, this is only one side of the story. There are many countervailing tendencies – including increasing corruption, the militarisation of the police services, and the social conservatism of Jacob Zuma – that point away from a deeper or more radical development trajectory. Nevertheless, some of the policies developed in the post-Polokwane period suggest that the potential for a more progressive agenda is greater than Marais anticipates.

Third, Marais's analysis offers a powerful critique but does not consider what needs to be done except in the most general of terms. He seems to be unable to conceptualise the kind of reforms that would deepen the progressive character of the transition. Again, this may be (despite his protestations in the final paragraph of his book) because he is seeking substantive ruptures rather than the structural, snowballing reforms more compatible with the Gramscian strategy that he professes to support. These are the only kinds of changes that are feasible for the moment but they hold the potential of slowly altering South Africa's future.

This question is discussed further in Chapter Seven of this book. For now, it is sufficient to note that the two defining characteristics of the state of the nation at the current moment are the continued racialisation of identities, and the growing socio-economic inequality created largely by the increasing wealth of those, both black and white, at the upper end of the class hierarchy. While existing scholarship has illuminated much of the transition and its development trajectory, perhaps the primary question is why this state of affairs continues to prevail in South Africa. This question is fundamental not only for scholars, but also for the architects of the transition. Solutions will not be found until there is a comprehensive understanding of why and how South Africa has evolved in the way that it has. Moreover, a comprehensive answer to this question requires investigation beyond descriptions of institutional architecture or policy contours and their effects. It requires an explanation of why these have taken the forms that they have; in effect, it requires an investigation of the politics of the transition.

Explaining the transition

Scholarly literature on the South African transition has been published in two waves. The first wave, produced and published in the years leading up to and immediately after the 1994 elections, took a programmatic and descriptive form (Adam and Moodley, 1993; Atkinson and Friedman, 1994; Friedman, 1993; Slabbert, 1992).[11] This was partly understandable given the contemporariness of the transition and the desire among (and opportunities provided to) scholars to participate in the process of crafting a legitimate, democratic political order.[12] Although this was useful for describing the events, and arguing for one or another ideological or programmatic solution, much of this scholarly literature was unable to provide a comprehensive analysis. In fact, it lacked analytical focus, which prevented it from explaining why particular choices had been made, what forces and factors had prompted these choices, or from outlining the likely results and limitations involved.

This then prompted a second wave of material, published around and in the years following South Africa's second democratic election in 1999. This literature, which was ideologically more diverse, advanced two methodologically different sets of explanations. The first critiqued earlier accounts that had focused on actors such as elites, political parties, and social movements (Bond, 2000; Desai, 2002; Hirsch, 2005; Marais, 2001; Terreblanche, 2002). The second, including the work reflected upon earlier by MacDonald (2006), Seekings and Nattrass (2006) and Marais (2011), tried to integrate structural and agential variables with varying levels of success.

This methodological schism mirrors the divide in the international literature on democratic transitions and their reversals. Much of the early scholarly literature on what Samuel Huntington (1991) termed the 'Third Wave' of democratisation, rejected the inevitability thesis of the structuralist accounts of democratisation of the 1950s, 1960s and 1970s, including the work of Lipset (1960), Moore Jr (1966), Schmitter (1974) and O'Donnell, (1979). Instead it focused on agential variables, and in particular on political elites (see, for example, Di Palma, 1990; Higley and Gunther, 1992; O'Donnell et al., 1986). Soon these scholars, too, came under criticism for presenting excessively voluntarist explanations (see Karl, 1990; Munck, 1994; Remmer, 1991; Rueschemeyer et al., 1992).

Then a new wave of integrative explanations emerged, focusing on both structural and agential variables. Two of the earliest examples were Huntington's (1991) *The Third Wave* and Ruth and David Collier's (1991) *Shaping the Political Arena*. Huntington distinguished between causes and causers of democratisation. The former refers to structural variables – the performance and legitimacy of authoritarian regimes, global economic growth, changes in the doctrine of the Catholic Church, changes in the policies of the United States and the European Union, and the impact of the technological revolution – that define the contexts of various transitions. The latter refers to the individual actors whose strategies, decisions and behaviour promoted democratisation (Huntington, 1991).

Similarly, albeit in a very different ideological vein, Collier and Collier (1991) explained the political systems in eight Latin American countries as a product of attempts to incorporate the working class into their societies. The number of workers had grown dramatically through the first half of the twentieth century. However, the specific forms of integration attempted in each country were dependent 'on the dynamics of intra-elite politics and choices by actors within the state' (Collier and Collier, 1991). Both studies therefore integrated structural and agential variables in their analyses of regime transitions.

I attempt to locate my own analysis in the methodological tradition of these more integrative studies, and aim to understand the role of political actors within specific structural conditions. Just as significantly, I borrow heavily from the work of Huber et al., (1997) who argue that particular clusters of power – class interactions, the nature of the state, and state–society relations – are responsible for shaping the conditions of democratisation and the possibilities for consolidation. Like Hein Marais's (2011) study, my analysis focuses on the balance of power as a variable informing the choices and decisions of actors in the South African transition. Unlike Marais, however, I conceive the balance of power as having evolved during the transition period. In my view, two distinct configurations are evident in the transition to date. The first informed the parameters of the settlement at the dawn of the transition, as well as the policies of the Mandela and the early years of the Mbeki administration. The second was an evolution that culminated in the Polokwane conference, and which has subsequently enabled certain choices and constrained other possibilities during Zuma's presidential tenure.

The nature of South Africa's transition was defined not only by the culmination of the resistance and reforms of the late-apartheid and early negotiations period (the transition's liberalisation phase), but also by the transformations that resulted from the collapse of the Soviet Union, including globalisation and the integration of production processes around the world (Marglin and Schor, 1992; Mittelman, 2000; Stiglitz, 2002).

The configuration of power at this key moment in South Africa's history was Janus-faced. One the one hand, there was a political stalemate between apartheid's rulers, the National Party, and the ANC – a condition that Dankwart Rustow saw as necessary for the genesis of democracy (1970).[13] The National Party's leverage was, of course, the military capacity of the apartheid regime which far exceeded that of the liberation movement. The ANC, on the other hand, had the legitimacy it derived from the fact that it had the support of the majority of the population. These competing strengths and the failure of the two organisations to neutralise one another (as they had attempted to do in the 1980s and early 1990s) effectively created a political stalemate.

On the other hand, despite the illusions of activists and union-aligned academics, the corporate sector had decidedly more economic leverage than the union movement. The collapse of the Soviet Union legitimised various market-policy prescriptions and the economic transformations that flowed from the integration of production systems around the world greatly enhanced the leverage of the corporate sector vis-à-vis unions and other social actors. The only resources available to the union movement were its capacities to strike and to influence its members' votes, and given its historical alliance with the ANC and the lack of alternative political options, neither of these capacities could be used to effect the change they might have wanted to see. This, then, was the balance of power that defined the negotiated settlement and the policy parameters introduced during the Mandela and Mbeki eras, both of which are discussed in more detail in Chapters Two and Three.

This configuration of power has evolved since, and underwent its most significant, yet subtle, change at the Polokwane conference in 2007. Here Jacob Zuma challenged Thabo Mbeki for the leadership of the ruling party and the nation. The institutional foundation for Zuma's campaign was provided by the ANC Youth League, COSATU and the SACP. The union federation and the SACP had been marginalised by Mbeki since the adoption of GEAR in 1996. They had fought back in multiple ways, including struggles around working conditions, campaigning for the provision of antiretroviral medication to people living with HIV and AIDS, challenging South Africa's policy on Zimbabwe, and protesting the failures of service delivery. From 2005, this struggle took the form of a succession battle and ultimately culminated in the defeat of Mbeki at the Polokwane conference in 2007.

Zuma's victory was therefore as much a victory for COSATU and the SACP. But while this has enhanced the leverage of these organisations within the Zuma administration, their positions are still heavily contested. The corporate sector retains enormous influence, particularly because its control over the lever of investment is seen as a precondition for growing the economy. Moreover, there are many within the ANC who resent the increased influence of the left, and prefer the more traditional, market-oriented strategy of the Mbeki era. Yet the relatively enhanced voice of COSATU and the SACP, together with global shifts towards a neo-Keynesian economic agenda as a result of interventions to address the 2008 economic recession, has created a relative parity in the balance of power between labour and the business community. This fragile and contested parity has nevertheless opened up policy options within the Zuma administration that are discussed in more detail in the chapters that follow.

A brief outline of the book

In the next chapter, Chapter Two, I focus on the post-apartheid state and its deficits in relation to accountability and service delivery. Beginning with an analysis of the debates that took place during the constitutional negotiations, I explain how these shaped the institutional contours of the post-apartheid state. I then attempt to explain why South Africa's ruling political elite is so unresponsive to its citizens, focusing particularly on how the electoral system, and the fact that there is no viable opposition party, affects the dynamic of accountability within government. The post-apartheid state's dismal record in terms of service delivery is explored with attention being given to the powers of different tiers of government, the particular character of affirmative action, the effects of cadre and factional deployment, as well as corruption. I end the chapter by identifying the essence of the accountability and service-delivery challenges facing the post-apartheid state.

The political economy of democratic South Africa is discussed in Chapter Three. I first describe the evolution of the state's economic policy, and analyse the political variables, including the particular configurations of power that informed its policy choices as well as their social impact throughout the democratic transition. I then analyse the economic policy debates that have occurred within the Zuma administration, identifying the contending factions, their respective leverage capacities, and the likely evolution of economic policy in the years to come. Reiterating what many have identified as South Africa's key challenges – unemployment, inequality and poverty – I note that unless these are comprehensively addressed they herald further social polarisation and political instability.

In Chapters Four and Five, I consider dynamics pertaining to the business community and civil society. In Chapter Four, I consider the prospects for a social pact between labour, business and the state. The failure of a similar initiative in the 1990s is accounted for with reference to the balance of power in those years. Drawing on international examples, I show that social pacts have been successful only where there is parity in the leverage capacities of business and labour. While relative parity between these sectors has emerged in the post-Polokwane period, the possibility of realising such a pact is being undermined by the state's failure to manage popular expectations, which, as a prerequisite, require the containment of the crude consumptionist practices and enrichment desires of both the political and economic elite. This is identified in the chapter's concluding reflections as another of the serious challenges confronting contemporary South Africa.

In Chapter Five, I investigate how these dynamics play out within broader civil society. The chapter begins with an examination of the impact of democratisation and liberalisation on civil society and its attempts to address South Africa's contemporary challenges. In particular, I note the deracialisation and pluralisation of civic activity in the post-apartheid era. I then consider the state's responses to civic activity, and how these have led to a situation in which neither the state nor radical activists understand the need for civic plurality, and therefore continue to imagine and demand homogenous (if differing) responses from citizens. I conclude by arguing that it is precisely the plurality of civil society, and its multiple engagements with the state, that has the potential to produce the checks and balances required for the consolidation of democracy and the achievement of inclusive development.

South Africa's engagements with the wider world are discussed in Chapter Six. I identify the source of post-apartheid South Africa's foreign policy as being embedded in the character of its political elite – second-generation nationalists who desire a deracialised and global order but recognise their relative powerlessness to effect this outcome. Their specific response has been to engage with the international system, aiming to subvert it from within. This has required enhancing their own leverage which they have sought to achieve by focusing on the stabilisation and economic development of Africa, establishing strategic alliances with other developing nations such as Brazil, China, India and Russia, and advocating for the reform of international institutions such as the United Nations, the International Monetary Fund and the World Bank. In practice, standing up for the rights of citizens has been traded off against the requirements of attempting to reform the international system or addressing historical inequities. It is in this context that the domestic and international human rights community has become increasingly outraged at South Africa's foreign policy. The Zuma administration has attempted to address this 'rights deficit', most notably via its support for UN Resolution 1973, which was meant to protect civilians in Libya. But the subsequent successful pursuit of regime change by NATO forced South Africa onto the defensive as it faced criticism from some members of the ANC, various African nations and other developing countries. This re-opened debates on South Africa's foreign-policy direction, and revealed the divisions between the South African government and the human rights community. I conclude that, with imagination, it should be possible for South Africa to simultaneously pursue the twin agendas of human rights and historical redress in the international arena.

Two chapters bring the book to a close: Chapter Seven is aimed at activists and political leaders, detailing an alternative political agenda and programme for democracy as well as inclusive development that stems from my analysis. Each of the preceding chapters concludes with a challenge. In Chapter Seven, I reflect on how these challenges can be addressed as part of a cohesive political programme. Chapter Eight, by contrast, is directed at both the academy and the intelligentsia. In it, I consider the lessons of the South African experience for theories of democratic transition, social change and conflict resolution. In this regard it reflects critically on the analysis of scholars associated with the progressive nationalist, liberal and social justice traditions, detailing how the intellectual divide between these scholarly communities can be bridged. This, the chapter argues, is essential if the intellectual foundation for democracy and inclusive development is to be established and consolidated across the globe.

The substantive analysis offered in the pages that follow explains political developments, and the evolution of the democratic transition in South Africa as the outcome of political choices of actors conditioned by the balance of power within which they operate. This does not mean that these actors are powerless to prevail against the realities of the context and moment. Indeed they can, and I discuss examples of this, such as the 'sunset clauses' proposed by Joe Slovo during the negotiations process. Thus, while I attempt to explain how South Africa reached its current suspended historical moment – which Achille Mbembe (2012) describes so well as 'caught between an intractable present and an irrecoverable past; between things that are no longer and things that are not yet' – I also propose an alternative political agenda for South Africa and outline what needs to be done to bring the country closer to the social democratic vision encapsulated in South Africa's Constitution.

2

Governance, political accountability and service delivery

There was little that united South Africans at the dawn of their democratic transition, but if there was anything – other than the desire to avert a civil war – it would have been a yearning for political accountability and service delivery. South Africans may have meant different things by these terms, but there was nevertheless a general desire across racial, class and gender divides for a political elite and a state that would be responsive to the needs of its citizens. Yet, by 2013, public opinion across the breadth of the political spectrum concurred that there was both a lack of accountability and a general shortfall in service delivery in South Africa. How did this come to pass?

Much of the debate about these issues has focused on institutional design and the quality of the country's human resources. Thus, since 1994, state officials have regularly redesigned state institutions and the relations between them, with a view to enhancing their effectiveness (Presidential Review Commission, 1998; Swilling et al., 2008). Poorly trained officials have been blamed for the inefficiencies and training and development programmes have thus been introduced (Fraser-Moleketi, 2002). Critics of government have condemned the ruling party's policies of cadre deployment and affirmative action for leading to the appointment of inappropriately skilled personnel and bloated administrative systems (Democratic Alliance, 2012b; *The Economist*, 3 June 2010).

The ruling party's allies have commented on these issues too – see, for example, the call by Zwelinzima Vavi, the general secretary of the Congress of South African Trade Unions (COSATU), for the scrapping of the country's provinces (*Business Day*, 21 December 2011; Paton, 2012).

But, while institutional design is important, it alone cannot account for the malaise affecting South Africa's governance and political landscape. After all, societies with similar institutional and governance frameworks have fundamentally different service delivery and accountability outcomes. Federal Germany, for example, is far more accountable and efficient than federal Nigeria. Similarly, unitary Britain is more accountable and efficient than federal Nigeria. Clearly, therefore, it is necessary to look beyond institutional design to understand the variety of governance and political outcomes in different societies. Comparisons can be useful, but they cannot replace an understanding of a particular social context and an investigation of how this affects the performance of institutions, individuals and state officials.

Whereas institutional design is a key variable in understanding outcomes, its feasibility and appropriateness should not be generically determined. Rather, the relevance of particular institutions should be contextually determined and grounded; that is, their appropriateness should be assessed in relation to the particular needs and characteristics of the society they serve.

An assessment of the South African government's institutional lethargy must, therefore, look beyond the debate about institutional design to highlight the dilemmas generated by our social context (including the policy and behavioural choices of our political elites and other actors) and consider how these have contributed to the situation the country finds itself in. Before proceeding with this, however, it is useful to briefly outline the institutional architecture and governance structures that have been developed by the political elites, and in particular the African National Congress (ANC), for the South African state.

The construction of the post-apartheid state

Contemporary South Africa's institutional architecture and governance arrangements developed in three distinct phases, which are discussed in more detail in the next three sections of the chapter. The first phase occurred in the negotiations process, which produced the Interim Constitution of 1993. The second phase took place through the deliberations of the constituent assembly, which produced the Constitution of 1996. The third phase comprised the institutional and administrative reforms introduced by Thabo Mbeki at the start of his presidential tenure in 1999. Although Jacob Zuma has since introduced some further reforms in 2009 – establishing new ministries and expanding ministerial appointments from 28 to 34 – these have been mainly administrative in nature and have affected the form of the state rather than substantively changing its inner workings. Thus South Africa under Zuma, despite all the pretensions of his administration, is very much a product of the Mbeki era.

Phase one: the negotiations process

The negotiations began with the unbanning of the ANC on 2 February 1990 and the release of Nelson Mandela on 11 February 1990. Three bilateral meetings between the former ruling party, the National Party and the ANC over the course of that year produced the Groote Schuur Minute, the Pretoria Minute and the DF Malan Accord. These three agreements enabled the release of political prisoners, the granting of immunity in respect of political offences, the lifting of the state of emergency, and the suspension of armed struggle by the ANC. Although the formal negotiations began on 20 December 1991, when the Convention for a Democratic South Africa (CODESA) held its first plenary session, tangible progress eluded the negotiators until 1993.

The reason for this is that two very different constitutional visions vied for supremacy in the negotiations process. The first, advanced by the National Party, was influenced by consociational theories, advanced most notably by Dutch theorist, Arend Lijphart.[1] Lijphart's general thesis is that a comparison of experiences of democracy indicates that majoritarian principles and organs of governance may not be compatible with plural societies. He maintains that because of the ethnic or class divisions in such societies, political contests manifest themselves in group terms. In such cases, political parties represent the interests of particular groups and voter preferences are determined more by group loyalties than by the policy preferences of individual voters. The largest group within plural societies is then guaranteed dominance in electoral contests, its party permanently occupies political office, and tends to monopolise state resources. Lijphart (1977) argues, therefore, that majoritarianism undermines the democratic principle of rotation in office and denies minorities the opportunity to form majorities. Moreover, he suggests that majoritarianism often leads to minority groups becoming frustrated with the democratic process and engaging in struggles to undermine it. In his view, civil strife is the likely result of majoritarianism in plural societies.

To avoid this scenario, Lijphart recommends that minority groups be guaranteed a share of resources and a say in the political destiny of their societies. He makes a number of recommendations in this regard (1977: 25–44). First, he argues for the entrenchment of power sharing in all the electoral organs of the state. He proposes that this be achieved by ensuring: a proportional system of representation so that all significant groups are represented in the legislature; that the executive be comprised of a mandatory coalition of representatives of all significant groups; and that the right to a mutual veto[2] on vital matters is granted to representatives of all groups within society. Second, Lijphart recommends that public funds and positions in the civil service be proportionally allocated between the various groups. Third, he advises that a high degree of internal autonomy be granted to groups that require it and that this may involve the establishment of a federal state if significant groups within the society are geographically concentrated. It should be noted that Lijphart's vision, as reflected in these recommendations, assumes that the principle of rotation in office is more fundamental to democratic practice than the right of majorities to govern.

In any case, in the mid 1980s, Lijphart applied much of his vision to South Africa, describing the country as a plural society with multiple ethnic divisions. He argued that black solidarity was a temporary phenomenon, and that universal suffrage and competitive elections in a post-apartheid South Africa would facilitate the reassertion of ethnic identities within both the black and white communities (Lijphart, 1985: 20; 36).[3] Majoritarian democracy, he maintained, would be catastrophic for the country. It would promote civil strife and undermine the stability of post-apartheid South Africa. He therefore recommended a consociational democratic system for the country, including elements of power sharing, the proportional allocation of public resources and civil-service positions, and a federal state (1985).

Lijphart's vision became the National Party's constitutional platform. The party proposed a three-tier government with legislative and executive authority at all levels. It insisted on the establishment of a constitutional state governed by a charter of fundamental rights that would guarantee the independence of the judiciary, ombudsman, auditor-general, public service commission and the Reserve Bank (South African Government, n.d.) It also demanded security of tenure for civil-service employees (NP, n.d; South African Government, n.d.). For the National Party, participatory democracy, interpreted as power sharing, was to be reflected in a bicameral parliament, the first elected by universal suffrage based on proportional representation, and the second to be composed of equal numbers of seats for all regions. In addition, the party proposed a multiparty cabinet operating on the principle of consensus; a three-person presidency with an annual rotation of the chairpersonship. Regional government would have legislative and executive powers, operating on similar consensual principles, and with complete authority in certain constitutionally defined areas. The party also proposed a local government dispensation that qualified the franchise so that property owners, lessees and ratepayers had two votes and ordinary residents had only one.

The ANC's proposals, on the other hand, were influenced by traditions of democracy as theorised and practised in much of the Anglo-Saxon world. On the basis of these traditions, which were consistent with the majoritarian elements of the ANC's earlier national democratic vision, the organisation rejected power sharing in favour of majority rule. The ANC recognised the rights of minorities, but maintained that these could be protected through a bill of rights and a system of proportional representation. The political participation and representation of individual citizens, they insisted, should not be determined through ethnic, racial or any other 'group-related' categories. Democracy, according to the ANC, essentially meant that the views and decisions of the majority must prevail within society. They argued that minority parties should accept this and try, through vigorous opposition, to attract new voters who would enable them to develop into a majority (ANC, n.d).

Like the National Party, the ANC advocated a three-tier system of government, but with a unitary rather than a federal flavour. While there was to be a bicameral legislature, the universally elected national assembly was to have primary power in enacting legislation. Executive authority was to reside in a single president who served as head of state. The ANC's proposals insisted on 'a strong and effective central government', with responsibility for foreign relations, defence and internal security, as well as economic, fiscal and tax policy. They also demanded 'the creation of a national policy framework and the furnishing of resources for eradicating racism and racial practices, and for the tackling of the vast problems of education, health, housing, nutrition, employment and social welfare' (ANC, n.d.: 2, 9).

The ANC's proposals regarding provincial and local government were also located within a majoritarian and unitary framework. Unlike in the National Party's federal proposal, the provinces were not conceived of as fully autonomous, but rather as areas that exercised 'concurrent authority with the central government' (ANC, 1992a: 18; see also Skweyiya, 1992). While the ANC hoped to harmonise the powers of provinces with those of the central government, it insisted that, in cases of conflict, national legislation should prevail. Similarly, local government's powers were to be circumscribed to function within the framework of national and regional legislation. For the ANC, the overall purpose of the local dispensation was to bring 'government closer to the people' without granting local authorities the powers that would enable them to reproduce apartheid policies and racial inequalities.

The two sets of proposals clearly indicate the political chasm that existed between the ANC and National Party. While the former wanted to establish a majoritarian democracy, the latter insisted on a consociational one. Both visions were perfectly consistent with the desires of their advocates to protect and advance the interests of their respective constituencies. For the ANC, majoritarian democracy would enable it to use the levers of government to advance the interests of the black community. For the National Party, consociational democracy would provide it with constitutional mechanisms to protect the white community. The ANC hoped to use a majoritarian system of government to advance policies that would undermine apartheid's inequities. The National Party hoped to use a consociational system of government to contain those same policies, thereby retaining the material and political advantages conferred by apartheid's inequities.

Not surprisingly, the two constitutional visions hit a deadlock when they came up against one another in the negotiations process. As noted, a political stalemate prevailed for much of 1992. It was broken in the aftermath of two events. The first was the Bisho massacre, which took place on 7 September 1992 in what was then the bantustan of Ciskei. The massacre brought an end to the campaign of rolling mass action that the ANC launched when it withdrew from the negotiations process after the Boipatong massacre of June 1992. The Bisho massacre, and the mass campaign that preceded it, not only provided emphatic evidence of the breadth of popular support for the ANC (demonstrated through the four million workers who participated in a stayaway called by the organisation and its union partner, COSATU), but it also emphasised the apartheid state's enormous military capacity. Thus, despite bringing millions of people onto the streets and keeping them away from work,[4] the stayaway had no effect on the regime's military capabilities. The Bisho massacre dramatically illustrated the fact that, despite the military pretensions of some ANC members, 'the Leipzig option'[5] was not a possibility for South Africa.

Just two weeks after the Bisho massacre, these realisations were underscored in the Record of Understanding signed on 26 September 1992, whereby all parties committed themselves to an elected constitution-making body, fixed time frames, and adequate deadlock-breaking mechanisms. Moreover, the National Party's pledge to release the approximately 400 remaining political prisoners, and to rein in the Inkatha Freedom Party by banning the display of cultural weapons (assegais, spears and other traditional military instruments) at its marches, also assisted the ANC in appeasing the more militant sectors of its constituency. But the concessions made by the National Party were by no means one-sided.

Compromises were also required of the Congress Alliance, and these were outlined in a new political position adopted by the ANC in November 1992. This was the second significant shift that broke the deadlock in the negotiations process. A stalwart of the ANC and the SACP, Joe Slovo, introduced the policy debate in August 1992 in his contribution to the *African Communist* entitled 'Negotiations: What Room for Compromise?' He insisted that the article presented his views alone, but it was common knowledge that most of the ANC negotiators at CODESA shared his perspective.[6] In any case, Slovo advocated a series of concessions to facilitate a breakthrough in the negotiations. These involved: (i) a 'sunset clause' that would provide for compulsory power sharing for five years; (ii) bilateral agreements with the National Party on regional powers; (iii) a general amnesty; and (iv) a commitment to respect existing employment contracts and retirement compensations in any future restructuring of the civil service (Slovo, 1992).

Although such concessions were of a qualitative nature, Slovo maintained that they were politically acceptable since they would not prevent the state from advancing to a full non-racial democracy in future. Slovo also justified the need for these concessions by outlining his perception of the balance of forces at that time. His references to the ANC as the major negotiating adversary and the apartheid state as an undefeated enemy, combined with his concern about the civil service (and particularly those in the South African security apparatus, including the police and defence force) potentially providing a base for a counter-revolution, suggests that he saw the situation as a stalemate. Given the realities of the ANC's political legitimacy, and the apartheid regime's control over the organs of security and administration, Slovo proposed that the ANC reconcile itself to the fact that 'the immediate outcome of the negotiating process will inevitably be less than perfect when measured against our long-term liberation objectives' (Slovo, 1992: 37).

Slovo's 'sunset clause' paper prompted an intense debate within the Congress Alliance. Members of the ANC's negotiations commission supported his analysis and proposals, and circulated a draft policy document entitled, 'Negotiations: A Strategic Perspective' (ANC, 1992b). Prominent ANC activists and leaders, including Pallo Jordan, Blade Nzimande, Harry Gwala and others came out strongly against the proposed concessions. Their argument and analysis objected principally to the notion of abandoning the ANC's aim to decisively defeat the apartheid government and destroy the apartheid state. They maintained that the balance of forces was not immutable, that it could be transformed by struggle, and by linking the mass of the people to the negotiations process (ANC Youth League, 1992; Gwala, 1992; Jordan, 1992; Nzimande, 1992).[7]

In November 1992, this polemical and sometimes fractious debate shifted off the pages of the *African Communist* and into the ANC executive. After three days of intense debate, the national executive committee swung decisively in favour of Slovo and the members of the negotiations commission and they adopted the commission's document as organisational policy. In a document entitled 'Negotiations: A Strategic Perspective' (ANC, 1992b), the organisation outlined its commitment to participating in a government of national unity, 'even after the adoption of a new constitution', and indicated its willingness 'to address the question of job security, retrenchment packages and a general amnesty ... [for the existing] armed formations and civil service'. The document also committed the ANC 'to bilateral discussions with the National Party ... [to] seek an understanding on the question of the powers, functions and boundaries of regions ... which the parties would pursue in the Constituent Assembly' (ANC, 1992b: 7–8).

The pace of negotiations accelerated from this point. Even the tragic assassination of Chris Hani, general secretary of the SACP, and the most popular ANC leader after Nelson Mandela, did not derail the process.[8] In fact, it had the opposite effect – increasing the pressure on the ANC to complete the negotiations process. (By this time, CODESA had been replaced by the Multi-Party Negotiating Forum.) Hitches in the multiparty talks were quickly resolved through bilateral discussions between the ANC and the National Party. Agreements achieved through bilateral discussions were pushed through at the multiparty talks using the principle of 'sufficient consensus'. By the end of 1993, the Transitional Executive Council was established in accordance with the Transitional Executive Council Act of 1993. Although the council's brief extended only to matters affecting the elections, in reality it served as a parallel government. Its powers were very vaguely defined, and this enabled it to intervene on practically any matter that it saw as potentially interfering with the holding of a free and fair election.

The details of the constitutional settlement are encapsulated in the Interim Constitution, which was adopted by the South African parliament in November 1993 and in two subsequent amendments gazetted on 3 March and 26 April 1994. The two amendments were the result of initiatives by both FW de Klerk (as leader of the National Party) and Nelson Mandela (as head of the ANC) to draw the Inkatha Freedom Party led by Mangosuthu Buthelezi into the elections.

The Interim Constitution established the parameters of South Africa's institutional and governance architecture. Moreover, it contained a mix of proposals put forward by both the National Party and ANC. While many of the National Party's proposals (such as a collective presidency, a minority veto and a federal state) were rejected, the Interim Constitution did enshrine the party's desire for power sharing through establishing a multiparty government of national unity at both national and regional levels, appointing De

Klerk as an executive deputy president, and requiring the majority party to rule in a spirit of consensus. Moreover, in accordance with the National Party's original proposals, the post-apartheid state was obliged to respect the tenure of civil servants, as well as guarantee the independence of the judiciary, the ombudsman, the auditor-general, the public service commission and the Reserve Bank. Similarly, although the Interim Constitution enshrined many of the ANC's specific recommendations, the majoritarian impulse of its original proposals was moderated through the establishment of the government of national unity, the enhanced representation of minority racial groups at local level (where a mixed electoral system results in both constituency and proportional representation) and the allocation of greater powers to regional and local authorities than are usual under a unitary government.

In the immediate aftermath of the first democratic general elections in 1994, a debate emerged in academic circles around the form of democracy that had been negotiated and was being practised in post-election South Africa. Lijphart suggested that the new constitutional arrangements represented a consociational form of democracy. He maintained that all of the basic principles that defined consociationalism were embodied in the Constitution:

- the government of national unity represented the 'grand coalition';
- group autonomy was guaranteed in the educational sphere through Article 32 of the Interim Constitution, which allowed for the establishment of educational institutions on the basis of a common culture, language or religion;
- proportionality was realised through the fact that the first elections utilised a proportional system of representation based on the party list; and
- the 'minority veto' appeared in the requirement that the final Constitution must be passed by a two-thirds majority of the constituent assembly.

Lijphart's only reservation was the weak form of federalism embodied in the settlement, but he was optimistic that the country would evolve stronger federal features (Lijphart, 1994).

While Lijphart's assessment of the South African political order as consociational was supported by US-based scholars such as Jung and Shapiro (1995) and Koelble and Reynolds (1996), it was contested by local academics such as Taylor (1994) and Friedman (1994). Taylor, for instance, insisted that the constitutional settlement met none of Lijphart's criteria for consociational democracy. He argued that the Interim Constitution, unlike consociational ones: directed fundamental rights solely at individuals without specifying group rights; did not enshrine a minority veto in the Cabinet; would not allow group autonomy to be realised in the weak form of federalism; and fell far short of realising the segmented education authority characteristic of consociational societies such as the Netherlands.[9] Furthermore, Taylor noted that voter preferences were not rigidly defined along racial lines, political parties could not be conceived as segmented organisations, and the grand coalition must be conceived not as a deal struck between ethnically established parties, but rather as a result of the support that political parties received in the April 1994 elections. Thus Taylor concluded: 'South African democracy did not represent an ethnic consociation; there was no exclusive space for the articulation of ethnic interests' (1994: 6).[10]

On balance, one has to agree with Taylor that Lijphart went too far in describing post-1994 South Africa as a consociational democracy. In addition to all the features that Taylor identified, it must be noted that the two-thirds majority required to amend the Constitution cannot be conceived of as a minority veto, because, as has been repeatedly demonstrated in national, provincial and local elections, the ANC has easily enough support to achieve the two-thirds mandate that it requires. Recognition of this fact was perhaps one of the reasons why the National Party eventually dropped its demand that compulsory power sharing be entrenched in the Constitution. Moreover, the National Party formally withdrew from the government of national unity in June 1996, and the final Constitution jettisoned all of the power-sharing concessions agreed to in 1993. None of this had any dramatic impact on South Africa's political stability.

Phase two: finalising the Constitution

In any event, the Interim Constitution was replaced by the Constitution of the Republic of South Africa (Act 108 of 1996), which was drawn up by the constituent assembly (comprised of both houses of parliament), ratified by the Constitutional Court, and signed into law by President Mandela on 18 December 1996. The post-apartheid state established by the constituent assembly involves a three-tier institutional and governance architecture under the authority of the Constitution.

The national parliament is a bicameral legislature, composed of the national assembly and the national council of provinces. The national assembly consists of 400 members, made up equally of members represented on parties' national and regional lists, and who are elected on a system of proportional representation. The national council of provinces comprises 90 members, 10 from each of the provinces, nominated by parties, but elected by the provincial legislatures in proportion to the regional representativeness of parties. Legislation, other than Bills relating to finance, may be introduced in either of the houses and passed by an ordinary majority. Should a conflict emerge between bills passed in the national assembly and the national council of provinces, such draft legislation is referred to a conference committee comprising members of all the parliamentary parties, after which it is referred to a joint session of both houses where it may be passed by a majority of the members of the legislature. The national assembly has primacy in financial legislation, and has the right to adopt such legislation (after a second review) even if the national council of provinces rejects it. Laws affecting the powers and function of provinces have to be passed by both houses, and require the consent of the majority of representatives from the affected provinces (Republic of South Africa, 1996: Chapter 4).

Executive authority is vested in the president, who is elected by a joint sitting of both houses of parliament. The president exercises this authority via a Cabinet s/he appoints. Cabinet

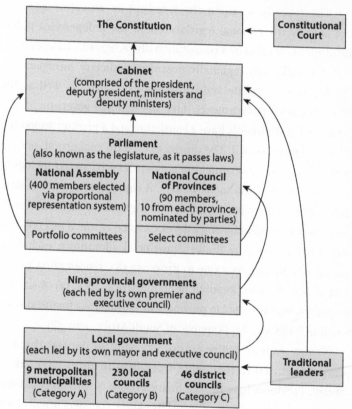

Figure 1: An overview of South Africa's governance structure

ministers account to parliament for the decisions and effectiveness of their ministries in two ways – firstly via portfolio committees in the national assembly and secondly via select committees to the national council of provinces. In addition to appointing and chairing the Cabinet, the president is responsible for appointing people to a range of independent institutions including the chief justice, the auditor general, the public protector and ombudsman, as well as commissioners to the Human Rights Commission, the Commission for Gender Equality, the Electoral Commission and the National Language Board.

Theoretically, a strong check is kept on executive authority not only by the national legislature and the independent public institutions, but also by a constitutionally recognised, independent, and nationally and regionally organised judiciary incorporating the supreme, appellate and constitutional courts, as well as the nine provincial governments. Like the national government, the provincial governments have a legislature and a premier supported by an executive council. The provinces exercise 'concurrent' powers with the national government in almost all social arenas including education, health, and social welfare. A significant amount of state expenditure is therefore channelled through provincial government, which is conceived as having a developmental as much as a political role. In the 2012/2013 Budget, provincial allocations, excluding conditional allocations, came to R309 057 382, representing 32 per cent of total revenue (Republic of South Africa, 2012: 52). A similar proportion was allocated to provinces in the previous financial year, totalling R288 492 831 (Republic of South Africa, 2011: 58).

Critics such as Butler (2009: 117) point to the fact that the provincial structure represents federalism in form rather than content. Provinces have limited financial powers with most of their budget made up of national transfers. These transfers are decided upon by a budget council, comprising representatives of the treasury and provincial finance ministers advised by the Finance and Fiscal Commission. Only 20 per cent of the provincial budget is spent on exclusive competencies – ambulance services, abattoirs, liquor licences and the like – as set out Schedule 5 of the Constitution. Thus the provinces spend most of their budgets on issues that fall under the concurrent jurisdiction of national and provincial government, and in which the former dominates largely through the mechanism of the ruling party (Butler, 2009: 114). All of this, critics argue, leads to a limited federalism and ensures that the structure of authority is similar to a unitary system of government.

The third sphere of government is the municipalities, where development dilemmas left by apartheid manifest in their starkest form. There are 282 municipalities divided into three categories. Category A covers the nine metropolitan municipalities – Johannesburg, Cape Town, eThekwini (Durban), Nelson Mandela (Port Elizabeth), Tshwane (Pretoria), Ekurhuleni (East Rand), Buffalo City (East London), Mangaung (Bloemfontein), and Msunduzi (Pietermaritzburg). To differing degrees, these are characterised by a diverse local economy, population density and a tax base (Nyalunga, 2006; see also Butler, 2009). Holding legislative and executive authority and empowered to collect funds via a tariff system for household services, these metropolitan municipalities sometimes have budgets larger than the provinces in which they are located. They are seen as development nodes, responsible for half of the country's population and two-thirds of its GDP (Parnell and Pieterse, 2010). This economic prominence has led to tensions between some provinces and their cities, complicating the 'coordinated governance' between the national, provincial and local spheres.

Category B and C municipalities represent local councils and district councils respectively. There are 230 Category B local councils or municipalities located around small towns and cities across the country. These are located within, and share authority with, the 46 Category C district councils. This collective decision making is meant to ensure that resources from the relatively well-resourced urban areas are transferred to their more impoverished surroundings, thus addressing historical inequities (Nyalunga, 2006). Yet almost two decades after the fall of apartheid, these same inequities continue to provoke blame and recriminations from all sides.

All municipalities elect councils every five years. The councils then elect a speaker, a mayor and an executive council. These elected officials interact with national and provincial government, and oversee the functioning of municipal executives and employees. A municipal manager is appointed to serve as chief accounting officer in each municipality. The municipalities are primarily responsible for the provision of services, including the delivery and billing for water and electricity, and waste disposal. In addition, they are meant to promote local economic development and achieve financial viability. This latter responsibility is what has made local governments the focus of citizens' wrath. Confronted with the challenge of financial viability, local government officials have prioritised cost recovery over the provision of services (McDonald and Pape, 2002; Naidoo, 2010). Challenging under any circumstances, this has been perceived as particularly insensitive in communities with high levels of unemployment and poor living conditions. Their rebellion has mainly taken the form of avoiding or refusing to make payments, and on many occasions it has exploded into violent popular protest. The resulting standoff has paralysed the municipal authorities and pushed many of them into financial and technical insolvency.

Phase three: state centralisation under Thabo Mbeki

The final evolution in the institutional architecture of the post-apartheid state occurred in 1999, at the dawn of Thabo Mbeki's presidential tenure. Following the recommendations of the Presidential Review Commission (led by Vincent Maphai), which identified the lack of coordination within government as the main obstacle to developmental efficiency in the state (Presidential Review Commission, 1998), a series of reforms sought to place the presidency at the heart of governance and public management. This involved the establishment of three new systems.

The first was a committee managed by an office within the presidency made up of cabinet members that clustered related national and provincial departments to enable coherent planning. The second was the Policy Coordination and Advisory Services, set up to consider proposed legislation prior to its review by Cabinet, and to monitor the implementation thereof. The third was a new Cabinet portfolio, a Minister in the Office of the President, to facilitate the management of the presidency's larger role. In effect, these reforms centralised power at the apex of the political system and diluted constitutional checks on executive authority.

As noted earlier, the Zuma presidency has so far not changed the institutional architecture in any fundamental ways. Zuma increased the number of Cabinet ministers to 34 and deployed two additional ministers in the presidency, one responsible for national planning and the other for monitoring and evaluation. But these adjustments have not fundamentally changed the broader institutional architecture, and the power and lines of authority within the state have continued as before.

In any case, despite developing an institutional architecture for the current South African state that was probably most appropriate to the circumstances of the post-apartheid moment – federal in form, but ultimately unitary in substance – the ANC government has been subjected to severe criticism for its lack of efficiency and accountability.

The erosion of political accountability

Democracy is essentially about producing political accountability. It is supposed to make political elites relatively more responsive to the collective interests of the citizenry. Democrats do not see democracy as a panacea for all evils. History is replete with examples of majorities that have supported autocrats and colluded in their own oppression or the oppression of others. However, when citizens wish to change their political circumstances, democracy can at least provide the leverage and mechanisms that make it possible for them to do so – either by encouraging existing political elites to become responsive to citizens' desires, or enabling citizens to replace political elites with more forthcoming and supportive leaders.

There is of course a huge debate about the essential aims of democracy. At one end of the spectrum are those who see it as enabling economic development and even social justice. Nowhere is this perspective captured more succinctly than by Amartya Sen in his book *Development as Freedom* (2000). Sen argues that political freedom (read democracy) enables economic growth and development by 'enhancing the hearing the people get in expressing and supporting their claims' (Sen, 1999: 5). At the other end of the spectrum, many scholars argue that the moral and ethical obligations imposed on democracies should be reduced. Nevertheless, even scholars who share Schumpeter's (1942) conception of democracy (Przeworski, 1999; Roemer, 1999; Shapiro and Hacker-Cordón, 1999), or other minimalist interpretations (Lijphart, 1977; Pettit, 1999), acknowledge that democracies should, in theory, establish relatively more robust lines of accountability between rulers and citizens than other political systems.

But democracies do not guarantee the responsiveness of elites to citizens. This is a weakness of Sen's work. He assumes that democracies always achieve a dispersal of power, promote a culture of discussion and debate, and ultimately enhance the leverage of citizens in their claims and demands on political elites. The growing literature on illiberal or delegative democracies (O'Donnell, 1993; 1994), or even neo-patrimonialism (Bratton and Van de Walle, 1994; 1997),[11] suggests the existence of too many formal democracies where this is not the case, and where representative political systems have been sufficiently weakened to enable power to be centralised in a leader or leadership with differing degrees of aversion to accountability. Thus political accountability cannot be taken for granted, but must be actively promoted in both new and established democracies.

The role of political uncertainty

A substantial body of literature addresses precisely this issue. Returning to the classical elements of democracy, various scholars highlight the need for competitive political systems to ensure that political elites remain accountable to their citizens. Robert Dahl (1966) made the case for democratic oppositions three decades ago in his pioneering study entitled *Political Oppositions in Western Democracies*. Indeed, his central thesis has not been persuasively challenged since then. Rather, it has been supported and corroborated by a range of other studies that followed the publication of his comprehensive work (Barker, 1971; Blondel, 1997; Epstein, 1967; Huntington, 1991; Moore Jr, 1989). Most recently, Dahl's thesis about the centrality of challenge and opposition for accountability in democratic systems has re-emerged in the work of Andreas Schedler. Following Dahl, Schedler (2001) argues that political uncertainty is the essence of democracy and draws a distinction between what he terms institutional and substantive uncertainty. He argues that the former, which he views as involving the rules of the game, is bad for democracy. The latter, which, relates to political elites being uncertain about their continuity in office, is good for democracy, as it is precisely this kind of uncertainty, Schedler argues, that forces political elites to become responsive to the needs and wishes of citizens.[12]

Of course, the uncertainty that Schedler promotes has to be conditional if it is to be systemically beneficial. It must occur within an overall context of commonality – a democratic constitution widely supported by the citizenry, for instance – if the uncertainty is not to produce instability and dictatorship. But if uncertainty emerges within such a commonality, then it has the net effect of dispersing power in the society. And it is precisely this dispersal of power that enhances citizens' leverage over political elites, thereby establishing a dynamic of accountability within the society.

But what facilitates substantive uncertainty and the associated dispersal of power? There are several mechanisms and factors that can be identified, and they will be considered in subsequent chapters. For now, two distinct sources will be focused on, namely: (i) the separation of powers and, in particular, parliamentary oversight over the executive, and (ii) the rotation in office that emerges from a viable parliamentary opposition. Both of these are seriously lacking in South Africa.

An electoral system that favours party leaders and the lack of a viable opposition

South Africa has a strong proportional electoral system at both the national and provincial level. This was strongly supported across the ideological divide at the dawn of South Africa's democratic transition because it enabled the maximum number of parties to be represented in the legislature. This positive feature, however, is counterbalanced by the empowerment of party leadership over rank and file legislative representatives. The fact that electoral votes are cast for a party rather than individual candidates, and that party leaderships largely determine parliamentary lists, severely weakens the accountability of legislative representatives to their constituencies (Gumede, 2012;

Mattes and Southall, 2004). Indeed, as the ninth COSATU congress recognised, accountability is structured hierarchically to party leaders, and this encourages individual legislative representatives to act, not with their conscience, but in line with party diktat (COSATU 2006). This has been tragically evident in the arms deal scandal in which legislative representatives, in violation of their constitutional mandates, colluded with the executive to cover up both ethical violations and corruption (see Feinstein, 2007).

The succession dispute between Mbeki and Zuma had the effect of loosening the ruling party's control for a short while. Ruling party MPs suddenly found their voices and asserted their legislative independence. In the last few days of the Mbeki presidency and in the first few months of the Zuma one, ministers suddenly found themselves having to account to the parliamentary portfolio committees. This led to more than one spat between portfolio chairs and ministers, the most high profile of which was the showdown between former defence minister, Lindiwe Sisulu, and the former chair of the portfolio committee on defence, Mnyamezeli Booi. But, as was evident in the controversy over the Protection of Information Bill, the ruling party soon reasserted control. Dissenting opinion within the ANC was brought into line as rebel MPs were hauled before disciplinary hearings. The effect of this has been to bully the legislature and undermine the constitutionally enshrined legislative check on executive authority.

The prospects for a viable opposition are no better. At present, South Africa has all the institutional characteristics of a robust democratic political order. Yet its political system cannot be interpreted as competitive. The ANC dominates overwhelmingly in terms of electoral support. The party increased its winning margin in each of the first three consecutive national elections, gaining 62.65 per cent in 1994, 66.36 per cent in 1999 and just shy of 70 per cent of the votes in 2004. In the 2009 elections, support for the ANC came down to 66 per cent. The ruling party lost support in every major province except KwaZulu-Natal, where it increased its support from 46 per cent to 63 per cent (Habib and Schulz-Herzenberg, 2011: 194). For a while the emergence of the Congress of the People (COPE) created some optimism that a level of fluidity might emerge in electoral support for parties. But leadership battles soon fractured the new party and led to a dramatic reduction in its appeal. Moreover, while the official opposition, the Democratic Alliance, increased its electoral support from 12 per cent to 16 per cent, and won control of the Western Cape province, it is still too weak to constitute a serious challenge to the ANC. Thus, South Africa has no viable political opposition, and there is no prospect of one emerging from the collection of parties currently represented in the national legislature (Habib and Schulz-Herzenberg, 2011; Habib and Taylor, 2001).

How do we explain this lack of viable parliamentary opposition? Political scientists of a conservative or liberal bent, many of whom are associated with the official opposition, tend to lay the blame on South Africa's electorate. Arguing that racial identity informs electoral behaviour, they hold that citizens are not willing to vote for a party with a white leader. This perspective has come under severe criticism in the post-1994 era. A range of scholars have offered alternative explanations of electoral behaviour suggesting that electoral outcomes can be accounted for, from a rational choice perspective, through an analysis of economic interests and popular evaluations of government.

In 2011, Collette Schulz-Herzenberg and I, based on the former's detailed doctoral study of opinion surveys and electoral results, accounted for the poor electoral performance of South African opposition parties in the 2009 elections through the notion of party imagery. We argued that

> Policies and electoral messages, the rhetoric of its leaders, their behaviour, the language used in meetings,

> its engagements in the body politic – essentially what
> are component elements of party imagery, or what
> Trilling describes as mental images that voters have of
> parties – is what determines whether voters perceive a
> party as inclusive of their interests, and thereby become
> open to the possibility of voting for it. (Habib and
> Schulz Herzenberg, 2011: 199–200)

We hold that the Democratic Alliance's imagery, one of representing minorities and the rich and privileged in society, may have enabled it to consolidate its support in its traditional constituencies and thereby win the Western Cape and continue as the official opposition, but suggest that this image will be a liability in its future endeavours to weave a national electoral majority. In a subsequent newspaper article on the 2011 local government elections, I lauded Democratic Alliance leader Helen Zille's efforts to transform the party's image, through appealing to liberation symbols, profiling a diverse, mainly female leadership, and using Xhosa together with Afrikaans and English at party rallies and in the media. All of this will hold the party in good stead and helps to account for the fact that its electoral footprint across the country had risen to 24 per cent by 2011 (*New Age*, 24/05/2011).

Zille's aggressive attempts to transform the Democratic Alliance continued apace after the 2011 local government elections, most notably through the appointment of Patricia de Lille as mayor of Cape Town and Lindiwe Mazibuko as leader of the opposition in the national legislature. Although these efforts are undeniably progressive, necessary, and nationally significant, the Democratic Alliance is unlikely to offer a serious electoral threat to the ANC in the short term. In the medium to long term, these changes may position the Democratic Alliance more favourably in the eyes of the entire electorate.

The only other prospect for a viable parliamentary opposition – a break in the Tripartite Alliance leading to COSATU and the SACP going it alone – is even more remote. In Chapter Seven, I consider the value of both a viable opposition party and a break in the Tripartite Alliance. For now, it is simply worth noting that such a break is not on the cards in the near future because neither the leaders nor the members of COSATU or the SACP would support such a move. In relation to COSATU, this has been consistently demonstrated via three surveys conducted between 1994 and 2006 by a group of scholars loosely associated with the Sociology of Work Programme (SWOP) at the University of Witwatersrand in Johannesburg. Each survey showed that more than two-thirds of COSATU's rank and file supported the alliance (Buhlungu, 2006).

Thus a viable parliamentary opposition is unlikely to emerge in the near future from either the current opposition parties or the COSATU/SACP axis within the Tripartite Alliance. This, together with the centralising effects of the proportional electoral system, blunts any possibility for the emergence of substantive uncertainty within the ruling political elites. The dynamic of accountability between the elites and citizens is likely to remain weak, with all of the concomitant consequences, including continued corruption, the aloofness of the ruling party, popular cynicism and sporadic revolts.

Behind the service delivery crisis

South Africa has been described as the protest capital of the world. Peter Alexander, Research Professor of Social Change at the University of Johannesburg, dates the current phase of local resistance to 2004, when 8 004 protests were recorded. Using data from a range of sources including the South African Police and Hotspots Monitor (run by a private research agency, Municipal

IQ), he notes that the number of protests increased to 10 437 in 2005. Whereas they came down slightly between 2006 and 2009, they have skyrocketed since Jacob Zuma came to power. Alexander estimates that in the first seven months of Zuma's presidency, local protests fuelled by service delivery and accountability concerns exceeded the total number in the last three years of Mbeki's rule (Alexander, 2010: 28). This leads him to conclude that the current phenomenon in South Africa represents a 'rebellion of the poor' (Alexander, 2010: 37).

Alexander's conclusion is shared by a number of academics (see Atkinson, 2007; Booysen, 2007; and Pithouse, 2007), who provide a rich empirical account of protests directed mainly at local government in contemporary South Africa. More significantly, the parlous state of the public service and its consequences for the legitimacy of the state and the living conditions of its citizens is recognised in both the *Diagnostic Overview* and the *National Development Plan: Vision for 2030* released by the National Planning Commission (NPC, 2011; 2012). Indeed, the *National Development Plan* makes a number of recommendations aimed at professionalising the public service (NPC, 2012: 408–443). These include:

- the appointment of a head of the civil service to whom heads of other departments should report on administrative matters;
- the development of a strategy to recruit graduates and enhance skills;
- appointments at lower levels to be determined simply on an administrative and merit basis;
- the clarification of the lines of accountability within the intergovernmental system and between departments and boards of state-owned enterprises; and
- the centralisation of large-scale and long-term tenders, and the banning of certain types of business activities by officials in an effort to strengthen the fight against corruption.

Despite the technocratic tenor of its approach, the plan does make some valuable recommendations but the state is unlikely to comprehensively address the malaise in the public service, unless it honestly acknowledges the root causes of its service delivery failures.

The commonly held view among a significant section of the citizenry, including powerful stakeholders such as the business sector, is that the public service is incapable of fulfilling its obligations because of a lack of capacity among civil servants – itself a consequence of affirmative action or the state's misguided cadre-deployment policy (CDE, 2009). It is argued that in such circumstances, corruption runs rampant and is not dealt with firmly because of party loyalties or inefficiencies in the system. As a result, citizens are denied basic services, become demoralised, and the post-apartheid democracy runs the risk of becoming delegitimised.

But is this diagnosis and prognosis not too easy? It assumes that the civil service under apartheid was adequately resourced and capable of delivering services to the citizenry. A fair body of evidence suggests that this was not the case (see Posel, 1999), and one needs merely to note that the apartheid state was organised to service a minority and suppress a majority; it was in no position to deliver on the aspirations of the post-apartheid regime. It is also worth bearing in mind that transforming the civil service such that it becomes demographically representative is important for the overall legitimacy of the system. It is thus difficult to sustain the argument that suggests South Africa would have been better off had the civil service been left intact.

Nevertheless, this should not prevent us from acknowledging the serious deficiencies in the public service, or that these derive partly from the policies and choices of the post-apartheid government. I would argue that there are four distinct causes of the malaise in the public service, two of which are identified by the National Planning Commission's development plan.

Blurred boundaries and lack of clarity between spheres of government

First, as the Commission recognises, the blurred boundaries between spheres of government, and the lack of clarity in the lines of authority between them, is a serious impediment to the efficient functioning of the civil service. It is worth noting that the lack of housing is one of the major causes of local protests. Although housing is a provincial and national responsibility municipal authorities are almost always the ones targeted in housing protests. This fact, together with the daily examples of disaggregated planning (where, for instance, housing infrastructure is coordinated by provincial government without due cognisance being given to the necessary water, electricity, sanitation and waste removal infrastructure, which is planned and managed by municipal authorities) suggests that there is a serious need for clarification in the roles and responsibilities of the various structures and spheres of government (NPC, 2012: 55–56; 429–442).

Corruption

Corruption is the second causal factor recognised by the National Planning Commission. It is worth noting that the Commission's plan bravely acknowledges that one of the biggest obstacles here is the lack of political will. It explicitly states that unless those who have been corrupt are dealt with efficiently and transparently, no matter how close these individuals may be to political power, state anti-corruption initiatives will never gain the legitimacy they need to succeed, nor will they facilitate the development of an institutional culture within the civil service that challenges and exposes corruption (NPC, 2012: 56–57). As mentioned earlier, the Commission proposed the reorganisation of the tender process so that large, long-term tenders are centralised at the national level where they can be subjected to greater scrutiny. It also proposed that civil servants be legally prevented from involvement in certain business ventures, and that the assets of corrupt officials be liable for seizure (NPC, 2012: 447–452).

Affirmative action and cadre deployment in the civil service

The third factor (and one that the National Planning Commission did not adequately address) is the impact of the implementation of affirmative action and cadre deployment on the quality of personnel in the civil service (see Terreblanche, 2012: Chapter 5). The Planning Commission clearly recognises the problem given its detailed discussion on 'stabilising the political-administrative interface' and its recommendation that lower-level appointments be made purely on a merit basis (NPC, 2012: 410–416). Unfortunately, the Commission does not comprehensively address the challenge posed by the conflict between appointing a civil service only on merit and one that is demographically representative. Of course, these are not mutually exclusive goals, but they are in tension, at least temporarily, in a society where skills sets remain largely racially defined as a result of the segregated educational opportunities of the past.

Perhaps this tension is best reflected in the work of sociologist, Karl von Holdt, who is also a member of the National Planning Commission. Von Holdt's path-breaking work on public hospitals, and Baragwanath Hospital in Soweto in particular, highlights the tension within the nationalist project between the imperative 'to establish a modern, effective bureaucracy', and the competing drive 'to subvert the dominance of whites and the apartheid system ... and promote the rapid formation of a new black elite' (2010: 5). The formation of a new black elite manifests itself in various ways, including: (i) a focus on staff mobility and class formation through mechanisms of affirmative action and black economic empowerment; (ii) an ambivalence towards skills as these are tied to racial power and inheritance; (iii) a continuous need to save 'face' which inhibits a frank understanding of the true state of affairs on the ground; (iii) hierarchical controls divorced from local institutional accountability; (iv) overall ambivalence towards authority, as reflected in the unions' assertion of power over the workplace; and (v) centralised budgetary protocols that are generally out of touch with real requirements. All of this, Von Holdt maintains, undermines the effectiveness and functionality of the post-apartheid bureaucracy, thereby compromising both its service delivery responsibility and the possibility for the emergence of a development state. His solution is the recasting of the nationalist imperative to make 'the needs of the people' its primary responsibility, while still enabling elite formation (2010: 24).

Two conclusions flow from this. First, the National Planning Commission's solution of giving senior officials full authority to appoint staff in their divisions, in the absence of the rewriting of the nationalist agenda, is unlikely to have the intended effect simply because these officials will also reflect the 'class formation' rather than the 'service delivery' imperative. Second, as Von Holdt implicitly recognises, affirmative action alone cannot be blamed for the state of the post-apartheid public service. Rather it is the coupling of affirmative action with conservative macro-economic policies and the infusion of a corporate ethic into the public service that collectively generated this state of affairs (Habib, 2004; Chipkin, 2008). Any transfer of skills and capacity, it should be borne in mind, involves two distinct processes: training and mentorship. The adoption of the Growth, Employment, and Redistribution Strategy (GEAR) circumvented this process (Streak, 2004). GEAR required cuts in state expenditure that meant a reduction in the numbers of state employees at the very point at which the state had to be demographically transformed. As black staff were being recruited to the civil service, incumbents, mainly white, were being allowed and even encouraged to exit the system. The net effect was not only a loss of institutional memory but also a sabotage of the skills-transfer process. The very people who could have played the role of mentors were no longer in the public service. Black recruits, particularly newly qualified young graduates from the universities, were set up for failure as they entered the public service.

This process has played out particularly tragically in the education sector. Driven by a desire to cut costs, the education department began to retrench teachers in the second half of the 1990s. Trying to avoid an adversarial process, it offered a voluntary severance package to teachers. Not surprisingly, the best teachers in the system took up the offer (Afrimap and OSF-SA, 2007: ix), leaving the least qualified teachers in the system. The capacity of the public education system declined significantly with consequences that we are still living with today. Von Holdt (2010: 22) graphically detailed a similar trajectory in public hospitals and concluded that the economic orthodoxy had had a 'destructive impact on the capacity (including financial capacity) of many service delivery departments such as Health'. Indeed, the process has played itself out in department after department in the post-apartheid state. The only ones that seem to have avoided this fate are the treasury and the South African Revenue Service (SARS), both of which have played crucial roles in relation to the economic ambitions of the post-apartheid state.

Cadre deployment has aggravated the situation. The ANC, ironically in this case, following the traditional Marxist revolutionary tradition that sees the state as merely an agency for capture by the party, established a deployment committee to manage the deployment of cadres to the public service (Mbeki, 2006b). Deployment of course happens in all countries and need not be antithetical to democracy. But if it is to be consistent with democracy, the boundaries for deployment must be established and respected. Simply put, deployment is permissible when it is confined to political appointments (ministers, deputy ministers) and the most senior levels of the public service (perhaps directors general). But the deployment of cadres undertaken by the ANC (sometimes with, and at other times without, the consent of the party leadership) has extended across the entire apparatus of the state.

In the post-Polokwane period, the problem has been further aggravated by factional rather than cadre deployment. Essentially, personnel in state institutions have been replaced not only by ANC members, but by members of whichever faction within the ruling party is in control of the particular state institution. Joel Netshitenzhe, previous head of the Government Communication Information Service, and one of the more authoritative voices in the Mbeki presidency, has suggested that this factional deployment has become a major obstacle to both state efficiency and the realisation of the development state because of the turnover in public officials, and the resultant loss of institutional memory that it promotes.[13] This is perhaps the primary reason why the National Planning Commission was prompted to highlight the need for a professional civil service, and recommend that senior officials be granted the authority to appoint staff in their departments, and that their reporting on administrative matters be directed to a head of the civil service (NPC, 2012: 55). In any case, in such circumstances where cadre deployment becomes the norm, party or even factional loyalty rather than skill sets become the defining criteria for state employment.

Added to this mix, has been the infusion of a corporate ethic into public institutions. To be fair, the principles of new public administration predated the ANC's ascension to power. Part of a worldwide phenomenon that emerged from schools of public administration in the United States and Britain, these principles have infected most parts of the public service sector across the globe. Their particular manifestations in South Africa have included an expansion of managerial layers within the state, a growing inequality in the remuneration between public sector managers and employees and the widespread use of quantitative performance management systems uncritically adopted from the private sector (Naidoo, 2008; Chipkin, 2008). With regard to the latter, quantitative benchmarks were established for transformation targets to which annual bonuses were tied. One of the perverse consequences of this was that it paid a public service manager not to appoint a white candidate to a vacancy, even if no black candidate was available, since employing a white candidate would compromise that manager's transformation targets and annual bonus. Despite the fact that such behaviour violates the very spirit of South Africa's Constitution, the quantitative character of the performance management system imparted to public sector managers a rationality that made it logical for them to leave vacancies unfilled rather than appoint white candidates to the positions (Bentley and Habib, 2008).

The net effect of coupling affirmative action with conservative economics and the infusion of corporate ethics into the public service was to severely compromise the capacities of the civil servants and hobble their ability to deliver services to citizens. Not only is the public service now saddled with employees who have severe deficiencies in their skill sets, but there are also too many individuals working for the state as deployees for other ends, including the procurement of state tenders. Corruption has spread throughout the system, further compromising the capacity of the state and delegitimising it particularly at local government level.

Inadequate resources

But one must guard against implying that the service delivery problematique is simply about corruption and the skills deficits of state employees. This then raises the fourth causal factor accounting for the dysfunctionality of public institutions (and this is another issue that the National Planning Commission does not sufficiently address), namely, the lack of adequate resources and the associate institutional crises that this promotes. This might seem surprising given the conventional wisdom that has developed in state, business and public administration circles suggesting resources are not the problem. After all, many departments regularly fail to spend their allocated resources and the state has run a surplus in a number of years (I return to this in Chapter Three). But failure to spend departmental budgets should not automatically lead to the conclusion that there is adequate resourcing, especially in public institutions that suffer from a capacity deficit. Von Holdt's study of public hospitals, cited earlier, offers dramatic empirical evidence not only of under-budgeting but also of the systematic under-financing of the public health system. Similarly, the earlier example of the education department's decisions, influenced by considerations underpinning GEAR, suggests that one should not conclude public institutions have sufficient resources to fulfil their mandate. Instead, the surpluses generated by the state in earlier years, or the small deficits they hope to achieve in years to come, may actually be indications of incapacity within the state. When this incapacity is adequately addressed, the lack of financial resources is likely to be recognised as a serious obstacle to effective service delivery.

In my view, therefore, a real analysis of the capacity deficit in the public service must look beyond the popular conservative view that it is simply a product of cadre deployment and affirmative action run amok. It also needs to see past the National Planning Commission's more technocratic analysis, which sees the problem as resulting from corruption and a lack of clarification of the roles of various state institutions. Instead, this analysis, while wary of the racialised tenor of some of the former explanations, and the narrow technocratic approach of the latter, nevertheless builds on some of their valid explanatory elements to conclude that the capacity deficits in the public service are a result of a complex array of factors. The most important of these are the blurred boundaries and lines of authority between spheres and institutions of government, corruption, inappropriately skilled public servants and inadequate allocation of resources. Furthermore, the skills deficit in the public service can only be substantively understood as a product of a nationalist imperative that prioritises class formation above service delivery as the key imperative of statecraft. The combination of cadre (and in some cases factional) deployment, an affirmative action policy that is coupled to a conservative macro-economic programme, and the infusion of a corporate ethic within the state, all contribute to the proliferation of vacancies in public institutions, the appointment of under-qualified personnel and the subversion of the mentorship that is necessary in any skills-transfer process. The net outcome has been a service delivery crisis that has compromised the image of the state and subverted its goal of ensuring inclusive and equitable development.

The challenge

The accountability deficit and service delivery crisis in South Africa cannot be understood solely through the lens of institutional design or human capacity. Indeed, the country's institutional architecture – which takes the form of a federal political system with lines of authority and delegation of powers typical of a unitary system – is probably the most appropriate for the South African context. On its own, changing the institutional architecture will not resolve the problems of accountability and state capacity. Neither will these problems be resolved by enhancing skill sets or even replacing the current civil service cohort with more technically trained and efficient personnel. The question that needs to be asked is why unskilled people were appointed in the first place.

In the preceding pages, I analysed the accountability deficit, describing how the electoral system enhances the power of ruling party bureaucrats and undermines the legislative arm of government;

that is, the authority of local MPs and parliament. I noted that the lack of a viable opposition party reduces the substantive uncertainty of the ruling party thereby weakening its responsiveness to citizens.

The lack of capacity in the civil service was explained through issues of institutional design, such as the blurred boundaries between spheres of government. Lack of capacity is, however, also a product of policy and behavioural choices such as the particular ways in which affirmative action has been implemented, the specific decisions with regard to the deployment of resources and the lack of political will to tackle corruption – all of which are related to the accountability dynamics that prevail in South African society. What to do about these issues is reflected upon further in Chapter Seven, where I discuss the elements of a political agenda that has the potential to consolidate democracy and enable the emergence of an inclusive development programme. Before this, however, it is essential to explain how the lack of accountability and the incapacities of the civil service have affected the policy choices and behavioural traits of political elites, and how these have determined the living conditions of ordinary citizens. One of the more important of these is South Africa's macro-economic policy, which I discuss in the next chapter.

3

The political economy of development

Economic policy has never been simply a technical, neutral exercise devised by impartial bureaucrats, and, in the modern world, the relationship between politics and economics has become ever more apparent and explicit. The nature of economic policy is determined by political variables and economic interests influence state priorities as much as the availability of material resources. Thus the adoption and legitimation of economic policies represents the advancement of political as well as economic interests, and the implications of economic policy are as much political as they are socio-economic. It can therefore be argued that the art of generating and implementing a particular set of economic policies is, at one level, merely 'the continuation of politics by other means'.[1]

This 'continuation of politics' acquires added significance in societies that are in transition to a new political order. Political transitions enable different social groups to enter the political arena in new ways, and this creates possibilities for significant changes in economic policy. South Africa's democratic transition is a typical example. The debate around future economic policies became one of the central contests between contending social groups and political organisations. The contest revolved around three key issues: growth, poverty alleviation and inequality. The goals of growth and poverty alleviation are widely shared across the political spectrum but political actors have very different views on how to achieve these goals. Some believe in unhindered markets, whereas others argue for market regulation and the containment of excesses, but almost all recognise the moral and strategic responsibility of tackling these problems.

Inequality is another matter. Many political actors, some explicitly and others implicitly, believe that inequality is part of the modern economic condition, and a necessary price to pay for economic growth and poverty alleviation. Chaudhuri and Ravallion (2006), for example, cite the examples of the United States, and more recently China and India, to sustain their argument. Others, such as Stiglitz (2012) draw on western Europe's social democracies and developing states in South East Asia, to argue that that inequality can be reduced with appropriate policies and interventions if it is twinned with poverty alleviation and sustainable economic growth.

Both perspectives are evident in the policy debates and public discourse in South Africa. But the appropriateness and relevance of these two perspectives for South Africa cannot be determined solely at a theoretical level; they must be considered in the light of contemporary realities. The country's social structures, the absolute levels of its poverty and inequality, their racial character, and the recentness of our political transition, make South Africa a fundamentally different place from the United States, western Europe, China, India and even the developing states of South East Asia. Further increases in economic inequality could have a very different impact on the social structure and political stability of the state, in part because its social inheritance was so unequal.[2] Inequalities polarise societies, and it is hard to imagine South Africa sustainably addressing its social pathologies – violent crime, the abuse of women and children, racial tension – or even HIV and AIDS and the service delivery crises without a sustained reduction in both inequality and poverty.

Perhaps this reality has ensured that the goal of addressing inequality has never been officially challenged within the African National Congress (ANC), even though some in the ANC's national executive committee, the presidency and the treasury may have harboured the thought. Yet, as two separate studies have shown, inequality increased significantly in the first term (1994–1999) and early second term (1999–2001) of ANC rule, (with the Gini coefficient rising from 0.672 to 0.685) and it has remained stable since then (Leibrandt et al., 2010: 18–19 and Van der Berg, 2010: 12). In terms of poverty, the picture is slightly less dismal. While the two studies show that poverty increased in the second half of the 1990s, this figure has subsequently declined, largely because of the massive expansion of social support grants (Leibrandt et al., 2010: 15; Van der Berg, 2010: 13).

But how can this disjuncture between the ANC's policy goals and actual outcomes be explained?

A critical reflection on economic policy in post-apartheid South Africa reveals three distinct phases in its evolution: (i) the implementation of the Growth, Employment and Redistribution Strategy (GEAR) from 1996 to 2001, pioneered by Thabo Mbeki and Trevor Manuel and implemented mainly during Mandela's presidency; (ii) the massive expansion of the social-support grant system, and the building of the black middle and upper classes during Mbeki's years as president (1999–2007); and (iii) the post-Polokwane period under Jacob Zuma (from 2008).

Several critics, particularly those of a more left-leaning perspective, would question this categorisation. For instance, Hein Marais (2011) and Vishwas Satgar (2008), despite their other differences,[3] agree that economic policy in the post-apartheid period has consistently reflected an attempt by the ruling class to restructure the terms of a new hegemonic growth trajectory. The difference between the three periods, they argue, is one of degree rather than substance. There is some basis to their argument, but by looking only for substantive ruptures in policy rather than more nuanced shifts, they miss not only the real impacts on the daily lives of citizens, but also the strategic opportunities that can be utilised to enhance the emergence of an inclusive development path in

South Africa. Before reflecting on these nuances, it is necessary to understand why the political elites in the post-apartheid era made particular choices and the implications thereof for citizens as well as for the ruling party and its leadership.

The shift to GEAR

Apartheid bequeathed a mixed economic legacy to South Africa. On the one hand, it created appalling levels of marginalisation and immiseration structured along racial lines. Not only was this morally reprehensible, but it also placed limits on the sustainability of the country's economic growth. Bantu education – one of apartheid's most notorious policies – compromised the development of South Africa's human resources, leaving a legacy of skills shortages that continue to burden the economy (Van der Berg, 2002). Similarly, the oppression and economic exploitation of the black majority stunted the emergence of a significant domestic market, thereby limiting growth in the manufacturing sector. As importantly, the industrialisation and economic development that was spurred on by the mining booms (first in Kimberly's diamond fields from 1867 and then on the Witwatersrand's gold mines from the late 1880s) and the peculiarly racialised forms of social and political rule that were developed to support these mines, imparted a minerals and energy orientation to the country's modernisation (Fine and Rustomjee, 1996). This skewed investments in the economy for over a century, leaving it an exporter of primary commodities that is competitive in manufacturing at the domestic and regional levels only.

On the other hand, South Africa inherited the continent's most advanced physical infrastructure. Its airports, harbours, railways, roads and electricity and water networks are some of the best not only on the continent, but also in the developing world. Moreover, its systems of banking, finance, higher education, information and law developed significantly, along with the skills sets of the country's white population. This led various scholars to conclude that South Africa was in a far better position than many other transitional societies to develop both a successful and efficient economy as well as a democratic polity (see Bratton and Landsberg, 1998; Shapiro, 1993).

Two economic visions vied for supremacy in the contest to transform South Africa's racially skewed economic inheritance. The first, advanced by the former ruling alliance, the National Party and the corporate sector, was a traditional neo-liberal economic programme that stressed the deregulation of financial and labour markets, the privatisation of state-owned enterprises and the integration of South Africa into the global economy. This perspective had its roots in the economic agenda that, in the late 1970s, brought together Afrikaner capital, the military and 'verligtes'[4] within the National Party behind then-president, PW Botha (Davies et al., 1985). This alliance fractured in the 1980s as a result of mass popular resistance, the state's response to it and the international isolation that followed. Botha's successor, FW de Klerk, subsequently re-established the alliance in the late 1980s and early 1990s, as he experimented with political liberalisation. After the unbanning of the ANC, the National Party put forward its neo-liberal economic agenda in *The Restructuring of the South African Economy: A Normative Model Approach* (Central Economic Advisory Services, 1993). Aiming for a GDP growth target of 4.5 per cent and a 3 per cent increase in employment, the party proposed a set of supply-side reforms, and the removal of political and social barriers that hindered the market. They argued that this would enable the economy to realise its maximum growth potential. The need for redistribution was acknowledged, but it was expected to occur inevitably (the trickle-down effect) as economic growth accelerated.

In the language of the ANC in the 1990s, this was labelled 'growth *with* redistribution'.

The second economic vision was advanced by the ANC and its allies. Rooted in the Freedom Charter, and understood as offering 'growth *through* redistribution', the aim was essentially a social-democratic one that involved, in the words of Joe Slovo, 'a mix between market and plan, with priority being allocated to the latter' (*Weekly Mail*, 30/03/1990). The vision was by no means coherently advanced. Indeed, ANC leaders issued an abundance of contradictory messages. Nelson Mandela announced his support for nationalisation soon after his release from prison, but just over a year later, in an engagement with corporate executives in the United Kingdom, he spoke out against it (*Financial Times* [London], 8/02/1992; see also Taylor, 2001: 60). Similarly, economic documents issued before the ANC's 1992 policy conference retreated from proposals related to firm controls on foreign investors that the organisation had adopted in 1990 (ANC, 1990a; 1990b; 1992c; see also Nattrass, 1994). Despite these contradictions, the ANC's economic policy proposals prior to 1994 were clearly distinct from those of the 'growth *with* redistribution' perspective.

The ANC's proposals were perhaps most coherently articulated in the reports published by the Macro Economic Research Group (MERG) and the Industrial Strategy Project, which were then the economic 'think tanks' of the Tripartite Alliance.[5] MERG advanced a ten-year plan with two distinct but equally long phases: the first led by public investment, and the second dominated by the private sector. It projected the creation of 2.5 million jobs in the ten-year life of the plan, and annual growth of 5 per cent in the second phase (MERG, 1993: 2). This growth rate was to be achieved by expanding the role of the public sector and by enabling the state to intervene to regulate the market so as to ensure that the basic needs of citizens would be met. In addition, the Reserve Bank was to be subject to political control so that monetary policy would support the state's developmental goals. The trade, corporate and industrial policy chapters of the plan were written by the Industrial Strategy Project. The focus was mainly on the manufacturing sector and it was argued that South Africa's growth prospects were largely dependent on developing a competitive export sector. The authors of these chapters were sensitive to the dangers posed by macro-economic imbalances and warned against the expansionary monetary and fiscal policies implicit in other proposals made by MERG (see Joffe et al., 1995; Kaplinsky, 1994). Nevertheless, despite these policy tensions, the ANC's proposals had a far more regulatory flavour, and were of a more social democratic hue, than those advanced by the National Party and the corporate sector.

Thus, on the eve of South Africa's first democratic election in April 1994, two distinct economic visions were being advocated. The Reconstruction and Development programme (RDP), which reflected the vision and many of the policies and targets put forward by MERG, served as the ANC's electoral manifesto. Thus many South Africans and external observers expected that, after decisively winning the election, the ANC would implement this developmental economic agenda. For a short while it seemed as if this would happen. Jay Naidoo, then general secretary of the Congress of South African Trade Unions (COSATU), was appointed by President Mandela as a minister without portfolio, but with responsibility for the RDP, and for marshalling government departments towards its implementation. But soon after the April elections ushered in the government of national unity, evidence began to emerge that the ANC in government was pursuing an economic agenda quite distinct from both the RDP and the proposals that had been put forward by MERG.

The first formal indication of this was the appointment of Derek Keys as finance minister. (Keys, a member of the National Party, had been chief executive officer of Gencor, which was then one of South Africa's largest mining conglomerates and which subsequently became part of the global resources company BHP Billiton.) Soon thereafter, the government of national unity, against the recommendations of MERG, enshrined the independence of the Reserve Bank and ignored the proposal put forward in the RDP that its board be democratised. Early in 1995, the financial rand (a separate currency for foreign investors that protected the country from currency volatility) was abolished, and four months later, in July 1995, exchange controls were eased further through asset-swap arrangements. These allowed South African corporations to invest abroad if they could secure an equal reciprocal investment in South Africa. Also in July 1995, Trevor Manuel, then minister of trade and industry, initiated an extensive liberalisation programme that dramatically reduced tariffs in a range of sectors, including vehicles, textiles, chemicals, electronics, metals, machinery and paper and furniture (*Business Day*, 13/06/1995). In December of the same year, Thabo Mbeki, then deputy president, committed the government to an extensive privatisation programme that included selling parts of Telkom, and South African Airways.

This neo-liberal economic agenda was formalised in June 1996 when the Cabinet adopted the GEAR policy, and symbolised in the closure of the RDP office, which had taken place three months earlier. GEAR followed the recommendations of a report that had been released by the South Africa Foundation – a corporate think tank (South Africa Foundation, 1996).[6] The report proposed cuts in state expenditure and the rationalisation of the public sector so as to reduce South Africa's budget deficit to 3 per cent by 1999. A series of deregulation measures were introduced, including the further liberalisation of foreign exchange and new allowances intended to attract foreign investment. Support for the privatisation of state assets was also reiterated (Department of Finance, 1996). All of this took place under the guise of supporting the RDP but, in its essential philosophical thrust, GEAR represented a fundamental departure from the ANC's 1994 election manifesto. Some scholars have questioned the labelling of GEAR as neo-liberal, on the grounds that it was accompanied by black economic empowerment and the passing of the Labour Relations Act (1995). Yet as Vishnu Padayachee and I argued in 2000, these do not 'negate the essentially neo-liberal character of the [government of national unity's] economic program. Rather, they can be seen as part of the contradictory impulses that sometimes accompany the application of neo-liberal economics, as has occurred elsewhere, including in Thatcher's Britain of the 1980s' (Habib and Padayachee, 2000: 253).

GEAR's economic impact was mixed. The programme did enable South Africa to strengthen its finances, lower its interest rates and bring inflation under control. The average annual growth rate between 1994 and 2003 averaged 2.8 per cent, up from 0.6 per cent in the last eight years of apartheid rule (Horton, 2005: 91). Inflation came down from an average of 15 per cent in the late 1980s and early 1990s, to an average annual rate of 5.2 per cent by 1999 (Van der Merwe, 2004: 1). Government debt as a percentage of GDP, which stood at 49.5 per cent in 1996, hovered in this range until about 2000, and then dropped significantly to 33 per cent by 2004, and 22.3 per cent by 2007 (PCAS, 2008: 9). Debt-service expenditure decreased accordingly from a high of 5.7 per cent in 1999 to 3.9 per cent in 2004 (Horton, 2005: 3).

These fiscal gains came at a devastating social cost, however. As indicated earlier, levels of inequality and poverty increased dramatically in the years immediately after the adoption of GEAR, although poverty levels have since reduced slightly since the early 2000s. The presidency's own data acknowledges that the percentage of people living on less than R462 (US$54) a month increased from 53 per cent in 1995 to 58 per cent in 2000. In the same period, the percentage of citizens living on less than R250 (US$29) a month increased from 31 per cent to 38 per cent (PCAS, 2008: 26). Meanwhile, inequality as measured by the Gini coefficient actually increased from 0.672 in 1993 to 0.685 in 1999. Thus the share of national income of the poorest 10 per cent of citizens remained constant over this period at 0.6 per cent, while that of the richest 20 per cent increased by 0.8 per cent from 72.9 per cent to 73.7 per cent (PCAS, 2008: 23).

How can we explain the ANC government's abandonment of its developmental vision? Two broad explanations have been offered. The first, preferred paradoxically by elements on both the left and the liberal right, focuses on state elites. Many left-wing critics believe that the ANC has sold out, even if they sometimes acknowledge that the prevailing balance of power limited real possibilities for the party (see, for example, Bond, 2000; COSATU, 2006; SACP, 2006b; Terreblanche, 2012). Those on the liberal right, such as economist Iraj Abedian (2004), seem to believe that the ANC has finally seen sense.[7] Both explanations are deficient. They both assume a homogeneity of thought and behaviour among political elites that simply cannot exist in a society in which such a significant turnover in public representatives and state personnel has occurred. But perhaps the more serious criticism of these explanations is that their almost exclusive focus on agents and actors does not recognise or sufficiently integrate the fact that individuals, parties and movements are constrained in their choices by their institutional locations and by the balance of power at any given moment.

Scholars formerly associated with MERG advance a more nuanced, yet nonetheless flawed, account within this explanatory paradigm. Their account of MERG's failure to win ground in the post-apartheid state suggests that weak institutional and personal relationships existed between themselves, the ANC's economic planning department and those who were part of the negotiations process before 1994. The result, they maintain, was that key economic decisions were made without sufficient consultation with the progressive economists who had been mandated to develop an inclusive economic programme (Padayachee, 1995: 66–67; see also Padayachee, 1998). The problem with this explanation is its assumption that the adoption of economic policies is a technical and rational process that went off the rails in this case because ANC political leaders were not sufficiently aware of what they were doing. It assumes that more radical possibilities were available but that this was not apparent to political leaders. Yet this is just not true. Nowhere was this more succinctly captured than in Thabo Mbeki's 'The State and Social Transformation'.[8] In this document, Mbeki acknowledges that government debt, capital mobility and the global environment limited the post-apartheid state's room to manoeuvre. He therefore called for 'an abandonment of the wish for the total defeat and suppression of the class forces responsible for apartheid', and suggested instead the development of 'a dialectical relationship with private capital as a social partner for development and social progress' (ANC, 1996: 22). Mbeki was not alone in this view. Hein Marais too makes the point by quoting Gramsci, 'change happens within the "limits of the possible", and those limits were more constricting than the rhetoric of the day conveyed' (2011: 398). Yet, as demonstrated below, the limits were probably not quite as debilitating as Mbeki and Manuel made them out to be.

This then raises the second explanation for the ANC's abandonment of a developmental vision in the process of ascending to state power – and it is the one I prefer. This view suggests that the balance of power in both the global and national arenas was unfavourable to poor and marginalised citizens, and, as a result, state elites were conditioned to make the choices they did. Elsewhere, Vishnu Padayachee and I have delineated the variables that constituted the prevailing configuration of power, and thereby constrained the progressive possibilities in the early post-apartheid period (Habib and Padayachee, 2000). To summarise the state of affairs at that moment: Mbeki and other state elites confronted two diametrically opposed sets of interests that were advocating contrary policy choices. On the one side, foreign investors and the domestic business community were lobbying for neo-liberal economic policies – including privatisation, deregulation, financial and trade liberalisation, and low budget deficits. Their leverage: investment. On the other side, the broader citizenry were demanding poverty alleviation, service delivery and transformation. Their leverage was their votes. The citizens were, however, weakened by the racial structure of the political parties that existed, and the fact that none of these posed any real threat to the ANC (Habib and Taylor, 2001). In this context, the pressure exerted by foreign investors was perceived as 'more real' or immediate, and Mbeki opted to accede to their demands first, which led to the adoption of GEAR.

This explanation has been presented simplistically for explanatory effect. The point is that particular power configurations lay behind the state's decision to adopt GEAR (Alexander, 2002; Habib and Padayachee, 2000; Marais, 2011). The power relations that prevailed in the early to mid 1990s, as defined by the balance of class power, the nature of state–society relationships and global power configurations, put pressure on ANC leaders, configured their choices and prompted them to adopt and implement GEAR.

What then were the parameters of possibility in the years immediately after the 1994 national election? Although the parameters of possibility are dealt with in more detail in Chapter Seven of this book, some reflections are offered here because if we cannot identify viable alternatives, the analysis automatically degenerates into a 'structural inevitability' thesis. Perhaps a useful way of doing this is for me to recount an engagement I had with then finance minister Trevor Manuel about this issue. Our communication was occasioned by an article I had written on universities, in which I lamented the effects on higher education of the conservative macro-economic policy adopted in the early years of the transition. Manuel challenged me via an email, asking what I would have done had I been in his place and given the realities of the moment. I responded by detailing 15 issues that I would have approached differently. He responded of course, and the email banter went on for a few weeks. Essentially, my argument was that while the pursuit of a radical economic agenda was not possible, a weakened version of a social democratic agenda would have been feasible and indeed was expected by both the business community and other stakeholders.

Among my suggestions were: (i) a less aggressive approach to cost recovery; (ii) a more measured approach to tariff reductions and a liberalisation of exchange controls; (iii) a more active industrial policy agenda; (iv) a focus on both small-business development and an incomes policy; (v) an explicit statement in favour of employment creation within the mandate of the Reserve Bank (as presently exists in the United States Federal Reserve); (vi) a rejection of both partial privatisation of important parastatals and the relocation of South African corporations on the London bourse. None of this was fundamentally different from what MERG proposed. My contention with MERG is not that its policy recommendations were problematic, but that it lacked an understanding of the politics required to turn its recommendations into state policy.

Such a politics would have had to neutralise the leverage held by big business. Only two situations could have achieved this. The first was a democratic threat to the ANC from a viable challenge on the left, organised either by the union movement (as occurred in much of western Europe) or by the Communist Party (as occurred in Kerala, India). The second was a mass popular rebellion capable of unsettling both the ruling political and economic elite (as occurred in Malaysia in 1969). A democratic threat from the left was made impossible by the consensus within the Tripartite Alliance and the progressive intelligentsia, that an inclusive development agenda could best be realised through a united front centred on the ANC. A popular insurrection was also impossible in South Africa in 1994, especially given the failure of the uprising that had been attempted in Bisho two years earlier. In this context, perhaps the abandonment of the RDP should have been anticipated.

The leadership of the ANC must still be held accountable, however. It is one thing to be forced by the realities of the moment to temporarily compromise one's economic agenda. It is quite another to wholeheartedly buy into a conservative macro-economic programme and then start to believe that it will achieve the ends it promises. The enthusiasm with which the ANC leadership implemented GEAR, and its rhetoric throughout that period, suggests that the latter was at play. Trevor Manuel's implementation of tariff reforms in 1994 greatly exceeded the requirements of the World Trade Organization's General Agreement on Tariffs and Trade.

Moreover, other choices were within the 'parameters of possibility'. For example, the ANC could have insisted that South African conglomerates retain their primary listing on the JSE, as the Australians did in the case of BHP Billiton. Empowerment resources could have been directed at developing small and medium enterprises instead of enabling politically connected figures to buy shares in large corporations. The Alliance's explicit project was to create a black bourgeoisie but the choices that were made turned this from a project of broad-based economic empowerment into one which led to the enrichment of a small political elite.

All of this makes the implementation of GEAR very different from the sunset-clause reforms proposed by Joe Slovo (discussed in Chapter Two). Slovo's proposals responded to the reality of the moment, but were designed to be temporary and to open up possibilities for empowerment. In contrast, GEAR locked down South Africa's extreme inequalities and polarised the society. Whereas the sunset clauses can be described as transformatory, GEAR's agenda cannot even be seen as self-contained or reformist. It represented a regression in social terms for South African society.

Political polarisation begins

The implementation of GEAR had devastating consequences not only for the citizenry, but also for the political evolution of South Africa. Essentially its implementation polarised the political spectrum. On the one hand, its consequences (either directly, or mediated through departmental policies it spawned, such as the policy on cost-recovery related to basic services) provoked a series of social protests across the country that has been ongoing since around the turn of the millennium. Sixteen of these movements were studied by a group of scholars under the auspices of the Centre for Civil Society at the University of KwaZulu-Natal (Ballard et al., 2006). They concluded that these 'social movements' had the effect of unsettling political elites, 'prompting a sustainable shift in state policy in the interests of South Africa's poor and marginalised' (Ballard et al., 2006: 415).

On the other hand, GEAR consolidated political polarities within the ANC and the Tripartite Alliance. Its adoption by Cabinet, and its subsequent endorsement by the ANC and the two houses of parliament, required the marginalisation of COSATU and the SACP. Both organisations raised objections, hesitantly at first, and subsequently more vociferously, about issues as diverse as economic policy, HIV and AIDS, as well as foreign policy towards Zimbabwe and Swaziland. This opposition ultimately culminated in their decision to throw in their lot with Jacob Zuma and form, together with the ANC Youth League and the KwaZulu-Natal branches of the ANC, the institutional platform on which Jacob Zuma was able to effect the palace coup that took place during the ANC's national electoral conference at Polokwane in 2007.

Despite the bravado displayed by the ANC leadership, most notably when Mbeki (and Mandela before him) challenged intra-party critics to leave the Alliance (Mbeki, 2002), the burgeoning of community protests combined with internal tensions and revolts unsettled Mbeki and his ministers. In his 'State of the Nation'

87

and other addresses, Mbeki repeatedly warned, often through the words of poets such as Langston Hughes, of the rage of the poor should their interests not be catered for. In his inaugural address to South Africa's third democratic parliament in 2004, he formally acknowledged that not enough had been done for South Africa's marginalised in the first decade of democracy (Mbeki, 2004a). He then laid out a comprehensive set of policies and targets that were intended to facilitate service delivery and address the poverty that so many South Africans are mired in.

Neo-liberalism with a human face?

The realisation of GEAR's consequences facilitated a gradual but significant shift in economic policy during Mbeki's presidency. The shift manifested itself at a number of levels.

First, social expenditure expanded massively, particularly in the form of social-support grants which went up in real terms, and were extended to include many more people. The number of recipients of such grants increased from 2 687 169 in 1999 to 6 476 587 in early 2004, and then to an astounding 12 386 396 by late 2007 (PCAS, 2008: 28).[9]

Second, state intervention came back into vogue in relation to black economic empowerment and a major infrastructure development programme was initiated. With regard to the former, the government became increasingly sceptical of the corporate sector's commitment to deracialisation, especially after the setbacks experienced in the wake of the 1998 financial crisis.[10] It therefore introduced new legislation that included the establishment of equity and transformation targets in industry charters. In 2004, a similarly activist stance was adopted by the state in relation to infrastructure development, with the launch of a R780 billion (US$91 billion) programme, partially directed towards preparations for hosting the 2010 soccer world cup. As Faulkner and Loewald (2008: 33) demonstrate, infrastructure investment increased rapidly from a '40 year low in 2001 ... to an annual rate of 12.4 per cent in per capita terms'. Much of this was directed through state-owned enterprises and the privatisation rhetoric of the late 1990s suddenly disappeared.

As the government's rhetoric changed, the need to correct for market failures became a priority, with poverty alleviation and even inequality reduction being given as much emphasis as growth. Not everyone recognised this. Many on the independent left gave little credence to the shift in the state's rhetoric and social policy (see, for example, Bond, 2004c; Desai, 2005; Hart, 2005). But some did. By 2004, the left within the ANC, including in COSATU and the SACP, were convinced that a significant reappraisal was underway within government. Their conclusion was based on an evaluation of the 2003 annual budget, which they argued indicated significant shifts in favour of infrastructural investment, a public-works programme and increased social expenditure (COSATU, 2004; Cronin, 2004). The corporate sector seemed to concur. Tim Cohen (2004), corresponding editor at *Business Day*, commented in this period that the ANC had lost faith in the business community and was beginning to pursue a more interventionist, state-led economic strategy. Some academics had already arrived at this conclusion. For instance, as early as 2001, Vishnu Padayachee and Imraan Valodia concluded that government's economic stance changed during the second post-apartheid administration (Padayachee and Valodia, 2001).

In my view, however, this perception was too unqualified. There was indeed a shift in favour of investment in infrastructure and increased social expenditure during Mbeki's presidency. But GEAR largely remained in place. Mbeki's (2004a) address to parliament, which heralded the shift to a more state-interventionist strategy, remained silent on rigid fiscal policies, on commitments to financial and trade liberalisation and on the narrow focus of monetary authorities on inflation. Indeed, in his address to the outgoing parliament three months earlier, in which he reviewed the ANC government's performance over its first ten years in power, Mbeki concluded that there was no need for policy shifts (Mbeki, 2004b). The failure of poverty alleviation and sustainable development, as well as the inadequacy of service delivery, was, in his view, the result of poor implementation. Thus, the presidency's review of the first decade of South Africa's democracy (PCAS, 2003), while acknowledging that unemployment had gone up, and that delivery had been most significant in areas where the state had retained predominant control, nevertheless concluded that government had delivered as well as was possible. The review argued that the tight fiscal reign was part of a far-sighted strategic manoeuvre to stabilise finances so that increased spending on social expenditure could be realised when this had been achieved.

The presidency's review is open to question on at least two levels: (i) the assertion that the shift in policy was part of an original long-term vision has to be challenged; and (ii), the view among government technocrats that the shift was a product of an incremental learning process, whereby officials corrected for earlier policy failures (Hirsch, 2005), also warrants further critique. Both views deliberately ignore the fact that the outcomes projected by proponents of GEAR in relation to increased employment, investment and the like, did not materialise (Habib and Padayachee, 2000). Moreover, both views are based on the assumption critiqued earlier, that policy making is primarily the outcome of a rational process involving policy technocrats and state officials. Finally, both views ignore Mbeki's concern about the rage of the poor, as well as the role that social struggles and intra-Alliance battles played in generating his anxiety (Hart, 2005).

There is a third level on which the presidency's analysis of its first ten years must be criticised for asserting that all was well in terms of economic policy. It was this perception that led to the South African government declaring budget surpluses of 0.3 per cent and

0.8 per cent of GDP in 2006 and 2007 respectively (PCAS, 2008: 9), at a time when the broad definition of the unemployment rate in the country hovered at 36.4 per cent (PCAS, 2008: 21).

The central contradiction

The problem lay in the presidency's analysis of South Africa as constituting two economies: one modern, efficient and internationally competitive; and the other informal, marginalised, poor and overwhelmingly located in black communities. While this analysis was appealing at face value, the usefulness of this model was questionable. It enabled the presidency to assume that the first economy required no intervention and that only the second was in need of policy reform and social assistance. Yet, as Archie Mafeje demonstrated in the early 1970s, in his critique of 'dual theories' of economic development, South Africa is not a special case in this regard, and 'dual theories become a mere apology and not an explanation' for this socio-economic outcome (Mafeje, nd: 66). Thus, Mbeki's dual-economy analysis did not enable the presidency to understand that the policies and functioning of the first 'economy' were precisely what was creating poverty and immiseration in the second (Terreblanche, 2005).

Of course, apartheid had established two sectors in South African society; one white and privileged, the other black and disadvantaged. The ANC's explicit mandate was to facilitate the transcendence of this racial divide. Instead, however, while the economic and social policies it pursued in the first decade of its rule began a process of deracialising the first sector, these same policies simultaneously increased the size and aggravated the problems of the second. Increasing the state's social expenditure did not solve the problem. In fact, as long as South Africa's industrial, trade, monetary and fiscal policies retained their neo-liberal flavour, they worked against the social expenditure components of the national budget. This contradiction has lain at the heart of the ANC government's policy ensemble since 1996, and it continued throughout both of Mbeki's terms in office, even though the state's economic policy began a slow drift to the left during his second term.

The contradiction manifested itself very clearly in the Mbeki administration's performance. Annual GDP grew progressively larger from 2000 and reached 5.1 per cent in 2007, driven in part by the booming global economy (PCAS, 2008: 5). Formal employment began to take off from 2003, and broad unemployment decreased from 42.5 per cent in early 2003 to 34.3 per cent in late 2007 (PCAS, 2008: 21). Poverty levels dropped, partly because of the new jobs, but mainly as a result of the massive increases in the number of people receiving social grants. Between 2003 and 2007, the poorest 10 per cent of the population increased their per capita real income from R921 ($107) to R1032 ($120) (at 2007 constant rand prices), but their share of total income remained at 0.6 per cent. Thus, the excessive levels of inequality, which increased in the second half of the 1990s because of GEAR, have since remained constant.

The fears and warnings of the editors of the 2003–2004 edition of the *State of the Nation* had been borne out. We argued that the combination of progressive policy in some arenas and a conservative macro-economic policy in other spheres had begun to deracialise the apex of South Africa's class structure. We noted that black professionals and entrepreneurs, in particular, were benefitting while poor and marginalised people were struggling. We concluded that despite President Mbeki's desire to transcend the dichotomy between the two 'nations' he constantly spoke about, the policies of his government would not achieve this. Instead they would lead to a deracialisation in the first 'nation', while leaving the second exactly where it was (Daniel, Habib & Southall, 2003: 20).

As noted earlier, it is my view that the unhappiness and inequalities generated by GEAR, as much as concerns about Mbeki's leadership style, account for his unceremonious ousting as head of the ANC in December 2007. Nine months later, the party's new leadership forced him to resign as president seven months prior to the national elections that would have ended his term in office. These political developments opened up the possibility for a further shift to the left in economic policy.

Groping towards social democracy

As indicated earlier, there is a widespread assumption in the progressive literature that Jacob Zuma has introduced no radical changes in economic and social policy during his time in office (Bond, 2008; Satgar, 2008), and some scholars have correctly recognised that slow but significant shifts to the left had already begun under Mbeki himself (see Marais, 2011: 440–441). While highlighting the continuities evident in economic policies over the first two to three decades of ANC rule illuminates one element of the contemporary South African story, it does not tell the whole story. One cannot equate rupture with change and conclude that no ruptures means that no significant changes occurred. Indeed there is substantial evidence to suggest that South Africa's economic and social policies have shifted in important ways. The question is whether this shift is of a qualitatively different order, and is capable of at least beginning to address the challenges of inclusive development and reducing inequality, poverty and unemployment.

This question must also be considered in the context of the observations made in Chapter One, on how the configurations of power have evolved in South Africa since 1994. I suggested in Chapter One that the configurations have evolved in significant ways. The evolution process has occurred in two phases. The first occurred in the late 1990s and in the early 2000s with the emergence of widespread social struggles. This, together with the divisions in the Tripartite Alliance provoked by the adoption of GEAR, unsettled the political elites and prompted them to expand the reach of social-support grants.

The second phase of the evolution process was defined by the ANC's national electoral conference that took place at Polokwane in December 2007, when the alliance of social forces that underpinned Jacob Zuma's ascent to the helm came to the fore.[11] Support for the Mbeki administration had unravelled as a result of Mbeki's personal behaviour, and the fact that his policies had failed to generate inclusive development. As noted in Chapter Two, Mbeki's support base – the intelligentsia, as well as the black components of the urban middle and upper-middle classes – abandoned him in the final years of his tenure. They believed that he was manipulating state institutions for his own ends, had become a racial chauvinist, and lacked empathy for citizens, particularly those living with HIV or beleaguered by crime. The result was a downward spiral in his popular support (Gumede, 2007).

Ultimately, however, Mbeki's defeat resulted from the rebellion within the ANC and the Tripartite Alliance against the nature of South Africa's transition. As noted earlier, Zuma's candidature was cemented not only by his own popularity, but also by popular revulsion to the Mbeki administration. This aversion was in large measure propelled by the fact that important quarters of the ANC and the Tripartite Alliance believed that the corporate sector and a narrow band of politically connected black entrepreneurs had been the primary beneficiaries of the transition (COSATU, 2006; SACP, 2006b). This prompted a diverse alliance of internal organisational stakeholders to throw in their lot with Zuma. The alliance comprised a mix of nationalists and socialists, black economic empowerment

(BEE) entrepreneurs, the ANC Youth League, COSATU and the SACP.

The ejection of Mbeki from the presidency inevitably empowered the grassroots within the ANC who increasingly realised that political leaders should be accountable to them and could be replaced if they were not responsive to their interests. More importantly, COSATU and the SACP's leverage increased significantly because they had provided a significant share of the institutional platform required for Jacob Zuma's ascendance to power. This is not to imply that COSATU and the SACP rule the roost within the ANC or the presidency, as some business leaders have come to fear (Bell, 2009). Indeed, the corporate sector has retained significant power and leverage. In effect, what occurred was that the power differential in favour of business that prevailed under Mbeki's reign eroded slightly in favour of a more equitable balance of power – both within the ruling party and in the country as a whole. In my view, this has, in turn, constrained the behaviour and choices of political elites and begun to condition the evolution of political and economic life in South Africa.

This new, more equitable balance of power was immediately evident in the Zuma administration's responsiveness to public and stakeholder opinion, especially in his appointments to Cabinet and other important economic portfolios. Business was concerned that Trevor Manuel would be ejected, and that there would be too fundamental a change in economic policy. The left, mainly represented by COSATU and the SACP, were concerned that too little change would take place – that Manuel and company would retain control of economic policy and that alternative voices would not be heard.

Zuma's appointments appeased both sides. Manuel was retained in a new portfolio within the presidency (national planning) and Pravin Gordhan, who had completed a sterling performance as commissioner of the South African Revenue Service, was brought in as finance minister in an effort to appease the markets. But these appointments were coupled with those of Rob Davies as trade and industry minister and Ebrahim Patel as minister of economic development. Davies and Patel have strong connections with the SACP and COSATU respectively.

A similar appeal to multiple stakeholders informed Gill Marcus's appointment as governor of the Reserve Bank. A stalwart of the ANC, Marcus had previously served in the treasury and her sojourn in the private sector involved not only chairing the board of a mining company, but also that of South Africa's largest bank (ABSA), a majority share of which was subsequently bought by Barclays.[12] Marcus's appeal transcended the boundaries of the corporate sector however, and both COSATU and the SACP welcomed her appointment. Her strength lay in the fact that she had never been fundamentalist in her economic or ideological perspectives. She was perceived as pragmatic, consultative and less pompous than her predecessor (Tito Mboweni) and thus appealed to multiple stakeholders.

The net effect of this mix of appointments was to introduce a plurality of thought in the corridors of economic power that gave several stakeholders the prospect of influencing policy. This more equitable balance of power was also reflected in a deepening of the shift to the left in economic and social policy that had begun with Mbeki. This has been evident at a number of levels. For example, social support grants continued to be expanded, notably by Cabinet's 2009 decision to extend the age limit for beneficiaries of child-support grants from 14 to 18. The higher education and training sector has also seen a renewed focus on making tertiary education more affordable and on rebuilding the training college sector to enable it to absorb a higher proportion of the three to four million unemployed youth who are not at university (Nzimande, 2009). The health ministry has become much more responsive, especially in relation to the HIV and AIDS pandemics, and in its commitment to developing a national health insurance scheme (Department of Health, 2011).

But the most dramatic evidence of the deepening shift to the left emerged on the economic front and became evident at multiple levels, including in both fiscal and monetary policy. In the midst of the global economic crisis, the last national budget drawn up by Trevor Manuel as finance minster and the first two budgets drawn up by his successor, Pravin Gordhan, expanded the fiscal deficit to 7.3 per cent, 6.2 per cent and 5.3 per cent of GDP in 2009, 2010 and 2011 respectively (Gordhan, 2010a; 2011; Manuel, 2009).[13] Spending on social and economic development increased accordingly in areas such as the maintenance of the infrastructure programme, social-support grants, rural development, education and healthcare. Yet most commentators – including those representing business – acknowledged that this expansion of the fiscal deficit was necessary and manageable.[14] And, in comparison with those of South Africa's main trading partners, it was much more conservative (Isa, 2009). Similarly, interest rates have maintained a downward trajectory under the Zuma administration, although they are nowhere near COSATU's demand that they be reduced to 3 per cent.[15] Moreover, although the Reserve Bank's formal mandate has still not been extended to include employment creation, an open letter (and subsequent statements of clarification) written by the finance minister, Gordhan, to Marcus as governor-general of the Reserve Bank on 16 February 2010 did intimate that factors other than inflation should be considered in determining the Bank's decisions in difficult economic times (Gordhan, 2010b; see also *Business Day*, 19/02/2010). Although cautiously phrased to reiterate the Reserve Bank's traditional mandate, the letter did put on public record that the management of South Africa's monetary policy had subtly changed under Marcus to include variables such as employment and growth in order to prioritise price stability.

Perhaps the strongest indication of the government's shift to the left has been the adoption of the *Industrial Policy Action Plan 2011/12–2013/14* (Department of Trade and Industry, 2011) and *The New Growth Path* (Department of Economic Development, 2010) pioneered by Rob Davies and Ebrahim Patel respectively. The *Industrial Policy Action Plan* (informally known as IPAP2) was developed through the Department of Trade and Industry and has as its goal the creation of 2.4 million jobs by 2020. The plan aims to achieve this by (i) harnessing and regularly recapitalising key institutions responsible for public financing (such as the Industrial Development Corporation, the Development Bank and Khula Enterprise Finance) to ensure that they support development projects and strategies; (ii) revising procurement legislation so that those doing business with government are compelled to behave in ways that favour development outcomes; (iii) deploying trade policies in ways that protect and promote jobs while penalising companies that engage in anti-competitive practices. The business sectors targeted for this kind of state support and intervention are: automotive components, minerals beneficiation, pharmaceuticals, tourism, business services, clothing and textiles, metal fabrication, capital and transport equipment, green energy, agro-processing linked to food security, aerospace, as well as nuclear and advanced materials (Davies, 2010; Department of Trade and Industry, 2011).

The New Growth Path squarely sets its target as the reduction of South Africa's economic inequalities. To achieve this, a set of policies with two distinct goals are recommended: enhancing the livelihoods of those at the bottom of the economic ladder and temporarily and voluntarily constraining the incomes of the upper-middle classes and the elite. To enhance livelihoods at the bottom, policies that facilitate increased employment have been proposed. These range from infrastructure and skills-development programmes, through to a competitions policy, a looser monetary agenda, as well as small-business promotion and financing. Here again, the streamlining of development finance institutions is envisaged to help achieve these objectives (Department of Economic Development, 2010).

While most of these policies have generated significant support from stakeholders, the policies directed at the elite end of the economic spectrum – relating to reforming black economic empowerment initiatives and voluntarily capping remuneration and bonuses – have come in for heavy criticism, even though these are envisaged as being voluntary. These measures are expected to be implemented through negotiations with the relevant business associations, as was achieved in the wake of the Marikana massacre where 34 striking miners were killed by police (*Business Day*, 19/10/2012; *City Press*, 20/10/2012).

Reforming the black economic empowerment agenda is widely supported in the public domain, but is likely to meet heavy opposition from the mandarins who stride the corridors of political power, including some members of the ANC's national executive. In any case, the *New Growth Path* acknowledges that, as presently structured, black economic empowerment merely drives enrichment for the politically connected, rather than empowering the majority. The plan recommends that the state's empowerment resources be redirected primarily towards supporting small businesses and new entrepreneurs. If implemented, this would not only empower individuals and ensure that transformation is more inclusive, it should also enhance the competitiveness of the South African economy (Department of Economic Development, 2010: 33–34).

In response to its proposals for remuneration and bonus caps, COSATU criticised the *New Growth Plan* on the grounds that the implementation of the wage freeze would be effected through businesses, and would end up being directed only at workers, thereby increasing economic inequalities (Baleni, 2010; *Business Day*, 26/11/2010). Representatives of the business sector, and opposition parties such as the Democratic Alliance, warned that bonus and wage caps had the potential to drive away skilled executives and foreign investment (Harris, 2010; *Financial Mail*, 25/11/2010; *Times*, 28/02/2011).

Both sets of criticisms are open to challenge. If COSATU fears a one-sided application of the wage freeze, can it not get its structures to monitor this at the industry level? As for concerns about an exodus of skills and investment, are these not just scaremongering? Reports indicate that levels of remuneration and living standards among executives in South Africa are on par with, if not higher than, those of their peers in the United States and Europe (*Sunday Times*, 10/07/2011). And why should investors fear remuneration caps? After all, shareholders have repeatedly expressed concern about executive remuneration and bonuses.[16] If the remuneration of both executives and employees were structured to contain corporate wage bills, and simultaneously stimulate productivity, shareholders would reap significant benefits. Thus the arguments put forward by business representatives and the official opposition conflate the interests of shareholders with those of the executives. If they distinguished these interests, they might see that voluntary remuneration and bonus caps – which have been successfully implemented in several market economies, including Ireland and the Netherlands, may indeed have some merit in the South African case.

But there is a more serious criticism of both the *Industrial Policy Action Plan* and the *New Growth Plan*. While the intention behind both plans (to stem the tide of South Africa's de-industrialisation) must be welcomed, only three of the sectors identified in the plans – namely, tourism, agro-processing, and clothing and textiles – have any real hope of creating new jobs in significant numbers. Since unemployment is South Africa's single biggest problem, should the state's collective focus not shift to addressing this crisis? In my view, this requires an industrialisation strategy capable of absorbing large amounts of unskilled and semi-skilled labour. In addition, it is worth acknowledging here that no amount of training is likely to transform the majority of those who have been deprived of adequate schooling into skilled entrepreneurs capable of competing successfully in the global economy.

South Africa's economic strategy must, therefore, be both multifaceted and logically sequenced. Certainly some policies need to be directed at the employment of new graduates emerging from school and tertiary education, but significant attention must also be directed at establishing industrial sectors capable of absorbing the unskilled and semi-skilled unemployed – those who were laid off in the last years of apartheid and in the first decade of South Africa's transition. Gradually, then, once the employment situation has stabilised, businesses and entrepreneurs should be prompted to progress up the value chain by producing products that would typically require more skilled workers. Obviously a balance has to be struck between employing new graduates and creating the conditions for the economy's competitive future on the one hand, and, on the other hand, devoting sufficient resources to addressing our greatest challenge, which is finding employment for semi-skilled and unskilled labour. Whether the implementation of the *Industrial Policy Action Plan* and the *New Growth Path* have the potential to achieve these objectives is highly questionable.

Nevertheless, there can be no doubt that the collective mix of economic and social policies pursued by the Zuma administration have a neo-Keynesian (that is, a social democratic) flavour – as distinct from the economic agenda pursued since 1994. This is evident even in the *National Development Plan – Our Future – Make It Work*, released by the National Planning Commission (2012) led by Trevor Manuel. Published just over a year after the *New Growth Plan*, and building upon it, this document announced the target of creating 11 million jobs by 2030. It also advocates similar goals of inclusive development and labour absorption, identifying similar business sectors as potential drivers of exports and employment, as well as a state-steered infrastructure programme to harness or crowd-in private investment (NPC, 2012: 145–155). The 2030 vision statement remains silent on remuneration caps and an incomes policy but this is to be expected given the diversity of interests represented on the commission that put it together. It is worth noting, however, that the plan supports a social pact among stakeholders, and that business representatives have indicated a willingness to engage on an incomes policy including executive remuneration (*Business Day*, 19/10/2012; *City Press*, 20/10/2012). Essentially, the economic recommendations in the *National Development Plan* reiterate the neo-Keynesian approach of the other two documents discussed above although there still is a significant difference on the issue of addressing inequality, which is discussed later in this chapter.

Acknowledging changes in economic policy

Critics who speak only of the continuities of state policy between the Mbeki and Zuma administrations do not do sufficient justice to the nuanced changes that have emerged. In addition, their concerns about Zuma's personal behaviour (including his predisposition to polygamy and his associations with individuals of dubious financial and ethical credibility), combined with his conservative attitudes on tradition and culture, have tended to infect their analysis of the economic and social policies that have emerged from his administration.

Clearly policy rupture has not occurred, but this does not mean that significant change cannot take place. Nor is it correct to assume that a conservative traditionalist is incapable of allowing the emergence and implementation of a progressive economic agenda. Rather we need to understand the policy developments for what they are: a continuation of the leftward shift in economic and social approach that began under Mbeki, which has deepened, strengthened and acquired an increasingly neo-Keynesian flavour under the Zuma administration. These nuances are significant if only because the new policies are beginning to explicitly and directly target inequality, poverty and unemployment. In this sense, they are proving significantly different to the mix of policies pursued since 1994.

This drift towards a neo-Keynesian economic agenda has of course also been enabled by a similar shift globally. The global economic crisis – the second most serious in a century – has weakened the global corporate sector, and this has enhanced the leverage of states and national political elites. This new configuration of power enabled a substantive change in the global macro-economic policy environment. Led at first by George W Bush, and then with increasing urgency by Barack Obama, the American establishment threw out the precepts of the Washington Consensus, and intervened significantly in the markets. United States banks were virtually nationalised via the largest bailout in history. Similar bailouts were facilitated for the motor industry and other conglomerates. Effectively, the American state addressed the financial crisis in exactly the way it, and the International Monetary Fund, has prevented developing nations from managing theirs. And the Americans were not alone. The governments of the United Kingdom, France, Germany, China, Japan and of almost every other major economy in the world undertook similar interventions. The net effect has been a shift of the global macro-economic environment in a neo-Keynesian direction (Blankenburg and Palma, 2009), thereby opening up possibilities for the emergence of development agendas across the world.

None of this must be interpreted to suggest that the neo-Keynesian orientation of economic and social policies in South Africa is uniformly supported. Indeed, this is clearly not the case. There are a number of countervailing trends. The first, and most worrying is corruption. As the National Development Plan recognises, this is reaching a scale that threatens the state's entire developmental programme (NPC, 2012: 446).

The second is that many technocrats within the state continue to support important aspects of GEAR. Most notable in this regard are the many in the treasury, the Reserve Bank and the National Planning Commission, who remain tied to rigid deficit and inflation targets that have the potential to compromise the neo-Keynesian agenda. Perhaps this is best demonstrated by reflecting on the debate between officials in the treasury, and in the trade and industry department, on the recommendations advanced by Dani Rodrik (2006). Rodrik, together with other scholars associated with Harvard University's Center for International Development, was commissioned to investigate the constraints on South Africa's growth prospects. His focus was on employment, which he recommended be addressed through an expansion of the export-oriented tradable sector that tends to employ low-skilled workers. This, he suggested, could be done through creating a competitive exchange rate, which would require the Reserve Bank to go beyond its narrow inflation-targeting regime, and incorporate tradable output, as well as employment, as criteria in its decision making. This recommendation was strongly supported by officials in South Africa's trade and industry department but strongly opposed by the treasury, which insisted on addressing the problem through a continued reliance on market measures, such as a competitions policy. The cautious approach adopted by finance minister, Pravin Gordhan (2010b), in his open letter to Reserve Bank governor, Gill Marcus, on the mandate of the Reserve Bank and his later reiteration of the government's commitment to achieve a 3 per cent deficit target by 2014 (2012a: 3), suggests that many in treasury remain sceptical of Rodrik's recommendations.

Contradictory approaches to inequality

In a similar vein, although there is much overlap between the *New Growth Path* and the *National Development Plan*, especially on improving the livelihoods of the poor, a fundamental philosophical difference is evident in the two plans on the issue of inequality. The *New Growth Path* hopes to address inequality by both expanding livelihood opportunities at the lower end of society and containing enrichment at the upper end. It hopes to achieve the latter through an incomes policy (inclusive of managerial and executive remuneration) and by redirecting black economic empowerment so that it becomes more broad-based. The National Development Plan, by contrast, supports the expansion of livelihood opportunities at the lower end, but is silent on containing enrichment and makes no mention of an incomes policy. Those who compiled the National Development Plan seem to imagine that it is possible to bring down economic inequalities simply by growing the economy, expanding employment opportunities and addressing poverty. Mainstream business, its economists and aligned research agencies share this view. This tension (some might suggest contradiction) in South Africa's policy ensemble has to be resolved if the neo-Keynesian economic orientation codified in the *Industrial Policy Action Plan* and the *New Growth Path* is to prevail and be sustained.

The resolution of this issue ultimately depends on how a third countervailing trend to the neo-Keynesian drift develops namely, the cracks that have emerged in the ruling party and within the Tripartite Alliance. By late 2012, the more public manifestations of these cracks included acrimonious engagements over the National Planning Commission (*Mail & Guardian*, 24/09/2009), leadership battles within various parastatals (especially Eskom and Transnet) (*Mail & Guardian*, 12/11/2009; *Daily Maverick*, 16/06/2010), and the debate about the nationalisation of South Africa's mines.[17] At the heart of these conflicts lie serious differences between nationalists and the left about where South Africa is with regard to its development, the goals that should be pursued, and the policies that should be advanced.[18]

Nationalists in the ANC, such as Billy Masetlha, Tony Yengeni, as well as Julius Malema and others within the Youth League (some say supported by wealthy beneficiaries of black economic empowerment), are concerned about the influence of communism (Letsoalo and Tabane, 2009). COSATU and the SACP, on the other hand, are concerned that the nationalists are increasingly motivated by the narrow aspirations of black economic empowerment as evidenced by their support for Bobby Godsell in the Eskom fallout with its CEO, Jacob Maroga (SABC News, 9/11/2009; SAPA, 10/11/2009).[19]

Essentially, the debate revolves around the meaning of national democracy. Nationalists within the ANC maintain that COSATU and the SACP are ignoring the fact that South Africa is in the national-democratic rather than the socialist phase of its transition. The left wing hold that the national-democratic phase should not focus on developing conservative black capitalists, but should instead move towards creating a social democracy and a mixed economy, in which inclusive development is at the core of the state's agenda (ANC, 2007). In other words, for the left, inclusive development, rather than narrow enrichment, should be the central motif of the national democratic phase of the transition.

If the drift to neo-Keynesianism is to be maintained, it is essential that COSATU, the SACP and social democratic elements in the ANC retain their political momentum. Moreover, the moulding of an economic consensus within the ruling party requires a bridging of the nationalist–left divide. This is perfectly possible. After all, national democracy is essentially about harmonising the interests of the black (and broader) capitalist class with those of citizens, as seen in social democratic societies around the world. This will, however, require political leadership from the president. It requires an engagement with intra-party stakeholders who are advancing different economic agendas, the establishment parameters for acceptable trade-offs, and the moulding of an economic consensus within the ANC. As of early 2013, the president has not yet demonstrated leadership in this regard. Many in the business community hope that Cyril Ramaphosa, the political architect of South Africa's Constitution, who was elected deputy president of the ANC at the party's 2012 Mangaung conference, may be able to play this role. But given that black economic empowerment has helped him to become the second-richest black businessman in South Africa, and that he was implicated in the Marikana tragedy by his shareholding and his representation on the board of the mining company, Lonmin, he may be too politically tainted to bridge the factional divides within the ruling party.

In the meantime, the economic challenges facing South Africa are growing. The employment gains made after 2003 have been reversed since the global economic crisis of 2008. By 2010, unemployment (using the narrow definition) stood at 25.3 per cent, 0.5 per cent more than it was in September 2003 (NPC, 2010: 21). Accusations and counter-accusations of who is to blame for this state of affairs dominate the public discourse and various kinds of populism have reared their heads. South Africa under Jacob Zuma has begun to feel similar to the last years of the Mbeki administration.

The challenge

In this chapter, I have questioned the progressive orthodoxy, which holds that South Africa's economic policy has been coherent and unchanged since 1994. I have demonstrated that while there has been no policy rupture in the post-apartheid era, economic policy has undergone significant changes over the first four post-apartheid administrations. During Mandela's term of office, economic policy (led by Thabo Mbeki and Trevor Manuel) was largely neo-liberal. This had catastrophic consequences for inequality, poverty and unemployment. The resulting social protests by civil society, and divisions within the Tripartite Alliance, prompted a gradual shift to the left in the Mbeki years. This manifested first at the level of social policy, and is evident in the massive expansion of social support grants. In the later years of the Mbeki presidency, particularly during his second term, economic policy drifted further to the left, with a focus on a state-led infrastructure development programme. Nevertheless, fiscal and monetary policy remained conservative under Mbeki, with a rigid focus on small national deficits and inflation targeting, both of which limited the parameters of what was possible.

The Zuma administration has not only continued this shift to the left, but has deepened and changed it in significant ways. The economic agenda, codified in the *Industrial Policy Action Plan* and the *National Growth Plan*, as well as being evident in the treasury's counter-cyclical budgets, is primarily focused on investment in infrastructure, revitalising industrialisation, creating an enabling environment for small and medium enterprises, driving agriculture, mining, tourism and green technologies, as well as broadening out black economic empowerment. All this is to be facilitated through the mobilisation of development finance, the implementation of industrial and competition policies that enable entrepreneurship, management of the exchange rate to encourage exports, continuing a counter-cyclical fiscal policy, and enhancing the country's education and research capabilities.

Economic policy under Zuma has thus developed a strong neo-Keynesian flavour. This shift has been contested and it (and indeed the state as a whole) is threatened by the levels of corruption in government and in society more broadly. But the ongoing commitment of many state bureaucrats and ANC political leaders to the budget-deficit policies and inflation targets of the GEAR years, as well as the divisions within the ANC and the Tripartite Alliance between nationalists and the left wing, also threaten the sustainability of the neo-Keynesian economic agenda. Its sustainability is dependent on the emergence of a political leadership capable of bridging organisational divides, moulding an economic consensus and developing an ethical value system within the ruling party. As of 2013, the existing political leadership does not have an inspiring track record in this regard.

4

The viability of a sustainable social pact

Social pacts have become a mantra of South Africa's political transition. Ever since the notion was mooted by Geoff Schreiner (1991; 1994) and Adrienne Bird (Bird and Schreiner, 1992), who were then senior officials in the Congress of South African Trade Unions (COSATU), the idea of a social pact has appealed to leadership figures in business, labour and the state. It is not difficult to imagine why. After all, a social pact promises the possibility of peace between warring social partners, a non-zero-sum outcome where all sides stand to gain at least part of what they desire. For an incumbent political elite, who needed to manage popular and stakeholder expectations and grow the economy, a social pact was a particularly attractive solution. But the romanticised expectations and euphoria surrounding the establishment of the National Economic Development and Labour Council (NEDLAC) in 1996 were soon dashed by the cold reality of everyday economics and politics. Within a year or two, business, labour, and the state were bickering over the Growth, Employment and Redistribution (GEAR) strategy, and almost all other government policies. A climate of political mistrust spread throughout the country during President Thabo Mbeki's terms in office, interrupted by brief attempts by the African National Congress (ANC) and COSATU to broker a kind of truce – usually around election periods.

Yet although hopes for a social pact were dashed, the idea retained its hold on the imaginations of many academics and leaders in business, labour and the state. Every now and then, therefore, the idea resurfaces. It arose for example after the upsurge of labour activism following the ANC's victory in the general elections of April 2009. At that time, driven by the biting effects of the economic recession, the global backlash against corporate executives' remuneration packages, and the fear that the ANC (including COSATU members deployed in the Cabinet and in government more broadly) was abandoning its roots and being seduced by the trappings of office, unions became more active and robust in their wage negotiations. Over the next few years, this led to a set of rolling public and private sector strikes. In 2010 20 674 737 workdays were lost – the highest yet recorded (Department of Labour, 2011: 26). Caught off guard, business and political leaders initially reacted by berating workers. ANC leaders, most notably the general secretary, Gwede Mantashe, accused workers of compromising the image of the Zuma administration (*Business Day*, 6/11/2009). Business leaders responded true to character, highlighting the threat of investment fleeing South Africa's shores (*Business Day*, 17/08/2010; *Black Business Quarterly*, 19/02/2011). In the midst of all of this, the notion of a social pact was again advocated by a number of leaders from all of the contesting stakeholder groups, as well as by academics and political commentators.

But is a social pact feasible in South Africa, and why did earlier attempts at forging such a pact fail?

To answer these questions, it is necessary to understand the political, economic and social conditions that enable social pacts to emerge and succeed. In my view, the South African literature on corporatism[1] and social pacts has not investigated this sufficiently. Indeed, much of the literature has been dedicated either to describing union (and business) behaviour (Adler and Webster, 1995), or offered superficial analyses of comparative cases with a view to identifying the adoption of a corporatist route in South Africa (Maree, 1993). However, before addressing the fundamental question of whether an equitable social pact that promotes sustainable inclusive development is viable for South Africa, it is fruitful to undertake a brief review of the idea of a social pact in South Africa, its institutionalisation through NEDLAC, and the successes and failures thereof.[2]

Social unionism and South Africa's first social pact

South Africa's democratic transition, like those of most 'Third Wave democracies' (Huntington, 1991), has been characterised by two distinct transitional processes: political democratisation and economic liberalisation. The goal of the first is representative government. The aim of the second is the integration of South Africa into the global economy. From the early 1990s, COSATU's leadership was refreshingly aware of the dilemmas spawned by this Janus-faced transition, and during the first few years of the negotiations period, they groped their way towards a new strategic vision.

To assist in this process, COSATU established the September Commission to inform organisational renewal and determine a strategic orientation for the federation, including its role in political alliances. The Commission premised its reflections on three possible scenarios for South Africa's future (COSATU, 1997). Scenario one, labelled 'the Desert', was defined as involving no economic growth, the ANC's abandonment of its Reconstruction and Development Programme, high levels of political instability and increasing industrial strife. Scenario two called the 'Skorokoro' (local slang for a clapped-out old vehicle) was distinguished by economic growth and modest delivery. In this option, racial divisions were imagined as likely to continue, but the black middle class would be empowered. The third scenario, known as 'Pap, vleis and gravy' (local slang for meat with all the trimmings), was defined as massive growth and development, with significant job creation and the delivery of services by the state as outlined in the Reconstruction and Development Programme. In this scenario, unions were imagined as engaging in joint decision making with business.

The September Commission viewed a combination of scenarios two and three as most likely outcomes for South Africa and argued for a programme of social unionism so as to increase the trade union movement's influence on the political and socio-economic outcomes of the transition. In the words of the Commission, social unionism is 'the strategy which will enable COSATU to ... proactively contest the transition ... The aim is to harness the organised power of COSATU, its capacity to mobilise, its socio-economic programmes and policies and its participation in political and social alliances to make important contributions to national, economic and social development' (COSATU, 1997). This was envisaged as occurring through COSATU's participation in the ANC and the Tripartite Alliance, in state institutions (including parliament and national, provincial and local administrations), in forums such as NEDLAC, in industry through bargaining councils and popular mobilisation and finally in civil society through alliances with civic organisations (Buhlungu, 2010). It was hoped, through this strategic orientation, to increase the influence of the working class so that labour could move to 'co-owning the transformation project' (COSATU, 1997).

The term adopted to describe this strategic orientation was 'social unionism' (COSATU, 1997). The term was borrowed from the writings of a number of sociologists loosely associated with the union federation, who since the late 1980s had toyed with terms such as 'strategic' and 'social' or 'social movement' unionism to describe the new path that COSATU was beginning to tread (Von Holdt, 1992; Webster, 1988; Webster and Von Holdt, 1992).

Within the discipline of industrial sociology these terms signal important conceptual differences. 'Social movement unionism' (or simply 'social unionism') is defined as 'a highly mobilised form of unionism which emerges in opposition to authoritarian regimes and repressive workplaces' (Von Holdt, 2002: 285). This concept is therefore often used to explain COSATU's involvement in the wider anti-apartheid struggle and its close relationship with the United Democratic Front in the 1980s and early 1990s and with the ANC after it was unbanned. 'Strategic unionism', refers to a form of unionism that involves itself in social pacts and seeks to strategically influence economic and social policy by participating in forums where such policies are formulated. Its objective is to influence policies to the advantage of workers and other marginalised communities. Strategic unionism emerged in South Africa during the early 1990s, when COSATU began to engage in economic policy discussions in the National Economic Forum. In the post-apartheid period, COSATU has continued this form of engagement and substantially increased its role in institutions such as NEDLAC.

The September Commission described the organisation's unionism as

> social in the sense that it is concerned with broad social and political issues, as well as the immediate concerns of its members. It aims to be a social force for transformation. Its goal is democracy and socialism. Its influence on society is based on its organised power, its capacity to mobilise, its socioeconomic programme and policies and its participation in political and social alliances. It is committed to workers control and democracy, and to maintaining its character as a movement. It is proactive and effective. It is able to negotiate and monitor complex agreements with government and employers. It is able to make important contributions to national economic and social development. (COSATU, 1997)

By focusing on both social and political issues, and on the negotiation of agreements with governments and employers, COSATU's definition essentially straddles the conceptual divide between social movement and strategic unionism, and largely reflects the practices that emerged in South Africa's labour movement in the late 1980s and early 1990s.

COSATU's strategic vision, as encapsulated in the term 'social unionism', has its roots in three related but distinct reflective exercises. The first of these was the attempt by a number of senior unionists and some labour sociologists to legitimise COSATU's increasing involvement in forums that also involved representatives of both the business sector and the state.[3] The exercise began with two articles mentioned in the introduction to this chapter, which were published in the *South African Labour Bulletin* by Geoff Schreiner and Adrienne Bird, and in which they argued that COSATU's participation in wider forums was an example of a social pact. They suggested that this sort of participation should continue, and intensify under when the new democratic government came into being (Bird and Schreiner, 1992; Schreiner, 1991). The two articles sparked a debate both within and outside the labour movement that continued for several years (see for example, Baskin, 1993; Callinicos, 1992; Desai and Habib, 1994; Godongwana, 1992; Schreiner, 1994; Shilowa, 1992). The debate culminated in COSATU's adoption of most of Schreiner and Bird's recommendations and an affirmation of the federation's participation in corporatist institutions.

The second reflective exercise, already mentioned in Chapter Three of this book, involved economists associated with the Industrial Strategy Project and the Economic Trends Group, who were contracted by COSATU to investigate an alternative, more labour-friendly industrialisation strategy (Gelb, 1991; Joffe et al., 1995). Their research also generated a fair amount of controversy since their recommendations were premised on the view that South Africa's economic growth depended significantly upon whether or not the country's manufacturing sector could be made internationally competitive. As noted in Chapter Three, their recommendations included the creation and development of South Africa's industrial beneficiation capacity, with a focus on manufacturing exports, and South Africa's integration into the global economy.

Finally, and ironically, the least controversial, was COSATU's decision to enter into a strategic alliance with the ANC for the 1994 elections. To be fair, the reflection, controversy and debates about this issue took place at the formation of COSATU in December 1985, and revolved around the question of whether or not it should form an alliance with the United Democratic Front.[4] In any case, COSATU's electoral pact with the ANC came with preconditions that the federation codified in the Reconstruction and Development Programme, which the ANC accepted and adopted as its electoral manifesto for the first democratic elections in 1994 (ANC, 1994).[5]

These three initiatives then, or at least their recommendations, combined with the work of the September Commission, formed the basis of what became known as social unionism. Social unionism in South Africa can thus be defined by three elements. First, it involves a corporatist strategy whereby the labour movement participates in forums or social pacts with the state and the business community. Second, it involves an assumption that integration into the global economy is inevitable, a realisation that maximalist outcomes are not possible, and that a strategic compromise between capital and labour is necessary. Such a compromise would involve a 'bargained liberalisation': 'liberalisation, because the changes involve opening up to the global economy; bargained, because agreements are subject to the institutionally structured interplay of societal interests' (Webster and Adler, 1999: 351). Bargained liberalisation, in this view, 'may provide workers and marginalised social strata with an opportunity to engage the state and capital over the form and pace of adjustment, allowing the extension of some measure of social regulation to those whose livelihoods are threatened by economic restructuring' (Webster and Adler, 1999: 351). Third, social unionism requires that COSATU align itself politically with the ANC. Such an alliance is legitimised through the conceptual banner of national democratic revolution, implying that the immediate outcome is a democracy defined essentially by the combination of a representative political system with a Keynesian-type economic strategy.

Social unionism's highpoint was, without doubt, the period between 1994 and 1996, and the labour movement recorded significant successes in these years. NEDLAC was established in February 1995, and the Labour Relations Act, which greatly enhanced organised workers' bargaining positions, was agreed to by the social partners, subsequently passed in the national parliament, and promulgated by the president in December 1995. A raft of other legislation, including the Skills Development Act, which benefitted workers in a variety of ways, also originated in this period even though some of it was only passed in subsequent years. And the final draft of the South African Constitution, promulgated in 1996, addressed many of the concerns raised by labour and enshrined socio-economic rights, even if these were restricted by the limitation clause.[6]

For a short while, it seemed South Africa might defy the odds and that social unionism would succeed. But this was not to last.

The symbolic turning point was the adoption of the GEAR programme, which occurred just before the September Commission published its three scenarios. GEAR violated all three of the central tenets of social unionism. First, it bypassed corporatist structures and was imposed by Cabinet without any discussion with the social partners (Adam et al., 1997; Alexander, 2002; Bond, 2000; Marais, 2001). Even President Mandela acknowledged this in his speech at COSATU's sixth national congress, saying 'It was unfortunate that here in GEAR we did not have sufficient consultation with other members of the alliance. In fact even the ANC learnt of GEAR when it was almost complete ... We ignored those who put us in power' (Mandela, 1997). Second, GEAR's economic strategy violated the ethos of compromise that forms the hallmark of social unionism (Adler and Webster, 1995; see also Webster and Adler, 1999).

And third, its passage indicated that the Tripartite Alliance was ineffective as a mechanism for ensuring COSATU's influence on the ANC. Indeed, the passage of GEAR suggested that COSATU's influence was waning.

If any doubts remained about this, they were quashed by the publication of Mbeki's 'State and Social Transformation' document (ANC, 1996: 22) as discussed in the previous chapter. This document spoke to the limits that the ANC was facing in its efforts to pursue a radical transformation agenda in the face of government debt, capital mobility and the global environment; it called for a stronger partnership with the private sector as a means to enable development. This call for a strategic alliance between the state and capital was a milestone. It signalled a significant departure from the ANC's traditional approach to alliances, which, until this point, had tended to prioritise labour and other marginalised sectors within the population.

The effects of this strategic shift and the adoption of GEAR were catastrophic for workers. Between 1985 and 2002, the share of workers' wages as a percentage of GDP declined significantly from 57.1 per cent in 1985 to 51.4 per cent in 2002. In the same period, profit share increased from 42.9 per cent to 51.4 per cent (Gelb, 2003: 21).[7] This trend was consolidated in the post 2003 era, as was demonstrated in a debate on the issue between Dick Forslund of the Alternative Information Development Centre, Loane Sharpe of ADCORP, and Brian Kantor of Investec. The debate was provoked by ADCORP's release of a study claiming that labour productivity had fallen in South Africa (ADCORP, 2011). Forslund challenged ADCORP's, Sharpe's and later Kantor's claims, arguing that wages had been 'one percentage point lower than the increase in productivity' (Forslund, 2011b; 2012). Sharpe and Kantor countered this by attributing GDP growth in post-apartheid South Africa to the mechanisation that has taken place rather than the efforts of workers (Kantor, 2011; Sharpe, 2011a; 2011b). In any case, all acknowledged that the wage share of GDP had decreased to 50.6 per cent in 2010, from the 55.9 per cent that it had been in 1994. Thus despite the democratic transition, workers were getting a smaller share of national income. Yet, as Forslund argued (using the cases of both the United States and Britain after the Second World War), it is only when real wages outpace labour productivity, and when the wage-share of national income increases, that inequality can be addressed significantly (Forslund, 2012). Clearly, this empirical data demonstrates that workers have benefitted far less than the corporate sector from the growth of the South African economy in the post-apartheid era.

The political consequences of this have been dramatic. As noted in Chapter Three, COSATU's relationship with the ANC deteriorated badly after 1996, and the trade union federation has since embarked on a series of high-profile stayaways against one or other aspect of government policy. Person days lost over this period increased from 650 000 in 1997 to 1.25 million in 2001 (Andrew, Levy & Associates, quoted in Devey et al., 2004). These public protests outraged the ANC leadership who challenged COSATU to leave the alliance (Mbeki, 2002). The political atmosphere within the ruling party became increasingly stifling, especially for left-leaning activists within the ANC who were pressured to toe the leadership's line. This culminated in 2002 with the public humiliation of South African Communist Party (SACP) leader, Jeremy Cronin, by Dumisane Makhaye, a member of the ANC's national executive committee, and Smuts Ngonyama, then the ANC's official spokesperson, for suggesting that the ruling party displayed some tendencies towards 'Zanufication' (Cronin, 2002).

The heady optimism among advocates of social unionism also dissipated as the implications of GEAR became evident. Their assessments on the prospects for unions and workers became more sober and realistic as the Mandela presidency came to its end.

A comparison of two articles by labour sociologists Glenn Adler and Eddie Webster on labour and democracy in South Africa makes this very clear. The first article (Adler and Webster, 1995) is largely an actor-based theory of transition, which prioritises agency over structure (although they would deny this). It demonstrates the central role played by COSATU in the transition and its evolution. The central message in this paper was that if the union federation continued to support a strategy of radical reform (by its participation in corporatist forums, the secondment of COSATU leaders to national and regional parliaments as ANC MPs, and participating in the formulation of the Reconstruction and Development Programme), then 'the South African transition may constitute the first significant challenge to the predictions of orthodox transition theory, [which suggests] ... that the democracy resulting from the transition process is conservative economically and socially' (Adler and Webster, 1995: 100).

Their second article, (Webster and Adler, 1999), was theoretically and conceptually more nuanced, recognising the conditioning effects of structures on actors. It also reflected on experiences of state transitions in both the developed and developing worlds.[8] Although their message was similar, that class compromise was still possible, they seem less sanguine about the chances of this happening in South Africa, and more aware of the structural pressures on the ANC to abandon the interests of workers and marginalised communities in favour of a compromise with the elite. The 1999 article still betrayed an exaggerated assessment of the capacities of the labour movement, as reflected in their conclusion that South Africa was in the throes of a class stalemate, but their article reveals that advocates of social unionism had moved on to a more sober assessment of prospects for a worker-aligned political dispensation.

But how is it that such politically astute labour leaders and experienced sociologists were so seriously misled in the early days of the transition? Why did the social pact that they advocated unravel so completely, and how did the social constituencies that COSATU represents lose so much ground in the democratic era? The answer to these questions lies in the motivations that drive the formation of social pacts.

Labour leaders cottoned on to the notion of a social pact in the early 1990s as a mechanism to legitimise their alliance with the ANC, the soon-to-be leaders in the state. Sociologists were driven by a similar desire to legitimise the decisions of the labour movement. As a result, little serious investigation was done of the conditions that generate such pacts and facilitate their success. Where comparative examples were examined, this was done in a fairly superficial way – describing positive outcomes experienced elsewhere and implying that these could emerge in South Africa, without an investigation of the specific conditions that facilitated these (Maree, 1993). Those studies that warned of the dangers of social pacts in the context of the economic and political climate of the 1990s were brushed aside as 'ultra-leftist' and 'academic' (Callinicos, 1992; Desai and Habib, 1994; Habib, 1997), although these too could have been more contextually grounded. As things turned out, the social pacts unravelled, the unions' political influence was weakened, and poverty and inequality increased. If this outcome is to be reversed, and attempts are to be made to launch a new social pact, it is imperative to understand the conditions under which social pacts emerge and succeed.

Understanding the emergence of social pacts

The international literature on corporatism or social pacts emanates from three schools, each of which advances a distinctive explanation for the prevalence of such arrangements in the modern world. The first, known as the historical continuity school, focused primarily on examples from Latin America. It argued that corporatist political initiatives in that region have their roots in a political culture that is historically grounded in hierarchy, status, and patronage. One of the more noted scholars from this school, Howard Wiarda (1981) argued that there is a distinct continuity between the pre- and post-colonial periods in Latin American nations; that is, that the nature of the society and the substantive character of the political and constitutional order extended, in an adapted form, from the pre-colonial into the post-colonial period. Thus, corporatism was conceived as having its roots in an elitist, historical, and authoritarian heritage and has having been imparted to the region by its colonial powers.

A second, related interpretation of corporatism emerged from the 'societal reflection school', which suggested that corporatist political arrangements were merely a reflection of the natural organisation of particular societies. Ronald Rogowski and Lois Wasserspring, two proponents of this view (cited in Stepan, 1978: 59–66), argued that it was natural for groups to emerge in socially segmented societies (although they excluded the state from their analysis of how such groups emerged), and that corporatist arrangements automatically emerge to govern the political interactions among these groups. Corporatism was thus seen as a natural political arrangement in socially segmented societies.

Stepan has critiqued both of these theories about the origins of corporatism. He argues that the 'historical continuity' explanation fails to account for the diversity of political outcomes in geographical areas that are considered to have experienced similar cultural influences (1978: 54). His principal argument against the 'societal reflection' theory is its treatment of society as an independent variable, and the political system as a dependent variable. It was this erroneous conception, he argues, that made it possible for scholars to conceive of group formation as a natural process that is not influenced by political factors.

An alternative explanation for corporatism and social pacts advanced by Stepan (1978) can be labelled the 'crisis response' theory.[9] According to this perspective, corporatist institutional arrangements are creations of states that are facing a time of crisis. Their imperative, following Schmitter (1974), is to create the conditions for the continued reproduction of capitalism through the incorporation of subordinate classes into formal political processes (Stepan,1978: 24, 25). Stepan analysed how the political programmes pursued by state-corporatist regimes in Peru, Brazil, Chile and Mexico had achieved this outcome. He then argued that the programmatic goal of elites in these societies was to achieve an 'integral security' that would serve to connect national security with development. State economic elites, he maintained, entered into alliances with the military and multinational corporations in order to achieve the social peace that was required for the realisation of their national development plans. Stepan also argued that corporatism appeals particularly to elites in the 'Third World' where 'there is a widespread elite fear that the old modes of domination are breaking down, and they search for new mechanisms to link the lower classes to the state and new formulas to legitimise such mechanisms' (1978: 58). He suggested that a corporatist and statist ideology was the natural political response of elites in Africa and Latin America, which rejected more liberal or Marxist ideas on the basis that these legitimise conflict.

Whereas Stepan's 'crisis-response' explanation focuses on the origins of state corporatism, it is also relevant to an understanding of the emergence of societal forms of corporatism. One application of this explanation to societal corporatism is Charles Maier's (1984) 'Preconditions for Corporatism', in which he suggested that the origins of societal corporatism in western Europe could be understood only within the context of the rise of mass labour movements and the political challenge that the unions presented to liberal constitutionalism. Maier contended that, during and after the First World War, the production demands imposed by the war effort, and the need to minimise labour unrest, prompted state elites to establish corporatist arrangements, which they maintained until after the Second World War. The eventual renegotiation of corporatist arrangements was motivated, Maier argued, by a sense of political and economic vulnerability experienced by state elites after the Second World War. Moreover, the imperative of rebuilding those Western economies that had been devastated by the war required industrial peace and wage moderation. Thus, social pacts were renegotiated and trade-offs were made, in which organised labour accepted lower wage increases in return for improved social protection (Hassel and Ebbinghaus, 2000; Pizzuto, 2006). These corporatist features were sustained in subsequent decades by the strength of social democratic parties and the legitimisation of a social democratic ideology that 'was built upon the premise of continued bargaining among class actors for political and social gains' (Maier, 1984: 49).

The contemporary revitalisation of social pacts in Europe since the early 1980s (particularly in Austria, Sweden, Norway, Netherlands and Belgium) and the establishment of new ones (in Portugal, Spain and Ireland) can also be accounted for using Maier's explanatory framework. Bieling and Schulten (2001) as well as Hassel and Ebbinghaus (2000) suggest that the newer pacts emanate from the imperative of enabling the process of European integration. They cite the demands made by the 1992 Maastricht Treaty for European economies to be restructured on a more competitive basis and for their public deficits and inflation to be brought under control. An alternative explanation is that political parties considered and established social pacts as a means to reduce the electoral fall-out likely to result from the imposition of economic adjustments and restrictive wage policies (Hamann and Kelly, 2006). Both of these explanations focus on political elites in moments of crisis and are therefore broadly compatible with the earlier accounts of inter- and post-war state and societal corporatism.

On balance, then, the 'crisis response' explanation seems to be the most useful one to apply to the rise of social pacts and societal corporatism in contemporary South Africa. The newly emerging ANC-aligned state elites believed that prudent management of the South African economy in the post-Cold War era was necessary for generating and maintaining business confidence, for enhancing the competitiveness of South African firms and for convincing the foreign and domestic business communities to increase their levels of investment in the productive side of our economy. They also recognised that prioritising these economic imperatives would not immediately address the material grievances of their main constituencies, nor would they deliver on the electoral promises made to voters. Recognising that COSATU, as the largest trade-union formation, had the capacity to destabilise this agenda by resorting to mass strikes and protests, they sought to neutralise this threat by going along with COSATU's proposed social pact and its corporatist strategy.

For its part, COSATU had been ideologically disarmed in the years immediately following the collapse of the Berlin Wall. This was dramatically captured by senior COSATU unionists Adrienne Bird and Geoff Schreiner (1992) in an article entitled 'COSATU at the Crossroads', in which they argued that the collapse of the Soviet Union necessitated a rethink of the meaning of socialism. They argued that the failure of the communist experiment proved 'that modern day economies ... do not permit the possibility that all functions of the market can be replaced. The market and private enterprise have to be allowed a significant role in a future socialist society' (1992: 23). It was on this basis that Bird and Schreiner proceeded to identify a range of corporatist institutions, including the National Economic Forum and the National Manpower Commission and suggested that these types of formations 'become permanent institutional features of a democratic socialist South Africa' (1992: 23–24). Social pacts, therefore, seemed to offer a reasonable compromise in a world in which more radical options were not on the cards. Furthermore, the idea of a social pact dovetailed neatly with the tradition of the Tripartite Alliance. A social pact was thus seen as a logical step forward for the Alliance under conditions in which it held state power.

The preceding theoretical reflections are useful in explaining the emergence of social pacts and the conditions under which they can be successful. Social pacts have helped to enhance the lives of ordinary citizens in democratic western Europe. In that context, however, the international threat of the Cold War, combined with the strength of the labour unions in those countries, predisposed international political elites (particularly in the United States) to facilitate western European development through the provisions of the Marshall Plan.[10] In other words, the prevailing international and domestic context created the political will among Western elites for the establishment of a Keynesian macro-economic environment, within which social pacts and social democracies were cocooned (Maier, 1984: 49; Panitch, 1986).

This must not be interpreted to imply that the social democracies of western Europe are homogenous. Indeed, as Esping-Andersen (1990) has demonstrated, significant differences exist, including widely differing social pacts and social welfare capacities. Nevertheless, despite their differences, their collective genesis lies in the Keynesian global economic environment and a domestic context in which labour was a significant political actor.

The use of social pacts in the more neo-liberal economic climate of South Africa in the mid 1990s was unlikely to lead to the same outcome. Indeed, as maintained by Adam Przeworski (1991) – and as shown by David Ost's (2000) case study of Eastern Europe – social pacts and corporatist institutions became mechanisms of co-option in this era. They paved the way for more conservative economic policies, increased political tensions and ultimately weakened the legitimacy of democratic regimes and their institutions.

The potential for a social pact in the post-Polokwane era

Is a social pact feasible in the post-Polokwane period? After all, as indicated in Chapter One, COSATU and the SACP are now in far more powerful positions. To briefly reiterate: the balance of power in South African politics changed significantly as a result of developments at the ANC's national electoral congress held at Polokwane in 2007. Mbeki's defeat and Zuma's victory installed a new governing alliance at the helm of the ANC and the state. COSATU, the SACP, and the left within the ANC constituted one of the more important, if not the core institutional elements within this political alliance, and their leverage within the state and its economic institutions has increased significantly.

This does not mean that the interest groups and social actors that held sway during the Mbeki era, namely the corporate sector and the black business community in particular, are no longer significant. Indeed, as indicated earlier, the corporate sector was highly influential in the appointments of Trevor Manuel, Pravin Gordhan, and Gill Marcus, and in the Zuma administration's continued commitment to inflation targeting and small budget deficits. The influence of black businesses has been evident in the fightback by nationalists within the ANC to contain the economic and leadership footprint of COSATU and the SACP.

Essentially the post-Polokwane era has witnessed the emergence of what Eddie Webster and Glenn Adler (1999) assumed already existed in 2000; namely, a stalemate between unions and the corporate sector, where the interests of neither can prevail within the state without being constrained by the other.

Nevertheless, as demonstrated in Chapter Three, this change in the balance of power manifested itself in a deepening shift to the left in economic terms. This is evident in increased social spending, maintained (at least in the first three years of the Zuma administration) through higher budget deficits. The shift is also evident in a more activist state within the economy. That is, through its regulatory power, the state has underwritten an active industrial policy and more interventionist general economic policies, while also focusing on an infrastructural programme managed through parastatals and financed in part by development financial institutions. The state has also engaged more robustly with the corporate sector and in particular with foreign investors. This was seen, for example, in the insistence by the departments of agriculture, forestry and fisheries, as well as trade and industry and economic development, that US-based Walmart's takeover of Massmart in 2011 be accompanied by guarantees of no job losses and skills transfers (*Business Day*, 3/08/2011).

Again, these shifts have not been uncontested, as evidenced in finance minister, Pravin Gordhan's commitment to realising an onerous 3 per cent budget deficit and a 38 per cent public debt to GDP ratio by 2014 (2012a: 3). But what I described in the previous chapter as the state's 'groping towards social democracy', still contains significant elements of a neo-Keynesian economic agenda and represents the most substantive economic shift to the left of the post-apartheid era.

The national shift to a neo-Keynesian economic agenda has been accompanied by similar developments at the global level. The 2008 economic crisis necessitated significant interventions in the economies of North America, western Europe, and even Asia including China, in order to avert the global economy sliding into something akin to the economic depression of the 1930s. This, together with the undermining of the 'Washington Consensus', which, in turn, delegitimised institutions such as the IMF and the World Bank (notably captured in Joseph Stiglitz's 2002 book, *Globalisation and its Discontents*) has enhanced the appeal of neo-Keynesian policy prescriptions in both the developed and developing worlds. The coinciding shifts to neo-Keynesianism at both the national and global planes helped to reduce external pressures on the South African government's economic shift to a more inclusive developmental direction.

This balance of power as of early 2013, combined with these broader structural dynamics and economic developments, is far more likely to allow equitable social pacts to thrive than was the case in the 1990s. But structural conditions alone do not enable the emergence of social pacts. Such pacts also require political will and leadership. Indeed, the importance of the role of agency cannot be overemphasised. As I indicated in Chapter One, history is never made simply by unconstrained actors; neither is it determined only by structural or historical conditions. Historical and political developments can only truly be explained through the interactions of actors within structures of power. Such power structures constrain individual behaviour and it requires imagination, political will and courage for actors to understand their constraining effects and to develop an agenda that speaks to the realities of the moment, yet opens up opportunities for further empowerment and development, thereby implicitly transforming the balance of power itself.

Two conclusions flow from these reflections. First, Seekings and Nattrass's (2006) proposal (discussed in Chapter One) for a low wage-growth strategy to be negotiated through a social accord, is effectively a nonstarter in the current context. Irrespective of the morality of the proposal, which I questioned earlier, it is also unworkable in strategic terms. Given COSATU's strength as the largest union federation in the country and its increased political influence, why would it agree to a social accord that would in effect, generalise and enhance the 'precariousness' of its members' existence (Franco Barchiesi, 2011)? Moreover, why would it do so in an environment in which its members have no access to the social net that is available to their counterparts in western Europe? In Chapter Seven, I interrogate the terms of a social accord that could resonate with the current balance of power, yet simultaneously address South Africa's unemployment crisis and protect the gains won by organised workers in the post-apartheid era. For now, it is worth noting that Seekings and Nattrass's solution is unviable because it essentially asks the labour movement, at the point of its greatest influence, to capitulate to what David Ost (2000) refers to as neo-liberal tripartism and effectively sacrifice the interests of its members.

Second, the reflections suggest that a 'Gramscian imagination' is required to capitalise on this moment, when the structural conditions and the broader environment are so facilitative of an equitable social pact. Unfortunately, such leadership has not been demonstrated on a consistent basis by the Zuma administration. Indeed, President Zuma's annual 'State of the Nation' addresses have been particularly uninspiring in this regard. Confronted with rolling labour strikes and service delivery protests, Zuma has responded by promising everything to everyone (Zuma, 2009; 2010; 2011b). There is little that anyone could disagree with in his formal speeches. He promised all stakeholders – business, labour, students, middle- and upper-middle-class citizens – what they wanted. But, by saying everything he, in effect, said nothing. He made no choices and exchanged no trade-offs. In the process, Zuma missed important opportunities to define his political administration and establish the essential preconditions for a social pact.

Social pacts, it must be understood, are established by state elites with the willing participation of the organisations linked to relevant interest groups and social actors. They are essentially about managing the expectations of citizens, workers and even the business community. To date, Zuma, his ministers, and the leadership of the ANC have failed in this. Essentially the ANC and government's responses have been unimaginative. Gwede Mantashe's characteristic response, for example, has been to chastise workers for compromising the image of the Zuma administration (*Business Day*, 6/11/2009). Trevor Manuel has accused the corporate sector of cowardice and asked it to stand up to the might of the unions (*Business Day*, 17/06/2009). President Zuma has remained silent or simply promised everything to everyone as noted. None of these responses have helped to manage popular expectations.

Astute political leadership requires a president, his ministers and other leaders to inspire a nation. President Zuma should have used his 'State of the Nation' addresses to identify the dilemmas he faces and recorded that he was not their architect. He should have recognised the hypocrisy of public debate in which workers are berated for asking for small increases in real terms, while CEOs and senior executives in the corporate sector enjoy overly extravagant remuneration packages. He should have explained that, while he recognises the need for wage increases, and sympathises with the economic plight of workers and ordinary citizens, he does not have the resources to immediately address their demands. Then he could have legitimately asked for time, provided what was immediately possible and established a process with representatives from all sides – in essence activating a social pact – to find a solution to the dilemma over the next three to five years.

To further legitimise the process, President Zuma could have led by example. He could publicly forego certain privileges to which his office entitles him and ask his ministers to do the same. He could then berate corporate executives for their lavish packages and ask them to temporarily forego their bonuses and take lower than inflationary increases. Not all would have listened, but the act of asking would make important symbolic statement. The president could argue that, in the economic recession, sacrifices must not only be made by workers, the poor, the marginalised and the ordinary citizens, but also by the rich and the upper-middle classes.

There are some who would, of course, warn of the dangers of alienating the business community and the likelihood of investors fleeing our shores. But is a mere request to be circumspect in executive remuneration packages likely to constitute a serious threat to investment? Note that the corporate sector invests to make profits. As long as a climate exists in which profits can be made, the business community will remain and continue to invest.[11] President Obama has berated American business executives for their lavish bonuses, remuneration packages and expense accounts. Prime Minister Cameron, President Sarkozy and Chancellor Merkel have done the same. Yet the South African government, with at least a half-a-dozen openly committed communists and socialists in its Cabinet, remained silent on the issue of excessive executive remuneration until 2010, some three years after the 2008 economic recession.

Then, when the request was finally made, both political and business leaders behaved in a manner that stoked citizens' anger and set back the management of popular expectations even further (Gumede, 2012: 27–28). Soon after taking office, ministers in Zuma's administration spent millions on new vehicles for themselves. The media has since reported scandal after scandal about the lavish travel and accommodation expenditures of senior officials and politicians, and exposed a number of cases of corruption and ethical violations involving senior politicians and high-profile officials within the Zuma administration. Some of the more high-profile cases, including those involving the commissioner of police Bheki Cele, public works minister Gwen Mahlangu Nkabinde and the minister of co-operative governance and traditional affairs, Sicelo Shiceka, were investigated and successfully concluded by Advocate Thulisile Madonsela in the public protector's office.[12] As if this were not enough, the Zuma administration has been tarnished further by his close family members – including his son Duduzane Zuma and his nephew Khulubuse Zuma – whose own ethical conduct and brushes with the law have created a perception that a crass personal enrichment exercise may be underway at the highest level of the state.[13]

Business leaders have, of course, bemoaned this state of affairs, but many have been implicated in their own enrichment exercises. The remuneration of executives in companies listed on the Johannesburg Stock Exchange or the Alt-X exchange increased by an average of 23 per cent in 2008 (*Financial Mail*, 15/07/2010). A similar 23.3 per cent increase was reported for executives in the top 40 JSE-listed companies in 2010 (*Business Times*, 9/07/20). These increases were recorded while many were challenging unions not to make excessive wage demands. In addition, a number of cases of CEOs receiving inflated bonuses created more scandal. For example, Whitey Basson, chief executive of the Shoprite-Checkers supermarket chain, received remuneration of R627.6 million in 2010 (*The Citizen*, 5/05/2011). Many other CEOs have received inflated bonuses, sometimes despite the fact that their companies performed sub-optimally in a given financial year. The defence often raised in this regard is that these levels of remuneration have little impact on the overall finances of a company or institution because they apply to such a small number of people. This rationalisation misses the point. The management of popular expectations requires some symbol of sacrifice from the political and economic elite. When the elite are perceived to be recipients of such lavish excess, not only does it prevent the management of popular expectations, but it also provokes ordinary citizens to demand more.

This is precisely what has happened since 2009. As noted, labour strikes increased dramatically with a record loss of worker days in 2010. Wage settlements were significantly higher than inflation (at 9.4 per cent, 8.2 per cent and 8 per cent in 2009, 2010, and 2011 respectively) (SARB, 2011: 16; 2010: 17). Public-sector wage settlements have been even higher since 2008, prompting Pravin

Gordhan to note in his 2010 Budget speech that the public wage bill, including the 2008 adjustments to the salaries of professionals, had virtually doubled in five years (Gordhan, 2010a: 20). In the same period, service delivery protests, targeted particularly at local government officials, have mushroomed around the country as citizens increasingly demand that the ANC fulfil its election promises.

In the wake of the Marikana massacre in August 2012, Zuma, his government and even the business community seemed to have gotten the message. After one of the high-level consultations involving the president and some of his Cabinet ministers, as well as business and union leaders, Zuma announced a voluntary pay cap for Cabinet members and corporate executives (*Business Day*, 19/10/2012; *City Press*, 20/10/2012). Simultaneously, however, a story broke in the media about the renovations to Zuma's personal homestead in Nkandla in northern KwaZulu-Natal costing taxpayers an excess of R240 million (US$28 million) (*City Press*, 20/10/2012; *Mail & Guardian*, 26/10/ 2012). The exposure provoked a public scandal. Once again, the personal excesses of political leaders compromised the management of popular expectations. In essence then, this political failure to manage expectations – both elite and popular – is increasingly snowballing to constitute a fiscal and developmental challenge for the post-apartheid state.

To sum up, the social pact attempted in the 1990s, the remnants of which still exist today, failed because the structural conditions of that time were not facilitative of equitable outcomes for all social partners. In essence, the social pact became a mechanism to co-opt and emasculate labour's demands. In the post-Polokwane era, however, these structural conditions have begun to shift – COSATU's leverage within the state has been enhanced, political and economic elites are less certain of their hold on power, and the global and national macro-economic environment is moving in a Keynesian direction – creating the potential for a social pact to succeed. Yet for this to happen, bold political leadership is required – leadership that is capable of managing the expectations of the citizens and workers, as well as those of the political and economic elites.

The ANC and government leaders have tried to manage the expectations of the former, but only tentatively tackled the latter. In addition, political leaders have shown reluctance to make their own sacrifices, and only since 2011 has Pravin Gordhan, the only senior figure in the Cabinet to do so, begun to make this a feature of his public remarks (*Business Day*, 27/10/2011). Moreover, paralysed by a fear of markets and their reaction, government leaders have been reluctant to rein in, even timidly, the expectations of business executives and the upper-middle classes. Again, this is increasingly and refreshingly being raised as a matter of concern by Gordhan. This is important, for as long as government fails to provide leadership in this regard, or is perceived as not doing so, it will fail to rein in popular expectations. Popular and privileged expectations are tied by an umbilical cord, and neither can be reined in without the other. Until this is done, no social pact will succeed. The irony is that whereas the social pact of the 1990s failed because of structural conditions, the one of the post-April 2009 era may be stillborn because of a failure of political courage and imagination.

The challenge

There is an urgent and collective desire in South Africa among political elites, business leaders and others to establish a social pact that would enable the management of popular expectations and allow available resources to be invested in a manner that facilitates inclusive development outcomes. So far, the political elites have had limited success in this regard. In my view, this is because they have not yet understood the two requirements for the establishment of a sustainable and equitable social pact, which are: (i) a relatively equitable balance of power between unions and the corporate sector that prompts the political and economic elites to make the necessary compromises; and (ii) the political will and leadership to manage both elite and popular expectations, without which the state cannot mobilise sufficient resources for long-term inclusive economic development.

Attempts to establish such a pact in South Africa in the 1990s failed because the balance of power between unions and the corporate sector was too unequal. State officials and corporate leaders were able to use the pact to try and co-opt and emasculate the labour movement. The latter, supported by local communities, rebelled both explicitly and implicitly and the pact unravelled, existing only in form by 2000. The 2007 ANC conference at Polokwane ushered in a new era, which changed the power relations between unions and the corporate sector to some extent. This has again opened up the prospect for the establishment of a social pact. However, although the structural conditions are now conducive to the success of such a pact, the political leadership seems to lack the will and imagination to effectively manage the expectations of both the workers and the corporations.

There is evidence that some political leaders, and, in particular the finance minister, Pravin Gordhan, recognise this and are trying to contain both elite and popular expectations, but until this agenda is pursued by a wider grouping of political and corporate leaders, the strategy is unlikely to succeed. A failure of collective leadership is likely to have disastrous consequences for South Africa's ability to build a future distinguished by inclusive development outcomes.

5

The evolution of state–civil society relations

Two very different visions permeate public discourse on state–civil society relations in South Africa. The first is well illustrated by the words of Zola Skweyiya who, when he was minister of social development, responded to a question about government's expectation of NGOs as follows:

> The basic twin expectations of government are that NGOs will firstly, continue to act as monitors of the public good and safeguard the interests of the disadvantaged sections of society. This performance of this social watch role requires both transparency and accountability on the part of NGOs. The government's second expectation is that NGOs will assist in expanding access to social and economic services that create jobs and eradicate poverty among the poorest of the poor. This requires cost effective and sustainable service delivery. (Zola Skweyiya quoted in Barnard and Terreblanche, 2001: 17)

The second vision is succinctly captured in the words of Ashwin Desai, an academic at the University of Johannesburg and one of the more prominent public intellectuals within the new social movements that have emerged in the post-apartheid era.

> For many of the activists ... working in different spaces and having different strategies and tactics, there was a binding thread. There was unmitigated opposition to the economic policies adopted by the ANC ... Activists

spoke of how the right-wing economic policies lead to widespread and escalating unemployment, with concomitant water and electricity cut-offs, and evictions even from the 'toilets in the veld' provided by the government in the place of houses. More importantly, there was general agreement that this was not just a question of short-term pain for long-term gain. The ANC had become a party of neo-liberalism. The strategy to win the ANC to a left project was a dead end. The ANC had to be challenged and a movement built to render its policies unworkable. It seems increasingly unlikely that open confrontation with the repressive power of the post-apartheid state can be avoided. (Desai, 2002: 147)

Both statements draw attention to some of the key problems in post-apartheid South Africa and express a wish to enhance the empowerment and living conditions of the poor. Both statements also reflect the institutional locations – in government and in civil society – of those who articulated them. But the absolute and categoric nature of what they envisage makes both statements unhelpful in conceptualising and understanding contemporary state–civil society relations. Implicitly, the statements portray South African civil society as homogenous; that is, they project a single set of relations onto the whole of civil society. But is civil society not plural by its very nature? And, should this plurality not infuse current understandings of state–civil society relations in post-apartheid South Africa?

The suggestions put forward in this chapter take as their starting point a definition of civil society that celebrates plurality. In other words, I recognise that the set of institutions within civil society reflect diverse and even contradictory political and social agendas and that state–civil society relations necessarily reflect this plurality. That is, some relationships between civil society actors and state institutions will be adversarial and conflictual while others will be collaborative and collegial. In my view, this state of affairs should not be lamented. Indeed, it is cause for celebration since it signifies the political maturing of South African society. Under apartheid, the adversarial–collaborative divide largely took a racial form. The bulk of 'white civil society' established collegial relations with the state, while the majority of 'black civil society' adopted a conflictual mode of engagement. This racial divide began to blur in the transition period as significant sections of the white community began to distance themselves from the apartheid regime. In the contemporary era, adversarial and collegial relations extend across the entire ambit of civil society so that, in this arena at least, the overt racial divide has all but disappeared.

Elsewhere I have defined civil society as 'the organised expression of various interests and values operating in the triangular space between the family, state and the market' (Habib and Kotze, 2003: 3). This definition conceptualises civil society as an entity distinct from both the market and the state. Of course, traditional Hegelian definitions of the term include the market, but Jean Cohen and Andrew Arato's (1992) comprehensive and defining work on the subject makes a coherent and persuasive case for why the market should be excluded from the definition of civil society. For Cohen and Arato, the actors in what they call 'political' and 'economic' society control and manage state power and economic production and this imparts to them a different strategic purpose and function from civil society actors. In their words, political and economic actors cannot 'subordinate [their] strategic and instrumental criteria to the patterns of normative integration and open-ended communication characteristic of civil society' (Cohen and Arato, 1992: ix). This then makes it essential for civil society to be analytically distinguished from 'both a political society of parties, political organisations, and political publics (in particular, parliaments) and an economic society composed of organisations of production and distribution, usually firms, cooperatives, partnerships and so on' (Cohen and Arato, 1992: ix).

Cohen and Arato's definition of civil society includes the actors and interactions in what Partha Chatterjee (2004) imagines as elements of 'political society'. Chatterjee distinguishes civil society – which he sees as the civilised expressions and interactions with the state of economic elites who reside in the cities of the developing world – from political society – which he views as the expressions and engagements of vulnerable groups (subalterns, as some prefer to call them) with the state via its local institutions and personnel (Chatterjee, 2004). Such engagements, Chatterjee argues, are not always democratic and may involve patronage,[1] clientelistic and other unethical, if not illegal, behaviour. But Chatterjee argues that these various forms of engagement are necessary if more vulnerable social groups are to survive the circumstances they find themselves mired in.

Care must, of course, be taken not to overly romanticise these groups or their 'survivalist' instincts. After all, what may be necessary for their short-term survival may also be detrimental to the long-term transformation of both the specific historical conditions within which they find themselves and the broader society in which they are located. In any case, Chatterjee is correct to include the role of these subalterns as well as their behaviour and interactions in an understanding of society. My own definition of civil society recognises this, and I include these actors and their activities within its ambit. Thus civil society is not interpreted here in its traditional western sense, as being defined by legitimate legal interactions with a democratic state. Rather it incorporates both the 'civil' and 'uncivil' components of all the collective endeavours that inhabit the triangular space between family, state and market.

Reflections on civil society in South Africa often describe its role in bringing about change, including its contributions to ending apartheid and its diverse engagements in the contemporary era. As indicated in earlier chapters, civil protests have influenced leadership changes in the ruling party as well as policy shifts within the post-apartheid state. But civil society has been impacted upon by the transition to democracy as much as it has informed its evolution. The policy choices of political elites, constrained in part by the balance of power within which they have found themselves, has influenced civil society organisations in both positive and negative ways. The net effect has been a transformation in the size and shape of civil society in South Africa. Before delving into the organisational contours of this civic transformation, it may be prudent to take up a historical lens and briefly examine the dynamics of civic engagement in the pre-1994 era.

Historical context

Contemporary civil society in South Africa is distinguished by the fact that it not only reflects the demographic realities of the society, it also transcends the racialised form of the adversarial–collaborative dichotomy that typified civic–state engagements in earlier epochs. This outcome is the product of a civic evolution that occurred in two distinct phases. Naturally these phases neatly coincide with key moments in the country's political evolution: the first with the liberalisation of apartheid which began in about 1978 and the second with the transition to democracy that is rooted in the first non-racial elections in April 1994.[2] The former facilitated demographic representivity by enabling a phenomenal growth in associational life in the country. Indeed, the distinctive feature of this period is not only the longitudinal growth of the civil society sector, but the formal emergence, or at least the surfacing in the political sphere of a significant part of it, namely black civil society actors who had hitherto been either banned or prevented from operating in the public arena. The later democratisation phase transformed the character and operations of civil society once again by creating new opportunities and challenges as the African National Congress (ANC) assumed state power in South Africa.

Before the political liberalisation of the late 1970s and early 1980s, the dominant elements in civil society were either pro-apartheid and/or pro-business. Agencies critical of the state and/or the socio-economic system were either actively suppressed or marginalised from formal political processes. The major political contest within formal civil society seemed to be between pro-apartheid institutions such as the Broederbond and the Nederduitse Gereformeerde Kerk on the one hand and liberal-oriented organisations such as the Institute of Race Relations and the National Union of South African Students on the other.[3] As the 1970s approached, anti-apartheid NGOs including trade unions and an array of organisations associated with the Black Consciousness Movement began to make their presence felt (Friedman, 1987; Marx, 1992).[4] However, their operations were more or less confined to South Africa's industries and townships, where they were continually harassed by the state and constrained by the miniscule resources that were available to them. Formal contestation and engagement within civil society and between it and the state was largely limited to 'white' civic associations.

This all changed in the late 1970s and early 1980s. Anti-apartheid elements within civil society resurfaced and, within a few years, became the dominant element within the sector. Two developments underpinned this growth in anti-apartheid civil society organisations. The first was the liberalisation of the political system unleashed in response to the 1976 Soweto revolt and implemented under PW Botha's regime in the early 1980s. This involved reform of the cruder aspects of grand apartheid, attempts to politically co-opt sections of the disenfranchised communities, and an allowance for some civic activity to emerge within the black population. It is indeed ironic that credit for facilitating the re-emergence of civil society, the institutions of which are most responsible for the destruction of apartheid, should go to the one of South Africa's most authoritarian political leaders. But such are the quirks of history.

In any case, the Soweto revolt in 1976, and the more general upsurge in protest including union activity throughout the 1970s, created a struggle between reformers and conservatives within the apartheid state. The former wanted to reform apartheid, make it compatible with the modernising imperatives of the economy and co-opt some elements of the black population by giving them a stake in the system. The latter wanted a recommitment to grand apartheid. The success of PW Botha and his reformist coalition in a leadership tussle within the National Party in the late 1970s created an opportunity for the reformist project to take off (Sparks, 1990).[5] A series of institutional reforms followed, of which a significant component included the recognition and legalisation of independent black unions and the establishment of a political space that permitted the re-emergence of anti-apartheid civil society (Friedman, 1987). Moreover, the state provided the rationale for mobilising this sector by proposing reforms that attempted to co-opt some and marginalise other elements of the black community. Anti-apartheid civil society was thus enabled and given a rationale for mobilisation, by the liberalisation of the apartheid state.

Not all of this was positive. In fact, very early on in the reform process the state began to actively repress elements within the anti-apartheid camp. But despite this repression, which became quite severe under the states of emergency of 1985 and 1986, anti-apartheid civil society formations retained their popular legitimacy. Thus, in September 1989, when FW de Klerk took over the leadership of the National Party in a palace coup, replacing PW Botha as president, and reintroducing or even extending the state's liberalisation initiative, the anti-apartheid movement rapidly re-emerged. By the early 1990s, the anti-apartheid camp had become the dominant element in the civil society sphere.

The second development facilitating the re-emergence of anti-apartheid civil society was the increased availability of resources to the non-profit sector in South Africa. On the one hand, human resources became increasingly available in the early 1980s as university students and graduates politicised by the activities of the 1970s,[6] as well as ex-political prisoners (many of whom were released in the early 1980s), came together in a myriad of ways to organise community and political activities and to establish non-profit organisations to support mass struggles. On the other hand, fiscal resources emerged from private foundations and foreign governments after the June 16 revolt had made its way across the television screens of the industrialised world. In addition, the increasing tempo of struggle within the country gradually compelled some local businesses and religious organisations to begin to underwrite anti-apartheid non-profit activity in South Africa (Stacey and Aksartova, 2001).

Two points need to be underscored in this very brief and cursory history of the emergence of contemporary civil society in South Africa. First, the historical overview provided supports two existing theories of how social movements emerge. Political opportunity theory (Tarrow, 1994) emphasises the opening of political spaces, while resource mobilisation theory (McCarthy and Zald, 1977; Tilly, 1978) focuses on resources and their availability to different social groups, to explain the rise of social formations. Both theories are helpful in understanding the emergence of contemporary civil society in South Africa.

The second point that needs to be stressed is that, although anti-apartheid civil society was borne within the womb of the apartheid state's reform programme, state–civil society relations tended to be highly adversarial throughout the 1980s. The reason for this is that the state's liberalisation initiative was not democratic or enabling.

Indeed, like all liberalisation initiatives in transitional societies, it must be conceptualised in relative terms. Thus, anti-apartheid civil society was treated with suspicion by the apartheid state. The legal environment, including the tax regime, while allowing anti-apartheid NGOs and community-based organisations to emerge, was nevertheless hostile to their operations. Similarly, the political and security environment remained repressive and became even more so after 1985. This hostility only changed after South Africa entered the democratisation phase of its political transition in the mid-1990s.

Civil society in the democratic era

Regime change doesn't always have significant impacts on society. But in South Africa the transition to democracy, which occurred in the context of globalisation, fundamentally transformed the society. In the process, civil society has been remoulded in significant ways, the effects of which are only now becoming evident. The most obvious outcome is the emergence of three distinct blocs in civil society, each of which is a product of separate transitional processes.

Creating an enabling environment

Political restructuring undertaken by the post-apartheid state to create an enabling environment for civil society largely influenced the first bloc, which comprises formal NGOs. Three initiatives are relevant here. First, the security environment was reorganised in significant ways. Repressive legislation was repealed and a political climate permitting public scrutiny and protest activity was established and sanctioned by no lesser authority than the Constitution.

Admittedly, legislative and behavioural blemishes have since emerged. Indeed, since 2000, there have been occasions when security officials and even some politicians have reacted to legitimate scrutiny and protest in ways reminiscent of their predecessors. Jane Duncan, for instance, has written and commented extensively on how post-apartheid South Africa's anti-terrorist legislation, the Protection of State Information Bill, and the militarisation of the police service under Zuma, limits legitimate civic protest and targets poor peoples' struggles to improve their circumstances (Duncan, 2007; 2010; 2012). Tragic manifestations of this include the murder of local community leader Andries Tatane in Ficksburg by police, when they attacked a protest march on 13 April 2011[7] and the massacre of 34 mineworkers by the police at Marikana in North West on 16 August 2012. Both incidents received massive publicity and highlighted the concerns of many grassroots activists who hold that repressive conduct is increasingly a feature of policing during local community protests. The police, Jane Duncan (2010) holds, are becoming securocratic in their approach and regularly abrogate the rights of poorer citizens who are actively involved in organising within their communities.

However, despite these real and ominous trends, any overall assessment has to concede that the current security environment is more enabling now than it has ever been in South Africa's history.

Second, the post-apartheid state moved quickly to pass legislation and adopt practices aimed at reorganising the political environment. Thus the Non-Profit Organisations Act of 1997 officially recognised civil society, created a system of voluntary registration for its constituents, and provided benefits and allowances for non-governmental and community-based organisations that undertake proper accounting and provide audited statements to government. A Directorate for Non-Profit Organisations was established in the Department of Social Welfare to co-ordinate these processes. In addition, the National Economic Development and Labour Council

(NEDLAC), the country's premier corporatist institution, was established with four chambers, the last of which aimed to cater for representation from civil society.[8] Perhaps most important in creating a new political environment, however, was the state's willingness to partner with NGOs in the policy-development and service-delivery arenas. As discussed later in this chapter, this opened up a new avenue of operations for certain kinds of NGO and fundamentally transformed their relations with the state.

Third, an enabling fiscal environment was created to facilitate the financial sustainability of this sector. This was, in part, forced on the state very early in the transition. NGOs confronted a major financial crunch when foreign donors redirected their funding away from civil society organisations in favour of the state. Again, legislation was passed and institutions were established to facilitate a new flow of resources to the sector. The Fundraising Act of 1978, which had limited the capacity of NGOs to raise funds, was repealed. Institutions such as the National Development Agency and the National Lottery Distribution Trust Fund were established with a mandate to fund legitimate non-profit activity. Tax regulations were reformed in 2000 and 2001 to grant tax-exemption to registered civil society organisations and to encourage the emergence of a philanthropic culture in the country.[9]

Not all of these initiatives have been an unqualified success. Indeed, the financing of non-profit activity by the National Development Agency and the National Lottery Distribution Trust has regularly been mired in controversy. The National Development Agency has been implicated in serious financial scandals and administrative inefficiencies and NGOs have regularly complained about not being able to access its grants, even though its primary mandate is to support such organisations (Funding Practice Alliance, 2011).[10] The National Lottery Distribution Trust has been criticised on similar grounds. In 2012, it faced controversy over financing a National Youth Development Agency youth festival and an event to celebrate the twenty-fifth anniversary of the Congress of South African Trade Unions (COSATU)'s, while ignoring many legitimate causes that directly benefit orphans, the aged and infirm, as well as other vulnerable groups (Democratic Alliance, 2012a). Critics have questioned the independence of both institutions and claimed that the allocations made by these agencies are too heavily influenced by the priorities of the state and the ruling party (Democratic Alliance, 2012a; Funding Practice Alliance, 2011). Nevertheless, once again, despite these challenges, the current domestic fiscal environment is more enabling of civil society organisations in South Africa than ever before.

The net effect of these legislative changes and restructuring has been the establishment of a fiscal, legal and political environment that has facilitated the development of a collaborative relationship between the state and formal NGOs. Such NGOs are increasingly contracted by the state to assist with policy development, implementation and service delivery. Donors, who sometimes fund such state–NGO partnerships, and who regularly advocate for the professionalisation and commercialisation of NGOs, have encouraged this. This shift to a service-related role has been contested, however.

The contestation was succinctly captured in an intellectual exchange between Max Price (1995) and Eddie Webster (1997), in the pages of the social science journal *Transformation*, soon after South Africa's first non-racial general elections. Price (who has since been appointed vice chancellor at the University of Cape Town was then the director of the Centre for Health Policy) warned of the dangers of too close a relationship between NGOs and the post-apartheid state. He argued that the democratic transition and the service relationships engendered between progressive NGOs and government departments, limited his centre's ability to link its research to the interests of poor and marginalised communities. He indicated that this was because the post-apartheid state treated the Centre for Health Policy as a technical research institute, and expected it to produce research reports on request (Price, 1995). By contrast, Eddie Webster (1997), then director of the Sociology of Work Project at the University of Witwatersrand, acknowledged the constraints experienced by his unit, but maintained that the project's opportunities to influence policy had been greatly enhanced by the new relationships facilitated by the political transition.

Despite Price's concerns, the structural pressures forging a more collegial engagement between NGOs and the post-apartheid state ensured that many of the NGOs that had played a role in opposing apartheid gravitated towards a service-related relationship with government. While this facilitated the financial sustainability of a number of these organisations, it came at a cost. The need for commercialisation and professionalisation blurred the non-profit/ profit divide and eroded the accountability of these organisations to the constituencies they professed to represent. As Rupert Taylor and I argued over a decade ago:

> The existing literature of the non-profit sector is replete with suggestions that NGOs are institutions that service the interests of the poor and marginalised. But can one really argue this when NGOs have become so commercially oriented and dependent on the resources of donors and the government? ... Can one really assert that [they are] community driven or answerable to marginalised sectors of South African society? (Habib and Taylor, 1999c: 79)

Counting the costs of neo-liberalism

The second and third blocs that have come to constitute contemporary civil society in the post-apartheid period are largely the products of processes associated with globalisation and its particular manifestation in South Africa. As indicated in Chapters Three and

Four, South Africa's integration into the global economy resulted in the post-apartheid government's adoption and implementation of neo-liberal policies at enormous social cost. Poverty and inequality increased, particularly in the late 1990s, and while economic liberalisation benefitted the upper classes of all racial groups, its effect on the lives of millions of poor and low-income families was devastating.

Civil society responded to this challenge by reconstituting itself in two very distinct ways. The first involved a proliferation of informal, survivalist community-based organisations, networks and associations, which helped poor and marginalised communities to simply survive the daily ravages of neo-liberalism. These include organisations that provide support for people with HIV and AIDS, informal orphanages, care structures for the aged, community gardens and the like. Care must be taken not to fall into the trap of much of the writing on the informal economy, and to celebrate these associations as representing the energy and vibrancy of South African society. Indeed, they must be recognised for what they are: a survivalist response of poor and marginalised people who have no alternatives in the face of a retreating state that has refused to meet its socio-economic obligations to its citizens. As I argued in the introduction to the first study on the size and shape of South African civil society (Habib, 2002: viii),[11] these informal, community-based networks increased throughout the democratisation era as a result of the government's failure both to address the scourge of HIV and AIDS as well as the ongoing crisis of unemployment.

The second response to the effects of neo-liberalism was the emergence of the category of organisations known as 'social movements' (Ballard et al., 2006). Social movements are a diverse set of organisations that network with one another to mobilise people around various issues. Some take the form of national campaign-based associations, such as the Treatment Action Campaign, which focused on challenging the state's policy on HIV and AIDS and on ensuring the provision of antiretroviral drugs to people with HIV. Others, such as the Soweto Electricity Crisis Committee and the Concerned Citizens Group, were located at the local level and in these cases organised against electricity cut-offs in Soweto and rates evictions and water terminations in Chatsworth and surrounding townships in Durban, respectively. Nevertheless, when compared to survivalist associations, social movements tend to be more formalised community-based structures, with distinct leaderships and memberships and they often have the support of a middle-class activist base. Moreover, their mode of operation is not survivalist; they are more political animals. Indeed, many have been established with the explicit political aim of organising and mobilising the poor and marginalised and contesting and/or engaging the state (and sometimes the corporate sector) around the implementation of neo-liberal economic and social policies. They aim to transform delivery and governance at the local level, and focus on changing the values and structures of the society within which they are located. As a result, they represent a fundamental challenge to the political status quo and its prevailing socio-economic dispensation.

These developments fundamentally changed the shape and size of civil society in South Africa. A number of studies have analysed components of this reconstituted post-apartheid civil society. With regard to the survivalist component, the first relevant study was coordinated by the School of Public and Development Management at the University of Witwatersrand, as part of a broader comparative project on global civil society that was managed by the Centre for Civil Society at Johns Hopkins University. This concluded that South Africa hosted approximately 98 920 non-profit associations in 1998. Of these, 53 per cent were found to be informal survivalist agencies organised and managed by individuals within poor and marginalised communities (Swilling and Russell, 2002: 20). Thus, in the late

1990s, NGOs and social movements constituted a minority within the South African civic universe, yet they received the vast majority of funding and other aid-resources deployed by government, the corporate sector, official development agencies and private foreign and domestic foundations (Swilling and Russell, 2002).

This significant survivalist footprint in South African civil society was also evident in a second study undertaken by the University of KwaZulu-Natal's Centre for Civil Society (Everatt and Solanki, 2007). Although focused on the state of giving in South Africa, the study's analysis of the flow of resources demonstrated the massive presence of survivalist organisations within the country's poor and marginalised communities. Its national survey indicated that 93 per cent of South Africans donated goods, money or time to development and/or poverty alleviation. The amount donated per month in 2003 came to R921 million, constituting an annual total of over R11 billion being targeted mainly at poor and vulnerable people (Everatt and Solanki, 2007: 51). An investigation of resource flows in poor communities demonstrated the continued emergence of informal organisations – stokvels, burial societies, remittance networks and the like – sustained by these resources, and directed towards providing collective services for vulnerable social groups (Seleoane, 2007). Such informal organisations enable communities to survive the devastating economic circumstances that they find themselves in.

An even wider set of research has focused on the new social movements component of civil society. The Centre for Civil Society at the University of KwaZulu-Natal also undertook the first large comparative study of post-apartheid social movements (Ballard et al., 2006). This study suggested that the institutional continuity between these post-apartheid movements and their anti-apartheid predecessors is limited and concluded that the newer organisations are a heterogeneous group defined largely by the poverty and inequality of the post-apartheid moment – itself bequeathed by the country's racialised history and the subsequent policy choices made by the ANC government. The study also argued that these movements are not simply 'spontaneous uprisings of the poor as is sometimes romantically imagined, but are dependent to a large extent on a sufficient base of material and human resources, solidarity networks, and often the external interventions of prominent personalities operating from within well-resourced institutions' (Ballard et al., 2005: 627). Many of these personalities do indeed have 'struggle credentials' – many having been activists in the anti-apartheid and/or union movements, who were subsequently marginalised for being critical of the strategic orientation adopted by the new government. But as the state's strategic orientation foundered in policy and service delivery failures, these activists regained their confidence, reorganised in their communities and became politically assertive once again.

Much of this analysis was reaffirmed in another study on social movements edited by William Beinart and Marcelle Dawson (2010) involving students from the University of Oxford. These researchers argued that while post-apartheid social movements 'echoed apartheid era mass mobilisation by being rooted in poor communities in the townships, sustaining a culture of discussion, of participation, and of the links between politics and community activity', they also 'operated in a transformed context, were beneficiaries of democratisation and had more freedom of organisation' (Beinart, 2010: 29). They also concluded that the new movements have had a positive effect 'by forcing key issues such as urban services and the right to antiretrovirals onto the political agenda' and by advocating for 'a broad citizenship, civic rights and democratization' capable of transforming the everyday lives of ordinary South Africans (Beinart, 2010: 30).

Both of these studies highlight the rights-based social struggles that predominated around the turn of the twentieth century. They do not capture the subsequent round of community protests, which Peter Alexander dates back to 2004 (2010: 37). As indicated in Chapter Two where I drew on Alexander's analysis, the more recent struggles are locally focused, fuelled largely by concerns surrounding service delivery or accountability, and mainly directed at municipal governments.

Scholars and social commentators such as Steven Friedman and Eusebius McKaiser (n.d.: 19) have questioned the description of these struggles as 'service delivery protests', suggesting that they are driven mainly by a desire 'of people at the grassroots ... to be part of the discussion on the way in which government is to serve them'.[12] While there is no doubt that a desire for participatory governance manifests in these protests, the repeated demands of protestors related to housing, water, sanitation and corruption suggests that service delivery concerns do play a significant part in defining their collective action. Moreover this need not mean that these citizens are 'unthinking passive recipients' as Friedman and McKaiser assume is the view of those who give these protests a service-delivery descriptor. Participatory governance and the state's delivery of services, which it is constitutionally obliged and has already promised to deliver, are not mutually exclusive goals and can reside comfortably alongside each other.

Various other scholars have noted that some of these protests are driven partly by factional fights within the ruling party (Alexander, 2010; Duncan, 2010; Kirshner and Phokela, 2010). This is, in part, a natural consequence of a widespread practice within the ruling party to deploy cadres to civil society organisations and groupings in local townships (Benit-Gbaffou, 2012; Piper and Africa, 2012). Nevertheless, while there is again no doubt that there is some spillover from factional battles within the ANC, these struggles cannot be solely attributed to internal battles within the ruling party. The struggles have independent autonomous roots in government's failure to enact promises made at election time, in the corruption of state officials, and in the excessive consumption evident in the lifestyles of local political elites at a time when those they are expected to serve are denied even the basics that their citizenship and residency status entitles them to.

Perhaps these social protests can be understood and explained as sporadic localised rebellions of the poor, driven by concerns around corruption, service delivery and accountability. In many cases, they are pragmatically directed at existing structures of the ruling party or at other organisations within the Tripartite Alliance, and aim to make dissident community voices heard within the corridors of power. In this sense, the protests are distinct from those that occurred at the turn of the century, in terms of their local focus and character. The social protests are also fundamentally different from the actions taken by survivalist agencies, as they typically aim to mobilise poor people in the hope of transforming delivery and governance at the local level.

In summary, the post-apartheid era has witnessed the 'normalisation' of South African society in a neo-liberal global environment. Poverty, inequality with the attendant problems of marginalisation and poor governance that the Washington Consensus's approach to globalisation and the Third Wave model of democracy have wreaked on other parts of the world, are now hallmarks of South African society. Civil society's response to these developments has been similar to that of civil society structures in other parts of the world; it has constituted itself into the three distinct blocs already discussed – NGOs, informal survivalist agencies and social movements. And this reconstitution has facilitated the evolution of a plurality of relationships between civil society and the post-apartheid state.

The state, civil society and the consolidation of democracy

The three constituent blocs in civil society have very distinct relationships with the state. At one end of the spectrum is a powerful set of service-related NGOs, which, as a result of the more enabling environment created by the democratic regime, have entered into partnerships with, and/or subcontracted to, the state. Other NGOs have used this same enabling environment to partner with other powerful stakeholders such as the corporate sector, international private foundations, and even the development arms of foreign governments. But the South African state is by far the largest fiscal contributor to developmental initiatives in the country (Swilling et al., 2008), and is therefore the primary interlocutor with the civil society sector. As such, the reflections below, which may often also apply to other important stakeholders such as the corporate sector, private foundations and international financial institutions, focus mainly on state–civil society interactions and relations. It should also be noted that in relation to NGOs, these interactions have largely taken an engaged and collegial form.

On the other end of the spectrum are community-based structures, which actively challenge and oppose what they perceive as the implementation of neo-liberalism. These organisations or social movements also have an explicit relationship with the state. This relationship, however, depending on the organisation and the issue area, hovers somewhere between adversarialism and engagement, and sometimes involves both (Bond, 2001; Desai, 2002). But even when engaging the state, the way in which they do so is qualitatively different to that manner in which formal NGOs would do so. Formal NGOs have a relationship with the state that is largely defined by their subcontractual role, whereas community-based structures engage the state on a relatively more even footing, as they attempt to bring about change through mobilising citizens, lobbying, challenging the state through court action, and even resorting to outright resistance.

Between these two sets of organisations lies the third set of structures, survivalist and informal, organised mainly in marginalised communities, and with no relationship to the state. These organisations are preoccupied with assisting people to survive the ravages of neo-liberalism. They receive no resources, nor do they covet recognition from the state. Instead, they are largely sustained by a flow of resources that are internal to these communities (Seleoane, 2007). Moreover, they are simply consumed with the task of surviving the effects of the state's policies. Indeed, it is doubtful whether the majority of these associations fully recognise the extent to which the plight of the communities they are located in, is largely a result of policy choices made by the political elites.

Of course, the distinctions between the three blocs of civil society are not quite as stark or rigid as they have been depicted here. In the real world, many organisations straddle the divide and blur the boundaries between one or more of the blocs. Some organisations, such as the Treatment Action Campaign, display, in the same historical moment, adversarial relations with the state on one issue, and more collegial relations on another (Friedman and Mottiar, 2006). Other organisations, such as the Homeless People's Federation, challenge and oppose some state institutions but have established partnerships with others (Khan and Pieterse, 2006). An important characteristic of the contemporary era is not the consistency of the message or practice within civil society organisations. Rather, it is that democratisation and globalisation have facilitated the reassertion of the plural character of civil society, and simultaneously undermined the homogenising effect that the anti-apartheid struggle had on the sector.

Most activists, politicians, and government officials recognise this plurality, at least at a rhetorical level. But for most, it seems that its meaning has not been internalised. Had it been, the constant demands from these actors, evident in the two statements quoted at the start of this chapter, for a single homogenous set of relations between civil society and the state, would cease. For state officials, and the leadership of the ruling party, the most appropriate relationship between civil society and the state is one founded on collegiality. In this view, service-related NGOs who contract with the state and community organisations that partner with the ruling party, are behaving in a manner that is conducive to democracy. Indeed, the ruling party has gone out of its way to reward such behaviour – mainly through providing access to corporatist institutions and other public-participation channels established by the state.

But, occasionally, the state intervenes more aggressively, manipulating its resources to benefit some organisations and undermine others. Perhaps the most notorious case of this to date was ESKOM's write-off of electricity arrears in Soweto. In this case, the then minister of public enterprises and now minister of justice, Jeff Radebe, convinced ESKOM to write off electricity arrears in the township in an effort to demobilise the Soweto Electricity Crisis Committee. The Committee had been gaining ground by assisting poor residents who had been disconnected for failing to pay their bills. To undermine the Committee, and to publicly demonstrate the benefits of alignment with the ruling party, ESKOM officially negotiated the write-off with the South African National Civic Organisation, a national civic body formally aligned to the ANC, (Zuern, 2006: 190–191). This blatant abuse of public resources by the state to influence the outcome of a competition between two civic associations, while rare, does graphically illustrate what the ruling party perceives as an appropriate state–civil society relationship, and the extent to which it will go to advance its model of state–civic engagement.

But the state is not alone in wanting to advance a homogenous state–civil society agenda. Radical activists within civil society also advance a homogenous vision, except for them the relationship should be adversarial rather than collegial (Bond, 2004c; Desai, 2002; McKinley, 2001). Of course this view is not dominant within civil society. Instead, the majority of activists in organisations such as COSATU, the Treatment Action Campaign and even the South African National Civic Organisation (SANCO) hold the view that the strategic priority of the contemporary era is to struggle for the soul of the ANC. They argue that the most effective strategy in this regard is to remain in partnership with the party but retain the independence and organisational capacity to take to the streets when necessary (COSATU, 2011; Cronin, 2002). Meanwhile in my view, and this is shared by my colleague Rupert Taylor, a strategic partnership with the ruling party has the systemic effect of consolidating existing power relations and enables state elites to be more responsive to the interests of black entrepreneurs and foreign and domestic capital. The antidote to this state of affairs is to break civil society's partnership with the ruling party, to reintroduce political uncertainty into the political system, and thereby foster greater responsiveness from political representatives to the interests of the poor and marginalised (Habib and Taylor, 2001).

This is unlikely to happen in the near future, however. As argued in Chapter Two, the trade union federation COSATU, the largest organised formation within civil society and one of the more significant institutional platforms that enabled Jacob Zuma's rise to power, continues to throw its lot in with the ANC. But its unhappiness with the ruling party, especially with regard to some of the ANC's economic policies, and with the enrichment and corruption scandals plaguing the Zuma administration, have led some COSATU leaders to consider developing additional partnerships as a means to pressurise the ANC to become more accommodating of the federation's interests. This strategic perspective is perhaps best expounded by Zwelinzima Vavi, COSATU's general secretary, who is fond of saying, 'you never win at the negotiations table what you have not won on the streets'. In any case, the perspective has manifested itself in a number of distinct initiatives. For example, in 2010, COSATU hosted a conference with a range of organisations from civil society, including many that are critical of the federation's alliance with the ruling party. Despite the differences between the various organisations on how they relate to the ANC, the goal of the conference was to explore avenues of collaboration.[13] COSATU has subsequently worked with civic associations to establish Corruption Watch in early 2012[14] and partnered with others in a campaign against the ANC's Protection of State Information Bill, which the ruling party railroaded through the national legislature.[15] In March 2012, COSATU led a massive national stayaway against labour brokers and the imposition of a toll system on the highways of South Africa's Gauteng province.[16] Vavi's public statement on the eve of this stayaway illustrates the federation's strategic intent. Addressing the middle classes, he urged them to join the COSATU marches if not against labour brokering, then at least to demonstrate their opposition to the toll system – a cause that resonated in these communities (*Business Day*, 6/03/2012). COSATU, it must be noted, had recognised the importance of going beyond its own base of organised workers and had begun to weave a multi-class alliance around issues on which it disagrees with the ruling party.

This too has been contested. The ANC has been unhappy with COSATU and with Vavi in particular.[17] ANC secretary-general, Gwede Mantashe, criticised COSATU for hosting the civil society conference and explicitly warned that the federation must not imagine that it would be able to unseat the liberation movement with a civic alliance as has happened in some neighbouring African countries (*Mail & Guardian*, 4/11/2010).[18] In a similar vein, the ANC criticised COSATU's stayaway, suggesting that the contentious issues could have been resolved at the negotiating table and that the federation was exaggerating the impact of toll roads on the poor (*Business Day*, 8/03/2012).

Within COSATU, tensions have emerged within the leadership especially on the issue of support for, and maintaining a positive relationship with the Zuma administration. Reports suggested that COSATU president, Sdumo Dlamini, and National Union of Mineworkers general secretary, Frans Baleni, were partial to continuing support for Zuma, while Vavi demanded that such support depend on concrete gains being made for the labour movement (*Mail & Guardian*, 9/03/2012). How this strategic battle plays out within COSATU will be important for the evolution of broader state–civil society relations in South Africa in the years to come.

Whatever the outcome, however, it is important to note that a single homogenous set of state–civil society relations is not conducive to the consolidation of democracy or the emergence of inclusive development. Neither the state's view of collegial state–civil society relationships, nor the adversarial alternative proposed by radical activists, would on their own facilitate a deepening of democracy, development or empowerment. It is the very plurality of civil society, and the consequent diversity of state–civil society engagements, that is beneficial for deepening democratic governance and inclusive development.

The informal, survivalist, community-based organisations enhance democracy at the simplest level because they enable ordinary people to survive. The establishment of more formal relations between them and the state would subvert their character and compromise this role.

The collaborative relationship with the state established by the more formal NGOs is largely a product of the services they render for the state. In a society confronted with massive backlogs and limited institutional capacity, this role can only be of benefit to democracy and development since it facilitates and enables service delivery to ordinary citizens and residents.

Finally, the adversarial and conflictual role played by the new social movements and other community-based organisations enhances democracy for it creates a fluidity in political support at the base of society. This can only be beneficial for it permits an ongoing reconfiguration of power that forces the state not to take its citizens for granted. It also effects a systemic shift to the left that may create the possibility for a more people-centred, neo-Keynesian oriented developmental agenda.

The challenge

Civil society has been as impacted upon by the democratic transition, as it has influenced its evolution. Civic mobilisation was critical not only for the unravelling of apartheid, and for some of the changes in policy of the post-apartheid state, but also for enabling the leadership change within the ruling party that occurred at the Polokwane conference. Yet the democratic transition – its political liberalisation and the neo-liberal bent of the economy's globalisation – has reconfigured civil society in important ways. Three sectors – NGOs, social movements and survivalist agencies – each with a distinct purpose, emerged and established different relationships with the post-apartheid state.

This diverse civil society facilitated a multiplicity of relationships with the post-apartheid state. This, of course, goes against what both political elites and radical activists would prefer. The former see institutional participation and collegiate relations with the state as conducive to democracy. The latter seek independence from the state and the ruling party so as to better mobilise the populace. Moreover, leadership figures in both the NGO sector and the social movements are cynical of one another's intentions. Despite this, however, it is precisely the diversity of state–civil society relations that is in the long-term interests of democracy and inclusive development. The diverse roles and functions undertaken by different elements of civil society collectively create the adversarial and collaborative relationships, the push-and-pull effects, which sometimes assist, and at other times compel, the state to meet its obligations and responsibilities to its citizens. Thus, a plurality of civil society organisations, and the diverse sets of relations that they engender with the state, offer the best guarantee of a consolidation of democracy in South Africa.

6

South Africa and the world

South Africa has served two terms as a non-permanent member of the United Nations Security Council. On both occasions its tenure was plagued by controversy. In the first term (2007–2008), human rights activists were demoralised by what they interpreted as the country's defence of 'rogue powers', when South Africa refused to support Security Council resolutions condemning and imposing sanctions on Iran, Myanmar, Sudan and Zimbabwe. Similarly, in its second term (2011–2012), activists were horrified by South Africa's stance on the crises in Côte d'Ivoire and Libya.

On Côte d'Ivoire, South Africa's official neutral stance was interpreted as implicitly supporting Laurent Gbagbo. This went against the decisions of both the United Nations and the Economic Community of West African States (ECOWAS) to recognise Allasane Ouattara as president after his victory in the country's national elections. On Libya, South Africa first supported Security Council Resolution 1973, which mandated the imposition of a no-fly zone to protect Libyan civilians against the army, but subsequently criticised the NATO-led bombing as an example of regime change backed by the West. In effect, the human rights community saw these positions as betraying the spirit of South Africa's own democratic transition and the international support that facilitated it (Human Rights Watch, 2012: 4; Neuer, 2007; Taljaard, 2009).

But is this label of betrayal not too simplistic a portrayal of South Africa's decision making? Is the suggestion that South African diplomats were simply appeasing the Russians and Chinese (Democratic Alliance, 2011) too lazy an explanation of South Africa's foreign policy? And is the same true of other explanations (see

Bischoff, 2003; Nathan, 2005; Zondi, 2012) that see South Africa's foreign policy as incoherent and inconsistent? None of these views engage sufficiently with South African government officials' explanations of their own decision making, or the concerns they have expressed about the abuse of multilateral institutions (such as the United Nations, the International Monetary Fund and the World Bank) by the world's largest and most dominant countries, including their lack of even-handedness and their hypocritical posturing.[1] While wishing to avoid being an unwitting agent of these great powers, however, one must be careful not to fall prey to politicians' rationalisations of their aloofness from the concerns of ordinary citizens or their own undemocratic behaviour, even if such elites are from the developing world. To avoid both scenarios, it is necessary to try to decode South Africa's foreign policy, to understand its philosophical and strategic underpinnings, and to locate this analysis in some comparative examples.

There have, of course, been a number of prior attempts to do this. Many of the studies (published in the late 1990s and early 2000s) tended to offer quite polarised assessments of South African foreign policy. On the one hand, African National Congress (ANC)-aligned intellectuals and activists portrayed South Africa's foreign engagements as progressive and as reflective of a human rights agenda (ANC, 1997; Landsberg, 2000; Mandela, 1993). On the other hand, liberal and Marxist critics concluded that South African foreign policy reflected realist calculations and sub-imperialist ambitions respectively (Bond, 2004c; McGowan and Ahwireng-Obeng, 1998; Williams, 2000). While these sets of analyses offer some useful insights, none provide comprehensive or persuasive explanations of South Africa's foreign policy practices.

A later set of studies (Adebajo and Landsberg, 2003; Daniel, Naidoo and Naidu, 2003; Landsberg, 2010; Le Pere, 1998; Schoeman, 2003) is less ideologically oriented and more useful in imparting an understanding of South Africa's foreign-policy engagements.

Drawing on the notion of 'middle powers' as applied in other parts of the world, these scholars advance the thesis that South Africa's status as a middle power predisposes it to multilateralism and partnerships at a global and continental level.[2] However, these same studies also describe South Africa as a 'pivotal state', as distinct from a regional or hegemonic power.[3] Regarding this as positive, they suggest that South Africa's pivotal status reinforces impulses within its foreign-policy elite to seek partnerships, and conclude that, on balance, the country has performed admirably on the African continent. Some argue that the only black spot on South Africa's foreign-policy record with regard to Africa, is Zimbabwe. In this case, analysts who usually advocate partnership suddenly recommend a robust and aggressive approach (see, for example, Daniel, Naidoo and Naidu, 2003).

Nthakeng Selinyane and I have critiqued these studies, suggesting that they suffer from 'the ideologically constraining effects of progressive orthodoxy' (Habib and Selinyane, 2006: 181). We argued that, in Africa, South Africa is neither simply another middle power nor a pivotal state, but that its aggregate capabilities – economic, diplomatic and military – automatically define it, at least in the present, as a regional power or hegemon. We suggested that this status not only imparts to South Africa a set of privileges, obligations and responsibilities that separate it from its African counterparts and from other middle powers (such as Canada and Norway), but that this status just as importantly defines South Africa's foreign-policy agenda and practice. Furthermore, the use of this conceptual lens is essential for understanding South Africa's foreign policy and international behaviour. Without this lens, analyses tend to explain the country's foreign policy decisions and engagements more simplistically – as a product of betrayals, or the respective presidents' personal friendships with one or other dictator, for example. However, such variables are not particularly illuminating when applied to South Africa's overall international position, the particular stances the country adopts on hotspots such as Zimbabwe, Sudan, Libya or Iran and its relations with newly emerging powers such as China, India or even with re-ascendant Russia. Confusion thus prevails around South Africa's foreign-policy agenda and about how it might evolve in years to come. Before considering the future, however, it is helpful to first describe the character, aspirations and strategic orientation of South Africa's post-apartheid political elite, and to show how these have influenced the country's foreign-policy decisions and practice thus far.

Foreign policy and second-generation nationalism

Classical realist scholars (such as Morgenthau, 1968) explain foreign policy as a product of a country's national interests. Neo-realists (see Waltz, 1979) view the structural location of nations in the international system as the key to their foreign policies. Liberal institutionalism, on the other hand, claims that elements such as business interests and political actors play a crucial role in configuring foreign-policy agendas (Keohane, 1986; Rosecrance, 1986). While the neo-realists' strength is that they point to the systemic constraints and conditioning effects of the balance of power in a given context, their theory is unable to persuasively account for foreign-policy behaviour in transitional societies, as it tends to ignore the impact of changing domestic values and the entry of new elites into a political system.

In South Africa's case, the ascension of the ANC to political office in 1994 led to a fundamental shift in foreign policy. And while this may seem to confirm the liberal institutionalist perspective, neo-realism's explanatory depth can be demonstrated in relation to the systemic conditioning of the South African political elite's foreign-policy behaviour. Thus it can be argued that both perspectives find vindication in the story of South Africa's foreign policy transformation.

The key political actor in this aspect of South Africa's story is, of course, the ANC and particularly its post-Mandela leadership as personified by Thabo Mbeki. This political elite is defined by two essential characteristics. First, like the founding fathers of newly independent African countries in the post-war era, they are nationalists whose overriding desire is to throw off the yoke of colonialism. Their anti-colonial agenda is reflected in a desire for racial equality and for a more equitably structured and just global order. As Thabo Mbeki (2006a) put it to the United Nations General Assembly, speaking in his capacity as chairperson of the Group of 77 and China:[4]

> Poverty and underdevelopment remain the biggest threats to progress that has been achieved, and the equality among the nations, big and small, is central to the survival, relevance and credibility of this global organization ... Madam President, when you correctly urge us to implement a global partnership for development, we the members of the G77 and China, who represent the poor people of the world, understand ... this common commitment for a global partnership for development cannot be transformed into a reality when the rich and powerful insist on an unequal relationship with the poor. A global partnership for development is impossible in the absence of a pact of mutual responsibility between the giver and the recipient. It is impossible when the rich demand the right, unilaterally, to set the agenda and conditions for the implementation of commonly agreed programmes.

In one sense, Mbeki is no different from Nkrumah, Nyerere, Nasser, or even Nehru. In another sense, however, he is fundamentally different. The second-generation nationalists, among whom Mbeki is one of the more articulate exponents, have witnessed the unravelling of the anti-colonial project. While some acknowledge the mistakes of earlier nationalist leaders,[5] they blame this unravelling primarily on the Cold War between the United States and Soviet Union, as well as the related and subsequent machinations of the imperial and ex-colonial powers (Arrighi, 2002; Lee, 2006). Second-generation nationalist leaders are thus acutely aware of their own countries' relative weaknesses and acknowledge that no anti-colonial agenda will materialise without a transformation of the power relations in the global order.

Three different responses have emerged from the second-generation nationalists. The first is one of appeasement. Exponents of this approach include Pervez Musharraf and Asif Ali Zardari of Pakistan, Hosni Mubarak of Egypt, Meles Zenawi of Ethiopia, Ellen Johnson-Sirleaf of Liberia and perhaps even Ian Khama of Botswana. Obviously these leaders have very different democratic credentials, but their strategic orientation, at least on foreign policy, is similar: namely, to form alliances with those who hold power, and win significant political and economic concessions (including foreign aid) for doing so. In a sense, such leaders may hope to emulate the success of the Asian tigers (even though their economic policies are very different), by entering into an alliance with the United States and other Western countries in exchange for significant economic and political benefits.[6] Sometimes, in exchange for this preferential treatment, these countries take on a variety of domestic or regional obligations.[7]

The second response is to adopt a militantly aggressive anti-imperialist posture accompanied by anti-American and/or anti-Western rhetoric. Exponents of this position include Hugo Chavez of Venezuela and Iran's theocratic leadership and it is also evident in the actions of Robert Mugabe and the leadership of Zimbabwe's ZANU-PF party. Obviously Mugabe himself does not qualify as a second-generation nationalist. As leader of one of the last anti-colonial transitions in southern Africa, he is very much a first-generation nationalist. But the economic meltdown in Zimbabwe and its internal conflict has led him and his party to adopt a similarly aggressive anti-Western posture. This is reflected both in his attacks on the opposition party in Zimbabwe, the Movement for Democratic Change (MDC) as 'British stooges', and in his assertion that Zimbabwe's economic and political crisis is the result of an imperialist assault on that country's freedom.[8]

The third response can also be explained through a focus on Zimbabwe, but this time articulated not by that country's own leadership, but by South Africa's former president, Thabo Mbeki, who was mandated by the Southern African Development Community (SADC) to mediate a political settlement in Zimbabwe. Despite the dominant perception of Western media, Mbeki was never enamoured with Mugabe. Indeed, while sharing the broad nationalist vision espoused by Mugabe, Mbeki was quite critical of the Zimbabwean president's conduct both domestically and internationally. This was clearly reflected in a paper Mbeki authored on Zimbabwe in mid 2001.[9] Arguing that the Zimbabwean crisis has its roots in ZANU-PF's decision to finance service delivery using high deficits and borrowed money, thus making the country dependent on the International Monetary Fund, Mbeki insisted that no amount of anti-imperialist rhetoric would resolve the crisis. Instead, he recommended a more strategically engaged orientation that involved Zimbabwe softening its stance on both the International Monetary Fund and the United Kingdom, the assistance of which Mbeki deemed necessary for addressing Zimbabwe's economic crisis (Mbeki, 2007a; see also Rossouw, 2008).

Mbeki's criticism of ZANU-PF provides a very clear exposition of the third response of second-generation nationalists. Reflecting a mix of principle and pragmatism, this response takes as its starting point the need to reform the global order, but recognises that such an outcome will not evolve from either appeasing or attempting to delink from the existing global powers. Instead, this response recognises the need to engage the global order with a view to understanding and subverting power relations within it. The focus is thus on developing mechanisms and alliances that enhance the leverage of those post-colonial powers that share this agenda. This response is, in a sense, the application of a neo-realist paradigm from the South; recognising the importance of power in configuring international and transnational outcomes, but realising that power is always relational, and therefore open to being subverted or transformed in the long term.

The literature on regional power refers to this strategic orientation as 'balancing'[10] but this label does not quite capture the complexity and nuance of this foreign policy practice. Thus while balancing involves both engagement and subversion, there is a fine line between engagement and appeasement, and for that matter between subversion and marginalisation. Where engagement ends and appeasement begins is hotly contested, particularly when it comes to economics.

The practice of the South African government since 1994 has shown characteristics of both appeasement and subversive engagement, as will be demonstrated in the next section. Nevertheless, despite the contradictions sometimes evident in its actual practice, ANC foreign policy is best explained through its adoption of a strategic orientation informed by both nationalism, and the fact that it is second-generation. The former identifies the goals and vision of the South African government. The latter defines its methodology, or the means by which it hopes to realise its ambitions. It is only through an understanding of its strategic orientation that one can make sense of South Africa's foreign policy practice. It is a practice that is frequently misunderstood and perceived as arbitrary, unprincipled, and incoherent. Yet, if one examines it within the conceptual underpinning used by its architects and practitioners, the country's foreign policy behaviour takes on a meaning and a coherence which, even if one disagrees with it, nevertheless has to be applauded for its sophistication and nuance.

It may also be worth noting that South Africa's foreign policy is not the only example of this neo-realism from the South. Brazil, India and even Turkey since 2009,[11] all display foreign policy practices that could serve as exemplars of this perspective. Again these countries are a diverse group with different democratic credentials and practices, yet their foreign policy engagements are increasingly directed at containing the power of the United States and its Western allies. If conditions do not permit this, then they at least attempt to redirect the West's agenda in ways that make it more compatible with their own. This does not mean that these nations always concur when faced with a concrete decision. On the Libyan crisis in 2011, for instance, Brazil and India abstained from the Security Council resolution sanctioning a no-fly zone, South Africa supported the resolution but opposed the subsequent NATO led-bombing and overthrow of Gaddafi, and Turkey supported NATO's agenda fully, including its regime-change activities. Yet despite their different approaches to this and other issues, all of these countries have become more active on the international stage and have established alliances with the potential to reform the regional and global order in ways that are more facilitative of their own agendas. South Africa's foreign policy narrative is thus one of many similar ones emerging in the developing world.

South Africa's foreign policy, 1994–2008

As mentioned, South Africa's democratic transition ushered in a fundamental transformation of its foreign policy. At the most basic level, the country moved from having an isolated, politically belligerent, regionally militaristic and globally defensive agenda to one that supports multilateralism and involves political partnerships, regional leadership, and global engagement (Landsberg, 2010). But this description masks the gradual evolution of South Africa's foreign policy and the development of its present strategic orientation.

In the initial years under Mandela, South Africa's foreign policy took on a naive, almost crusading human rights quality, that reached its zenith when Mandela called for opposition to Nigeria's Sani Abacha at the Conference of Commonwealth Heads of Government in 1995 for the hanging of Ken Saro-Wiwa and his compatriots, and in 1997 when Mandela negotiated with Mobutu Sese Seko on a South African navy ship off the coast of the Democratic Republic of Congo. The low point came shortly thereafter, as it became clear that South Africa's attempts to isolate Nigeria had failed. Thabo Mbeki then took charge, slowly but surely crafting South Africa's foreign policy credentials and reorienting its strategic direction.

Prioritising Africa

Since then, the ANC's nationalist impulses have led its leaders to prioritise Africa in four distinct ways. First, South Africa deploys an enormous amount of its diplomatic and military energy in stabilising the continent. This involves peace-building initiatives directed at facilitating negotiations between political and military adversaries. Between 1994 and 2012, South Africa was involved in initiatives to broker negotiations in Angola, Burundi, Côte d'Ivoire, Lesotho, Kenya, Mozambique, Sierra Leone, Sudan, Zimbabwe, and Libya. Its troops have been deployed to peace missions in several countries, including Burundi, the Democratic Republic of Congo, the Union of the Comoros, Eritrea, Ethiopia, the Central African Republic and Sudan. While many of these initiatives have yielded positive results, South Africa has overreached itself at times and its efforts have not always been appreciated. A case in point was Côte d'Ivoire where Mbeki was humiliated when his bona fides were questioned by

Ivorian rebels.[12] Similarly, in Zimbabwe, the main opposition party, the Movement for Democratic Change routinely questioned Mbeki's neutrality and even tried to get him replaced as the SADC's official mediator (*New York Times*, 14/02/2008). Nevertheless, even the Afro-pessimist magazine, *The Economist* (5/01/2006) has acknowledged the huge gains that have been made in stabilising Africa, and the central role that South Africa has played in this regard.[13]

Second, during Olusegun Obasanjo's tenure as president of Nigeria (1999–2007), South Africa and Nigeria set about reconstructing Africa's institutional architecture.[14] Both countries playing a leading role in establishing the African Union.[15] Mbeki and Obasanjo, together with Senegal's Abdoulaye Wade, were the primary movers behind the formation of the New Partnership for Africa's Development (NEPAD), including its peer-review mechanism[16] and the former two played a central role in selling NEPAD to the international community including the G8, the World Bank and the International Monetary Fund. South Africa has also played a leading role in revitalising the SADC.

McGowan and Ahwireng-Obeng (1998) have described the unequal and acrimonious engagements between South Africa and its immediate neighbours in the early post-apartheid period, including South Africa's refusal to renegotiate the unequal Southern African Customs Union Agreement in 1998, its trade battles with Zimbabwe between 1994 and 1997 and its stalemate with the latter in the SADC's Organ on Politics, Defence and Security. However, this political stalemate has since been replaced with greater co-operation and willingness to undertake regional interventions under the auspices of the SADC. Moreover, the more outlandish economic arrangements and terms have also been addressed, enabling the launch of the Southern African free-trade area at the twenty-eighth SADC Summit in August 2008. Nevertheless, South Africa's neo-liberal economic orientation in regional and continental matters, deliberated on further below, remains a matter of concern, especially given the potential for this economic orientation to undermine the emergence of an inclusive developmental agenda in Africa.

Third, South Africa has played a leading role in popularising African agendas within the international community, insisting that Africa's development be placed among the priorities of the G8, the United Nations, the International Monetary Fund, the World Bank, and the World Trade Organization (*Cape Times*, 7/07/2008). South Africa has also used its turns to chair the United Nations Security Council to prioritise African conflicts and their solutions.[17] It has played a leading role in demanding debt cancellations for the poorest and most marginalised of nations (BBC News, 25/11/2005; *The Economist*, 29/09/2005).

Through NEPAD, South Africa has enhanced Africa's investment environment, and played a role in attracting new foreign direct investment in the continent. This, together with the global boom in the resources sector, ensured that foreign direct investment in Africa increased from between US$2 to US$3 billion per annum at the beginning of the 1990s to US$87.6 billion by 2008 (UNCTAD, 2010: 2). From 2000 to 2004, Africa's average investment rate as a ratio of GDP was 20.7 per cent, while that of sub-Saharan Africa was 18.1 per cent, having virtually doubled over the previous decade (UNCTAD, 2007: 3). Moreover, even though foreign direct investment in the continent was seriously affected by the 2008 global economic recession, this stood at the relatively respectable level of US$54.4 billion in 2011 (UNCTAD, 2012: 6).

Furthermore, *African Economic Outlook* (OECD, 2012) indicates that the continent registered a 6.5 per cent growth rate in 2007, up from 6.1 per cent, 5.9 per cent and 6.2 per cent in the three preceding years (see also IMF, 2012b). While the 2008 economic recession impacted heavily on these figures, the continent returned a 5.3 per cent growth rate in 2010 (IMF, 2012a: 2). While North Africa was severely affected by political instability in 2011, falling to 3.3 per cent (IMF, 2012b: 82), sub-Saharan Africa continued its strong showing, and registered a 5.1 per cent growth in 2011 (IMF, 2012b: 87).

Fourth, South Africa has also led by example with regard to investing in the rest of Africa. Its corporate footprint has expanded exponentially in the post-apartheid era. By 2000, South African companies were active in 20 African countries, in sectors ranging from mining, manufacturing, energy, aviation, telecommunications, as well as research and development. From 1994 to 2000, South Africa's investment in the SADC region totalled $5.4 billion, outstripping British and American investment (Daniel, Naidoo and Naidu, 2003). This corporate involvement was supplemented by state investment: almost all of South Africa's parastatals expanded their operations on the continent. The scale of this investment is perhaps best captured in the activities of South Africa's state owned Industrial Development Corporation, which had funded 37 projects in 11 countries by 2004, and had an additional portfolio of investments under consideration that numbered 69 in 23 countries (South Africa Foundation, 2004: 18). The Industrial Development Corporation's work was supplemented by that of the energy parastatal Eskom, which became a key architect in the SADC's Southern Africa Power Pool, and transport corporation Transnet, which manages rail networks in 14 countries and trains port-authority officials across the continent. Finally, while South Africa was overshadowed by the investments of China and India after 2005, it has consolidated its foreign direct investment in Africa in the last few years and by 2012 was the second largest developing-country investor on the continent after China (OECD, 2012).

But this market activity has had a dark side too, in that it betrays the neo-liberal economic predispositions of South African (and other African) political elites. The economic policy prescriptions encapsulated in South Africa's Growth, Employment and Redistribution programme (GEAR) (discussed in Chapter Three) form the fundamental assumptions underpinning

NEPAD's economic agenda for the continent (Melber, n.d.). While this neo-liberal economic agenda has since come under attack in South Africa, forcing domestic economic policy to shift in a more developmental direction, similar shifts have not occurred elsewhere on the African continent. Thus, much concern has been expressed about the consequences of the unregulated march of South African corporations across the African continent (Bond, 2004c; Miller, 2008). Peter Vale, in his study of regional security in Southern Africa (2002), also bemoaned how quickly the new ANC political elites adopted the policies of their predecessors – maintaining rigid border controls, and using immigration and economic policies to discipline the movement of people – rather than promoting and consolidating on equitable terms the single regional economy that has developed over the last century. All of this confirms that developmental outcomes cannot be assumed from existing patterns of investment, and corporate and economic activity in Africa.

South Africa's engagement in Africa has provoked robust debate within the country's diplomatic corps and its universities about the country's existing and future role. As indicated earlier, some observers see South Africa as a pivotal state, rather than as a regional power, and suggest that its modus operandi on the African continent has been and should continue to be one of partnership (Adebajo and Landsberg, 2003; Daniel, Naidoo and Naidu, 2003; Landsberg, 2010; Le Pere, 1998; Schoeman, 2003). Nthakeng Selinyane and I, on the other hand, have argued that by virtue of its aggregate capabilities defined in economic, diplomatic, and military terms, South Africa is a regional power. In our view, it should be recognised as such, and given responsibility for stabilising and underwriting the continent's development (Habib and Selinyane, 2006). It should be noted that many of those who advocate the 'pivotal state' view tend to misrepresent hegemonic leadership. Hegemonic leadership is not about militaristic adventurism, as is often assumed, nor is it necessarily hostile to partnerships. Indeed, any careful study of global and regional hegemony demonstrates that partnership is as much a modality of hegemonic behaviour as other, more aggressive interventions. Selinyane and I have described the role of a regional hegemon as follows:

> Every hegemon is a pivotal state. But it has to be more. Hegemons not only aspire to leadership, and are not only endowed with military, economic, and other resources. They also have – necessarily – a political and socio-economic vision of their transnational environments, and a political willingness to implement such a vision. If that vision is one of security, stability, and development, as is often the case, then the hegemon undertakes to underwrite the implementation of these goals. Again, that does not mean that a hegemon does not have partners in this enterprise. It often does, but it takes responsibility in the last instance to ensure that the features of its vision are operationalised in the region it sees as its sphere of influence. More importantly, a hegemon should be prepared to compromise its own dominance in respect of market share, balance of trade, and military overlordship should that be in the interests of fulfilling this vision. (Habib and Selinyane, 2006: 181)[18]

In many ways, South Africa has already begun to play a hegemonic role. Sometimes it does so hesitantly, but is increasingly being forced to take on a leadership role in resolving national or regional crises and, once these have been addressed, to follow through by helping to manage the subsequent development challenges. South Africa has effectively played this role in Mozambique, the Democratic Republic of the Congo, Sudan and Zimbabwe.[19] It tried to play a similar role in both Côte d'Ivoire and Libya, with far less success. Nevertheless, as South Africa's confidence grows, we may see the emergence of an

African power capable of taking leadership in resolving problems on the African continent.

Fostering South–South and other alliances

The second-generation nationalism of the Mbeki administration also led it to foster a broader South–South solidarity. At the most basic level, this is reflected in support for national liberation struggles, including for what some analysts perceive as 'rogue states'. For example, South Africa is one of the more ardent supporters of the Palestinian struggle (much to the chagrin of Israel and the United States), and it has retained strong relationships with Cuba and Iran. In the 1990s, South Africa had similar links with Libya[20] – indeed South Africa was instrumental in facilitating negotiations between Libya and Britain that ultimately led to the lifting of sanctions against Libya, and its temporary rehabilitation in the eyes of the West. Similar solidarity has been extended to Iran, especially around its nuclear ambitions.

South Africa has also played a role in engaging and building relations with the African diaspora. This has included building strong relationships with the Congressional Black Caucus and the African-American lobby in the United States, as well as underwriting and hosting at least two African diaspora conferences in Jamaica since 2000. For similar reasons, the Mbeki administration provided ousted Haitian leader, Jean-Bertrand Aristide, with asylum in South Africa, against the wishes of Western powers and domestic human rights lobbyists.[21]

South Africa's solidarity with other national liberation struggles and countries of the developing world, reflect its desire to act as a bridge between North and South. In this, South Africa is motivated by the broader belief that a more equitable world is necessary for the full realisation of citizens' rights in the South, and by the Mbeki administration's more narrowly shared strategic calculation that this will only be achieved through a fuller engagement with the global order. As a result, South Africa has dramatically increased its institutional participation in mainstream multilateral organisations and in those of the South.

An early indication of the importance of power as a variable in conditioning foreign policy emerged when South Africa jettisoned its strategic relationship with Taiwan in favour of one with China. Taiwan's relationship with South Africa predated the transition and in the last few years of apartheid rule, Taiwan invested heavily in wooing the ANC in the hope of preserving its relations with South Africa.[22] But soon after the 1994 election, Mbeki suggested that it was in the national interest for South Africa to establish a strategic partnership with a rising China instead. He succeeded in this, and while he was initially criticised for this by some, no one can today seriously question the wisdom of his decision.

South Africa's relationship with China has since gone from strength to strength. Essentially, like many other African nations, South Africa has used its relations with China as a counterweight to both the United States and Europe and tried to wring political, economic and diplomatic concessions from all parties. Some analysts close to South Africa's foreign policy apparatus have recommended that South Africa join the Chinese camp (Le Pere and Shelton, 2007).[23] Mbeki (in my view, astutely) resisted this. South Africa under Mbeki was uncomfortable being the junior partner in either camp, preferring instead to retain South Africa's independence, play the powers off against each other, and thereby maximise development concessions both for the country and the African continent. In fact, as president, Mbeki was quite critical of Chinese engagement with Africa and suggested that it is akin to the colonial and neo-colonial relationships established by the European countries and the United States (*International Herald Tribune*, 28/01/2007). This unsettled the Chinese and seems to have had its intended effect as former President Hu Jintao quickly sought to allay such fears and to distinguish China's engagement from the practices of colonial countries (*Financial Times*, 7/02/2007).[24]

The counterbalancing diplomatic act that South Africa has with China, the United States and Europe is supplemented by two more formal alliances; the first with Brazil and India, in the India–Brazil–South Africa Forum (IBSA) established under the Mbeki administration, and the second with the two former countries and China and Russia – in the BRICS alliance – which South Africa joined in 2011 during Zuma's presidency.

IBSA emerged after the failure of the 2003 World Trade Organization conference in Cancun. Membership involves annual meetings on issues such as trade, investment, energy, security, transport, and higher education, as well as other common interests in global affairs that affect trilateral and South–South co-operation. Obviously the three sets of political elites hope to use this engagement to develop a more substantive collaborative global political agenda, believing that this has the potential to enhance their respective leverage capacities. Alden and Vieira (2005), however, criticise IBSA for not having a clear strategy. Daniel Flemes, on the other hand, suggests that the forum has had a significant impact in pursuing what he terms 'milieu goals' that reflect 'global responsibility' and 'shape the environment in which the state operates' (Flemes, 2007).[25] On a practical level, Flemes argues, this translates into their pledge to co-ordinate their activities and jointly promote, in international forums, the agendas of global peace, human rights, collective security and sustainable social and economic development. Flemes (2007: 25) acknowledges, however, that IBSA's lack of institutionalisation is a weakness, and recommends that consideration be given to enlarging the trilateral coalition either to include Russia and China, or Germany and Japan.

The association of emerging countries known as BRICS was originally established in 2008. South Africa was not among its four founding members but, in 2010, South Africa began lobbying to join the group, and was formally invited to join on 24 December of the same year.[26] Like IBSA, the purpose of BRICS is to facilitate co-operation among the member countries, and to enhance their collective leverage with a view to reforming international financial institutions and the global order. The group has expressed concern about the US dollar serving as the single major reserve currency (*City Press*, 25/03/2012) and its members have pledged to lend to one another in their own currency. They are also considering the establishment of a new Global Development Bank to further enable their co-operation and collective economic endeavours (*Financial Times*, 19/03/2012). In addition, South Africa hopes to draw on the fiscal reserves of its BRICS partners for US$480 billion in infrastructural development in Africa that is planned to take place by 2020 (Zuma, 2011a).

Increasing the leverage of developing nations

BRICS' and IBSA's collective concerns are not new. Indeed, they were evident at the 2003 World Trade Organization conference when the kernel of the G-21 lobby emerged to enhance the developing world's leverage capacities and to ensure that an unpalatable agreement was not forced through by Western powers. The next three rounds of the Doha Development Agenda ended without substantive agreement, thus imperilling the future of the World Trade Organization and undermining the legitimacy of the global trading system. The main sticking point was the concession on agricultural subsidies offered by the United States and Europe, with the G-21 believing that this was too far below the acceptable minimum to warrant further substantive concessions on their part (Flemes, 2007).[27] This was significant because it was the first time that developing nations had used their collective muscle to thwart the agenda and ambitions of existing economic powers.

This collective muscle was again evident at the United Nations Climate Change Summit in Copenhagen in December 2009, but this time the consequences were negative. Effectively the summit failed to achieve any of its substantive objectives. The weak final agreement – eventually brokered by the United States, China, Brazil, India and South Africa – recognised the scientific case for climate change, agreed on the necessity of retaining temperature increases below 2°C, but entailed no commitments for reducing carbon emissions necessary for the achievement of this goal (*The Guardian*, 19/12/2009). The impasse emerged because developing nations held the United States and Europe responsible for global warming and demanded that these powers make the bulk of concessions. The latter, in turn, pointed to the increasing carbon footprints of Brazil, China, India and South Africa and insisted that these countries also make significant concessions. The failure of the summit was ultimately laid at the door of the United States and the alliance comprising China, Brazil, India and South Africa. Neither side was prepared to make concessions that might compromise their economic ambitions (*The Guardian*, 11/02/2010). However, the fact that the United States ultimately brokered the final agreement with these emerging powers graphically demonstrates the enhanced leverage of the latter in the contemporary era.

Another challenge to the existing power structures emanates from attempts to reform the multilateral institutions. Again, South Africa has played a leading role in this. With different sets of alliances, including the African Union, IBSA and BRICS, South Africa has advocated for reforms of the quotas and board representation of the International Monetary Fund and the World Bank, as well as how their leaders are chosen. South Africa has also been strident in its criticisms of the powers of the United Nations Security Council and has pushed, again in alliance with others, for more equitable representation on this structure – that is, the expansion of the Security Council to include developing countries from Africa, Asia and Latin America. In the run-up to negotiations around these reforms, however, South Africa, unlike its Indian and Brazilian counterparts in IBSA, did not join the G4 nations (including Germany and Japan), which were supporting one anothers' candidacy for Security Council representation (Flemes, 2007: 12).[28] Instead, South Africa stood by the African Union's guidelines on equitable continental representation. The push for United Nations reform, and attempts to prevent the European Union and the United States from imposing their choice of leader on the International Monetary Fund and the World Bank, have not been very successful so far and these issues remain focal points of unhappiness in the developing world in relation to the global institutional architecture.

But perhaps South Africa's most controversial attempts to force reforms onto the multilateral system emanated from its decisions in the United Nations Security Council during its first term as a non-permanent member. In four moves that alienated the international and domestic human rights lobby, South Africa worked with China, Russia and other countries to prevent: (i) the adoption of a Security Council resolution condemning and imposing sanctions on the military leadership in Myanmar (ii) a similar resolution on the Mugabe regime in Zimbabwe; (iii) the condemnation of states using rape as a political and military weapon; and (iv) the imposition of sanctions on Iran for violations of the Treaty on the Non-Proliferation of Nuclear Weapons.

Its decisions in all four cases were motivated on grounds that the United States and European countries were either violating existing rules of the United Nations' system by tabling issues in inappropriate forums, or selectively targeting countries they were hostile to. Nevertheless, South Africa's decisions outraged the human rights community, which accused the country of betraying its own rich legacy of human rights struggle and of opposing the very traditions and strategies that enabled it to achieve political freedom (Neuer, 2007; Taljaard, 2008; 2009; Wines, 2007).

Clearly there is merit in this criticism. South Africa in its desire to get the United Nations to function equitably and fairly was, via these actions, sacrificing the human rights of people in Myanmar, Zimbabwe and Darfur. Elsewhere I have argued that, to make its position on Myanmar politically tenable, South Africa would have had to take the lead in calling for the isolation of the country's military rulers in the Human Rights Commission which, of course, it did not do (Habib, 2007). Nevertheless, it must also be said that the human rights lobby was being disingenuous by either not recognising, or being complacent about, South Africa's complaints concerning the manipulation of the United Nations by the permanent members of the Security Council (China, France, Russia, United Kingdom, and United States).

This, then, is the strategic challenge confronting the human rights community: how to distinguish its actions from those of the United States and other Western governments when the latter decide to use the abrogation of human rights in authoritarian states as a means to realise their own geopolitical goals? Ignoring the agendas of these governments turns the human rights community into willing or unwilling accomplices to the manoeuvrings of the world's great powers.

The United States and its allies have always selectively supported human rights. During South Africa's first term in the Security Council, the United States wanted action to be taken against Myanmar, Sudan and Zimbabwe, while it remained silent on Pakistan and Egypt, condoned the actions of Israel, and had strategic relationships with countless other regimes that have dubious human rights records including, Saudi Arabia, Kuwait, Libya (under Gadaffi), Equatorial Guinea and Gabon. Similar inconsistencies typify the behaviour of all five veto-wielding powers. A dramatic example of this was the action taken against Iran after

2002. The latter, as a signatory of the Nuclear Non-Proliferation Treaty, was denied the right to develop nuclear military capacities, but was entitled to develop a civilian nuclear industry. The five permanent members and other European powers in the Security Council, distrusting Iran's intentions, objected to its civilian nuclear programme suggesting that this is merely a pretext to develop military nuclear capability. Initially, at least until 2006, South Africa defended Iran citing its rights under the treaty. Subsequently, when Iran's military intentions became more evident, South Africa tried to serve as a bridge between Iran and other powers in the hope of facilitating a political solution.[29]

South Africa was not alone in trying to seek political answers. Brazil and Turkey, much to the chagrin of the United States and European governments, also attempted to facilitate a political resolution to the standoff between Iran and the West in 2009 and 2010. This involved getting Iran to send low-enriched uranium to Turkey in exchange for fuel for its nuclear reactor. However, the initiative unravelled when Iran insisted on its right to continue its 20 per cent enrichment programme, which violates the Security Council's resolutions (*The New York Times*, 16/05/2010). Nevertheless, the initiative, despite its failure to break the stalemate, and both countries' traditional opposition to the imposition of sanctions on Iran, demonstrate the widespread scepticism within the developing world about the United States and Europe's intentions vis-à-vis the Persian country.

South Africa's behaviour in this regard betrays disillusionment with the Security Council's track record on nuclear disarmament. It should be noted that, in 1995, South Africa played a crucial role in brokering support in the developing world for the extension of the Nuclear Non-Proliferation Treaty. But the Security Council's five permanent members, South Africa believes, did not fulfil their end of this bargain, which required them to reduce their nuclear stockpiles and begin a phased disarmament process. Indeed, South

Africa, together with its IBSA partners, has expressed concern about the failure of the Conference on Disarmament, and demanded the progressive elimination of nuclear weapons in a non-discriminatory manner (Flemes, 2007: 9). Instead, however, the spirit if not the legal precepts of the Nuclear Non-Proliferation Treaty were violated when the United States, France, and China tested nuclear weapons, and all three, plus Britain, modernised their nuclear arsenals. This kind of hypocrisy has not only imperilled the nuclear non-proliferation programme, it has also alienated countries such as South Africa and undergirds its international engagement on the Iran nuclear case. South Africa believes that as long as this pattern of behaviour prevails, the inequities and inconsistencies of the multilateral system will continue.

In any case, whatever the merits of the individual decisions, what is evident is that South Africa's foreign policy decisions are determined by a mix of traditional nationalist goals and a desire, common to second-generation nationalists, to subvert the way that global power structures operate. For the primary architect of South Africa's policy, Thabo Mbeki, such a strategy has the potential to ensure the realisation of the more equitable global order on which the development prospects of both South Africa and the African continent so depend. But is foreign policy under Zuma operating on the same philosophical and strategic premises, and how should South Africa's contemporary foreign policy be understood?

Continuities and discontinuities in foreign policy since 2008

The prevailing orthodoxy, both domestically and internationally, is that foreign policy under Zuma has lost its moorings. *The Economist*, for instance, taking its cue from Tom Wheeler, research fellow at the

South African Institute of International Affairs, argues that South Africa's contemporary foreign policy has no coherence, is caught between the contradictory values of national sovereignty and human rights and has resulted in 'a mishmash of unpredictable responses to apparently similar situations in different countries' (*The Economist*, 24/03/2011). The magazine is not alone in this view. Indeed, even astute observers such as Steven Friedman (2012) and Siphamandla Zondi (2012) have come to the same conclusion. But there is a danger of confusing incoherence with disagreement and mangled communication. *The Economist*, in particular, betrays a profound ignorance of South Africa's foreign policy and seems to assume that there is incoherence where it is more likely that its contributors simply disagree with South Africa's agenda. Moreover, as McKaiser (2012) notes, South Africa's Department of International Relations and Cooperation has done itself no favours by failing to effectively communicate the government's position on foreign policy issues.

There are, of course, some differences in the ways in which the Mbeki and Zuma administrations have managed international engagements but these are not of a substantive or strategic nature. It is worth bearing in mind that Zuma and many in his administration are also second-generation African nationalists. Furthermore, many in the Zuma camp were integral to the foreign policy apparatus established by the Mbeki administration. A significant continuity in foreign policy is thus evident between the two administrations, even though some faces at the top have changed.

This does not mean that South Africa's foreign policies are exactly the same as they were, but that the changes made have been within the parameters of the strategic framework established by the Mbeki administration. However, two significant differences are evident. The first is at the level of practice where the Department of International Relations and Cooperation has been given a freer hand to lead on foreign policy. Under Mbeki, foreign policy initiatives were often driven from the presidency, mainly by Mbeki himself, his advisor Mojanku Gumbi, and minister of provincial and constitutional development, Sydney Mufamadi. Zuma, by contrast, is happy to let his foreign minister, Maite Nkoana-Mashabane, lead on day-to-day matters, and he becomes directly engaged only when circumstances dictate a need for direct involvement from the head of state.

The second difference is perhaps more significant. As indicated, the human rights community consistently criticised the Mbeki administration's willingness to continually trade human rights off against broader strategic goals in the foreign policy arena. The Zuma administration has tried to address this issue while remaining consistent with Mbeki's broad strategic perspective. Thus, soon after Zuma's ascension to the presidency, his deputy minister of foreign affairs, Ebrahim Ebrahim, called in the Burmese ambassador to protest the continued house arrest of the country's most famous and popular opposition leader, Aung San Suu Kyi.[30] But South Africa's desire to address the human rights issue while remaining committed to broader strategic perspectives was severely challenged by the cases of Côte d'Ivoire and Libya.

The crisis in Côte d'Ivoire arose when incumbent president, Laurent Gbagbo, refused to recognise the declaration by his country's electoral commission that Alassane Ouattara had won the November 2010 presidential elections. Gbagbo then appealed to the Ivorian constitutional court, which overturned the election result and declared him the winner. Ouattara's victory was recognised both by the international community led by France and the United States as well as by the Economic Community of West African States.

South Africa was initially reluctant to endorse Ouattara. Concerned that the electoral process had not been duly followed, the South African government took a neutral stance, calling for an investigation into the elections, and suggesting that a government of national unity be appointed in the interim (*The Daily Maverick*, 19/02/2011). South Africa was heavily criticised for this stance as it went against the election outcome and favoured Gbagbo.[31] After being subjected to enormous pressure (including Zuma being personally lobbied by then French president Nicolas Sarkozy), South Africa eventually succumbed and, in March 2011, signed the mediation panel's recommendation to the African Union that Ouattara be recognised and that Gbagbo be forced to step down (*Mail & Guardian*, 11/03/2011). In April 2011, French, United Nations and rebel forces aligned to Ouattara overran the city of Abidjan, enabling the latter to assume power in Côte d'Ivoire. The decision by South Africa to reprioritise the democratic outcome over procedural issues signalled a shift in the country's foreign policy practice.

The Libyan case demonstrated this even more dramatically. The crisis was initiated by the Gaddafi regime's militaristic response to the Arab Spring protests that took place in Libya in early 2011. The conflict quickly descended into a civil war, which the Gaddafi regime tried to crush by ruthlessly bombing civilian neighbourhoods. The situation reached a crisis as Gaddafi's forces approached Benghazi – the country's second largest city and the heart of the civilian revolt – and the prospect of a massacre in the city became very real. In this context, the United Nations Security Council adopted Resolution 1973, which authorised all necessary means to protect civilians, imposed a no-fly zone over Libyan airspace, and mandated efforts to find a political solution to the armed conflict (O'Brien and Sinclair, 2011). South Africa, (unlike its allies Brazil, China, India, and Russia, which abstained from the vote), supported the resolution on the grounds that it was designed to save civilian lives.

In the weeks that followed, NATO members, and in particular Britain and France supported by the United States, changed the agenda from one of protecting civilians to seeking regime change. Arming the rebels, especially with support from neighbouring Qatar, and utterly destroying the Gaddafi forces with the use of aerial bombing, NATO paved the way for the rebels to overthrow the regime and ultimately kill the dictator. South Africa and the

African Union protested, claiming that this was a deliberate abuse of Resolution 1973 (O'Brien and Sinclair, 2011). Under the auspices of the African Union, South Africa then launched a number of attempts to broker a political solution in Libya, all of which failed, partly because of a lack of support from the NATO countries, but also because of the amateurish way these initiatives were carried out (including failing to visit or sufficiently engage with the rebel forces). In the end, the Libyan insurrection was ultimately interpreted as a significant victory for NATO and as a complete failure for both the African Union and South Africa.

Two responses to South Africa's foreign engagements emerged after this. The first one perceives South Africa's engagements as incoherent. The country was seen to have first sanctioned a United Nations resolution mandating the use of force and subsequently criticised its implementation once it came under pressure from the African Union. Explanations that NATO went beyond the remit of Resolution 1973 were met with incredulity, suggesting that South Africa exhibited a naivety unbecoming of a seasoned member of the international community (*Mail & Guardian*, 6/05/2011).[32]

The second response represents a retreat into an oppositional stance and a defence of sovereignty. Supported by a diverse grouping, such as the ANC Youth League, senior ANC members Ronnie Kasrils, Aziz Pahad, and Jesse Duarte, and prominent academics and intellectuals including Mahmood Mamdani, Shadrack Gutto, Vusi Gumede, Chris Landsberg and Wally Serote,[33] this perspective's most notable exponent is Thabo Mbeki (2012). Arguing that the United Nations Security Council and the Office of the Secretary-General had violated the mandate of the United Nations charter by sanctioning the United States, Britain and France's manipulation of Resolution 1973 to effect regime change in Libya, Mbeki has suggested that Africa's right to self-determination is increasingly imperilled. Maintaining that there was no evidence that the Gaddafi regime had either committed genocide, or was in the process of doing so, Mbeki argued that division among African nations enables such neo-colonial interventions by Western countries. He called on African leaders to guard the continent's independence and be mindful of their historical obligation to deepen democracy, respect human rights, and develop African capacity within the African Union and in other regional bodies to find African solutions to African problems (Mbeki, 2012).

Both responses must be challenged, and the question must be asked: is South Africa's seemingly inconsistent response – first supporting the resolution, and then criticising the coalition – as incoherent as its critics make out?

The challenge presented to the international community by the crisis in Libya was how to avoid repeating mistakes made in relation to the 1994 Rwandan genocide, and the 2003 invasion of Iraq. Rwanda represents the failure of the international community, including African countries, to intervene decisively when political authorities begin the systematic murder of their own citizens. Iraq represents the political adventurism of Western powers, and in particular the United States, being given the leeway to initiate regime change in countries that they unilaterally deem to be destabilising or dangerous. The dilemma that Libya (and Iraq) posed for the world was how to manage the tension between the responsibility to protect citizens and to respect the sovereignty of a nation. Even more importantly, the Libyan case raised the challenge of how to ensure that powerful nations do not opportunistically exploit a domestic crisis to effect regime change for their own economic or geopolitical interests.

In this context, South Africa's vote for Resolution 1973 was perfectly legitimate and responsible. Those who criticise it tend to forget that Gaddafi's forces were on the verge of entering Benghazi and that the world anticipated a blood bath involving the massacre of rebel forces as well as innocent men, women and children. Mbeki's assertion that this was exaggerated and would not constitute genocide, is beside the point. The issue is whether there was a reasonable prospect that Gaddafi's forces would use the incursion into Benghazi to stamp out the uprising at a significant cost to civilian lives. Gaddafi and his army's conduct up to that point suggests that this was a reasonable assumption, thereby confirming the legitimacy of Resolution 1973. The only alternative offered by critics of the resolution was the suggestion of a political solution. But political solutions – negotiated settlements – seldom take place when military forces are ascendant; they occur when there is a military stalemate. Essentially those who criticised Resolution 1973 were prepared to turn a blind eye to the massacre that was about to happen. They were willing to trade the principle of 'the responsibility to protect' for its alternative, 'respect for sovereignty'. In essence they were willing to see another Rwanda.

But preventing a 'Rwanda' should not make one complacent about invasions such as that which occurred in Iraq. In the Libyan crisis, many were rightly concerned that Western powers would quickly move beyond the mandate given to them under Resolution 1973, which limited the intervention to the imposition of a no-fly zone, and did not sanction regime change or the removal of Gaddafi. Mbeki (2012) was correct to note that Presidents Obama and Sarkozy as well as Prime Minister Cameron were all on public record as not only desiring Gadaffi's removal, but also actively pursuing it through their intervention in Libya.[34]

Allowing powerful countries to abrogate the principle of sovereignty sets a dangerous precedent, for it not only compromises the independence of developing countries, it also allows the international order to continue to be organised solely in the interests of the powerful. The global human rights community needs to be particularly aware of and sensitive to this, lest it becomes an unwitting accomplice to the machinations of the world's most powerful nations. Moreover, democrats should rarely, if ever, consider condoning the imposition of democracy through military means. Autocrats – and Gaddafi was one – must as far as possible be removed through democratic means and by their own people.

The implementation of Resolution 1973 allowed for this possibility. The imposition of the no-fly zone created, at least temporarily, a military stalemate in the east of the country. This would have been the ideal time for a political intervention. In my view, South Africa was therefore correct in both criticising the attempt by the United States, Britain and France to move beyond the mandate of Resolution 1973, and in launching a political intervention in Libya through the African Union. The strategic mistake it then made was that the political intervention should have happened at the point of the stalemate in Benghazi. Instead, Gaddafi's forces were allowed to recover before the intervention was initiated. In addition, it does seem that Zuma relied on charm in trying to convince Gaddafi to step down, rather than brokering a settlement and a transition on the basis of the leverage he had, namely: the ability to get the Western powers to back off, provided Gaddafi conceded to an internationally supervised election process and allow Libyans to choose their own leaders. South Africa's intervention in Libya was, therefore, not as incoherent as it may have seemed. Indeed conceptualising the no-fly zone and the political intervention as two phases in a single strategic intervention represents an innovative approach and one that was appropriate to the challenges confronted by the international community at the time.

Unfortunately, South Africa's implementation of its strategy left much to be desired. Two obvious mistakes were made. First, if the game plan was to avoid both Rwanda and Iraq, South Africa should have gone into the military coalition formally, preferably with its BRICS and IBSA partners. At the appropriate time, South Africa and its allies should have called for a halt to the military operations, and initiated a political engagement. It would have been much more difficult for the Western powers to proceed with regime change if a critical mass within its own coalition, including many from the developing world, had called a halt. All three Western governments were susceptible to domestic public opinion, and South Africa could have used this to keep the intervention to the agreed parameters.

This raises the second criticism, namely, South Africa's inability to coherently sell its strategy. Its public communication in this regard was dismal. South Africa's international relations department has acknowledged its limited capacities in this regard (see Masters, 2011), yet it repeatedly appoints staff who seem unable to enhance its communication capabilities. A cursory glance at the public discourse on this issue in New York, London, Paris, and even Pretoria, suggests that there was very little public understanding of what the political solution proposed by the African Union and South Africa entailed (McKaiser, 2011; 2012). South Africa's and the African Union's communication failures thus made it possible for the Western powers to easily win the hearts and minds campaign around Libya.

The solution proposed by South Africa would have meant that the international community need not make a false trade-off between the principles of the 'responsibility to protect' and the 'respect for sovereignty'. Moreover, the solution was perfectly compatible with South Africa's strategic orientation to foreign policy as developed by Mbeki, but without the rights deficit evident in its implementation during South Africa's first term in the Security Council. Mbeki's (2012) recommendation, with its implicit critique of the South African government's support for Resolution 1973, would reverse these gains. In other words, reprioritising the principle of sovereignty over that of the responsibility to protect would, in effect, weaken South Africa's foreign-policy strategy.

It is vital for the South African government and the human rights community to recognise the importance of three principles, namely: respect for sovereignty, the responsibility to protect citizens, and the need for systemic reform within the world's multilateral organisations. These principles must be seen as indivisible and should not be engaged with selectively. The principles are not mutually exclusive, and trading one off against the others delegitimises the whole system, thereby retarding the struggle for the realisation of human rights throughout the world and for the equitable development of all nations.

The challenge

South Africa's foreign policies and its engagements in the international arena are best understood as the product of a second-generation nationalist political elite who are cognisant of the country's weakness in the global order, and yet are intent on its deracialisation and restructuring on a more equitable foundation. As primary designer of the country's foreign policy, Thabo Mbeki prioritised an African-focused agenda and South–South solidarity, while establishing alliances and aiming to reform the world's most influential global institutions. These priorities have enabled South Africa to pursue its developmental and other interests more effectively. In doing so, South Africa has insisted on the appropriate use of the world's multilateral institutions, and has challenged the United States and other Western countries in their attempts to institutionally penalise autocratic countries outside their sphere of influence. This particular element of South Africa's foreign policy initially alienated the human rights community, as it entailed prioritising the principle of systemic reform over that of the protection of citizens.

South Africa's international engagement under Jacob Zuma has been defined by this same strategic orientation, although the new administration has attempted to compensate for the rights deficit that its implementation entailed under Mbeki. The failure of its strategy in Libya, including the overthrow and subsequent murder of Gaddafi as well as NATO's success in effecting regime change, provoked a degree of soul searching on the country's foreign policy and strategy. At the heart of this intellectual reflection is how to manage the inherent tension between the principles of sovereignty and the responsibility to protect citizens. Mbeki's (2012) recommendations in this regard implicitly reprioritise the former over the latter, and thus have the potential to weaken the legitimacy of South Africa's foreign policy. The empowerment of citizens of the developing world – the ultimate goal of the country's foreign policy – requires both a respect for sovereignty and a rights regime for citizens. Trading one off against the other is likely to ultimately compromise this goal. Is it therefore not essential to think more creatively so that the principles of sovereignty and human rights can be pursued simultaneously, and the collective empowerment of the citizens of the world can become a realisable objective?

7

What is to be done?

The title of this chapter, essentially that of Vladimir Lenin's (1902) famous essay, may seem pretentious but it is merely meant to indicate that the analysis of the preceding pages need not discourage leaders and activists from working towards the construction of a better society. This chapter defines the contours of an alternative progressive political agenda that recognises and flows from an understanding of the balance of power, without compromising the goals of democratisation, empowerment and inclusive development. This agenda involves two distinct tasks: (i) conditioning political elites to become more accountable and responsive to the concerns of citizens; and (ii) fulfilling the overall objectives of the Constitution when the provisions of different clauses come into conflict with each other.

The lack of accountability among the political elites towards citizens (or their greater responsiveness to stakeholders who hold more leverage than ordinary voters) has been identified as a problem in several chapters of this book. In Chapter Two, I engaged with the accountability deficit to explain not only the aloofness of the state and its adoption of policies that do not speak to the interests of ordinary citizens, but also the service-delivery problems that continue to plague all tiers of government. Similarly, in Chapter Three, the conservative macro-economic policy of the Mandela and Mbeki eras, and the continued resonance of this perspective in some quarters within the ruling party and the state, was shown to derive from the leverage of domestic and foreign businesses with their command over investment resources. In Chapter Four, I showed that the balance of power in favour of the business community explains the failure of the social pact of the 1990s. Attempts afoot in 2012 and 2013 to establish a similar pact are likely to come to naught unless political elites develop the will to challenge elite aspirations as much as they challenge those of ordinary citizens. And in Chapter Five, I explained that the evolution of civil society in the post-apartheid era can be seen as a response to consequences of the state's adoption of policies that reflect the inequitable balance of power.

The analysis in the preceding chapters also identified policies and political choices as having compromised the substantive fulfilment of the Constitution because of trade-offs made when different constitutional priorities came into conflict with one another. Three such trade-offs were explicitly identified. The first (discussed in Chapter Two) involved the implementation of equity policy and related legislation which reflect the trade-offs made by the ruling party in managing the tension between the goals of historical redress and national unity. The second trade-off (discussed in Chapters Three and Four) is implicit in the economic policies of the post-apartheid era, which reflect the tension between the constitutional objectives of economic growth and prosperity versus inclusive development. Finally, the political choices made in the implementation of South Africa's foreign policy (discussed in Chapter Six) has tended to prioritise systemic reform and historical redress over the rights of citizens, both of which are equally relevant and important objectives in the Constitution.

Thus, in attempting to identify the contours of an alternative progressive political agenda in this chapter, I set out to accomplish two tasks. The first is to consider how to engage with an unfavourable and inequitable balance of power, with a view to enhancing the accountability of the political elite to ordinary citizens, thereby making progressive outcomes more feasible. The second is to investigate what policies and political choices have the potential to enable the simultaneous pursuit of contesting constitutional goals, rather than requiring trade-offs that favour one over another. Before discussing these issues, however, it is necessary to identify the philosophical impulses that underlie such an agenda.

Reform or transformation

A long tradition permeates progressive socialist thinking about how to advance the interests of the workers and the poor in non-revolutionary contexts. Theorists and scholars associated with this tradition have essentially been bedevilled by the relationship between reform and revolution. In the early part of the twentieth century even the grand old masters confronted this dilemma. Rosa Luxemburg's essay, *Social Reform or Revolution* (1900), was about her intellectual battle (with Eduard Bernstein) to ensure that reforms were not divorced from revolution, but rather conceived as part of a continuum of struggle culminating in the latter. Similarly, Leon Trotsky grappled with this dilemma in his programme of transitional reforms (Trotsky, 1938/1981), and even Vladimir Lenin grappled with the role of reform processes, particularly in his 'Left Wing Communism: An Infantile Disorder' (1920/1964). But perhaps the greatest of the socialist theorists on this issue was Italian communist Antonio Gramsci, whose notion of 'hegemony' provided the intellectual inspiration for much of the European left in the second half of the twentieth century.

Gramsci's most significant intellectual contribution, articulated in his *Prison Notebooks* (1971), was his use of the term hegemony to explain the longevity of capitalist rule. The bourgeoisie, he maintained, rule not only through controlling arms and the armed forces, as well as the means of material production. They also perpetuate their domination through controlling the means of cultural reproduction, as manifested in the norms and mores of society and its institutions. Capitalism continues, he believed, because ordinary citizens, including workers, believe that it reflects the natural order of things.

Gramsci argued that if socialists desire an alternative order, they have to break through this 'common-sense view', and he identified two strategic projects for socialist parties: a war of manoeuvre, and a war of position. The former, for activists confronted with social conditions ripe for revolution, involves an assault on the state for political and economic power. The latter, he proposed, was the path for activists confronted with societies in which capitalism is dominant and the bourgeoisie holds sway. Here socialist parties had to methodically create counter-hegemony through the propagation of alternative ideas, norms and values. Essentially, Gramsci held that activists need to engage in a struggle for reforms that prepare the conditions for a future social revolution (Gramsci, 1971). As noted in Chapter Three, Gramsci maintained that change occurs within the 'limits of the possible'. The struggle was, therefore, not for just any type of reform, but rather for reforms that could serve as a bridge between the social realities of the present and the vision of the future. How to define such reforms was the challenge Gramsci identified for the socialist parties of his time. This same challenge confronts progressive South African activists today: what reforms have the potential to fully transform the social realities inherited from apartheid?

One of the earliest conceptual exercises addressing this question in relation to post-apartheid South Africa was undertaken by John Saul (1991) who, following Boris Kagarlitsky (1990), made the case for what he termed 'structural reform'. Saul defined structural reform as having a snowball effect, thus facilitating further reforms that collectively constitute a project of self-transformation. In addition, such reforms would be, in Saul's words, 'rooted in popular initiatives in such a way as to leave a residue of further empowerment – in terms of growing enlightenment/class consciousness, in terms of organisational capacity – for the vast mass of the population, who thus strengthen themselves for further struggles, further victories' (1991: 6).

Saul floundered, however, when it came to specifying which reforms could be defined as structural. Caught up in the euphoria of the transition, and the rhetoric of intellectuals, progressive academics and union leaders, he proceeded to give credence to a slew of policies that, by no stretch of the imagination, can be described as transformative (Desai and Habib, 1994).

Nevertheless, Saul's conceptual point of departure – structural reform – can be usefully harnessed to an understanding of how to advance an alternative progressive political agenda. For reforms to warrant the title 'structural' they must enhance the leverage of working and marginalised communities, diffuse power in favour of these social groups, and promote the accountability of political elites to the vast majority of citizens.

It is worth noting that this perspective is similar to that articulated by the SACP. In part two of a controversial discussion document released by its central committee in May 2006, entitled 'Class Struggles and the Post-1994 State in South Africa', the organisation argues that 'if it is to have any prospect of addressing the dire legacy of colonial dispossession and apartheid oppression, a national democratic strategy has to be revolutionary, that is to say, it must systemically transform class, racial and gendered power' (SACP, 2006b: 28).

It is probably true to say that most progressive thinkers in South Africa would agree with this perspective and conceive of reforms as part of a broader continuum culminating in social transformation. However, it is at this point that the consensus disintegrates. Progressive activists have long been divided on which actions, policies and strategies constitute such transformational reforms. Within the Tripartite Alliance, and sometimes even outside it, excessive focus has been placed on the role of agency and an inordinate amount of time is therefore spent on ensuring that the 'right people' get into positions of influence in both the ruling party and state institutions. As a result, too little attention has been paid to the structural configurations of power and the systemic checks and balances required for conditioning elite behaviour and decisions. An alternative progressive political agenda must prioritise engagement with the contemporary balance of forces, with a view to enhancing the responsiveness of political elites to the collective concerns of citizens and thereby reinvigorating the dynamic of accountability within South African society.

Reconstructing political accountability to citizens

Political accountability is not simply a product of good leaders and appropriate institutional designs. These are important elements, but they facilitate accountability between elites and citizens only when citizens have sufficient leverage over the elites to produce what I referred to in Chapter Two as 'substantive uncertainty'. Such uncertainty is usually the product of social mobilisation and extra-institutional action on the one hand and elite contestation on the other. Both political processes have the net effect of dispersing power within society. This dispersal is what enhances citizens' leverage over national political elites. It also has the potential to enhance the leverage of national political leaders over their international counterparts.

Since electoral reform would go a long way towards enhancing citizens' leverage over political elites, a number of civic actors and political parties have called for an overhaul of the electoral system. Indeed, the majority of those appointed to the Slabbert Commission, which was appointed to investigate the issue in 2002, recommended that the electoral system be changed to a mixed-member proportional system, with 75 per cent of legislative representatives elected from 69 multi-member constituencies, and the remaining 25 per cent from the party list, to ensure overall proportionality as per the mandate of the Constitution (Electoral Task Team, 2003: 12–30).[1] This recommendation reflected a popular view that while the national-list and proportional-representation system is fair and representative, it does not hold individual parliamentarians accountable to voters (Mattes and Southall, 2004). The express purpose of the Slabbert Commission's proposal was to enhance the influence of citizens on their representatives. The implementation of its recommendations had the potential to contribute to a political system that generates substantive uncertainty for the political elites. Unfortunately, the view of the majority of commission members was contested in a minority report, which favoured the status quo (Electoral Task Team, 2003: 62–73). The recommendations of the minority report were ultimately accepted by the African National Congress (ANC) government.[2]

A related but distinct development that has the potential to greatly enhance the accountability of the political elite is the establishment of a more competitive political system. This requires the emergence of a viable opposition party which, as Courtney Jung and Ian Shapiro (1995: 272–273) argue, is important in (i) providing a site where critics can coalesce and organise; (ii) facilitating a peaceful transfer of political office; (iii) protecting the democratic order from being delegitimated when citizens are unhappy, and (iv) enabling a variety of public-interest functions including the monitoring of government performance and corruption. As important for South Africa is the fact that a viable opposition party would enable citizens' votes to counterbalance the influence of other stakeholders, including domestic and foreign investors. A viable opposition party in South Africa could, therefore, enable a significant reconfiguration of power relations, encouraging political elites to become more responsive to the socio-economic interests of their citizens, including the poor and marginalised.

At present, South Africa has all of the institutional characteristics of a robust democratic political order, yet its political system is entirely uncompetitive. The ANC overwhelmingly dominates electoral support. More importantly, the largest opposition parties are unable to seriously compete with the ruling party because their support base is largely confined to South Africa's minority groups. Thus, it can be argued that a viable political system does not yet exist in South Africa and there is no prospect of one emerging from the collection of parties represented in the national parliament (Habib and Taylor, 2001).

The only alternative is for an opposition party to emerge from within the Tripartite Alliance. In 2001, Rupert Taylor and I argued that, as the natural political home of organised workers, the lower middle classes and the unemployed (that is, the most appropriate social base for such an alternative political project), the Congress of South African Trade Unions (COSATU) and the SACP represent the best hope for a viable parliamentary opposition party.[3] We also held that both organisations retain significant popular support as a result of their liberation credentials, and that COSATU was the only institutional actor outside of the business sector, with the organisational and financial muscle to underwrite the development of a viable parliamentary opposition (Habib and Taylor, 2001: 222).

But we also acknowledged that there were significant obstacles to such a split in the Tripartite Alliance – the most significant being that it was opposed by both the leadership and membership of COSATU and the Communist Party. The leaders feared that leaving the alliance would give the elite classes, both black and white, free rein to determine ANC policy (Marais, 2001). Jeremy Cronin, deputy general secretary of the SACP and current deputy minister of public works, explicitly argued as much in an interview he gave in 2004 (quoted in Habib and Valodia, 2006: 248). He contended that remaining in the Alliance prevents neo-liberal tendencies from dominating the ANC, and makes progressive victories more likely, especially as the global economy becomes increasingly beset by crises. The weakness in this perspective is that it assumes that policy influence occurs only via participation in internal forums. Yet as many studies demonstrate (and as shown in Chapter Five), policy can as easily be influenced by extra-institutional action and/or the deployment of other forms of leverage by social actors within society. After all, capital has been able to significantly influence ANC policy since 1996 ostensibly without a substantive presence inside the party (Habib and Padayachee, 2000). Moreover, as COSATU (2006) and the SACP (2006a; 2006b) have both conceded, their alliance with the ruling party did little to prevent the slide into neo-liberalism during the first decade of South Africa's transition.

Another factor preventing a split in the Tripartite Alliance is the overwhelming support for the alliance among workers and shop stewards. As noted in an earlier chapter, three surveys conducted since 1994 have convincingly demonstrated that the overwhelming majority of COSATU members support the continuation of the alliance (Buhlungu, 2006). Survey data cannot replace dispassionate analysis, however, and demonstrating that a majority of workers support the alliance does not address the issue of whether a break would strategically advance the agenda of the working and unemployed poor. After all, majorities have been known to support inappropriate or even incorrect strategic perspectives.

Nevertheless, while the rationale for a break in the Tripartite Alliance may be entirely logical, it has not happened yet, and developments at the ANC's Polokwane conference in December 2007 made this an even more remote possibility. COSATU was an integral element of the anti-Mbeki Alliance, and Zuma's win in the organisation's national electoral conference was as much a victory for COSATU and the SACP as it was for Zuma himself. Both COSATU and the Communist Party were duly rewarded with significant Cabinet portfolios, including those of economic development, trade and industry and higher education. While COSATU members may still be unhappy about some of the policies and about the corruption scandals plaguing the Zuma administration, the union federation has far more influence than it has had before. For the foreseeable future, then, it is unlikely that COSATU will seriously contemplate leaving the alliance or charting an independent path.

In this context, it is vital that COSATU maintain a critical distance and retain sufficient independent leverage to enable it to pressurise its alliance partners into taking its interests seriously. COSATU's general secretary, Zwelinzima Vavi, is clearly aware of this and (as argued in Chapter Five) is openly leading COSATU with a view to enhancing its influence by establishing additional alliances with civil society. The ANC is not particularly happy about this and has taken measures to contain what it perceives as Vavi's exuberance in this regard.[4] But it is worth noting that an independent and critical COSATU, willing to take on the state, is a necessary political condition for fostering a level of accountability within the ruling political elite. Although this is unlikely to compensate for a viable opposition party, it at least has the potential to keep ruling-party politicians on their toes.

In the longer term, however, the contradictions of governance under a restrictive fiscal regime are likely to overwhelm the Tripartite Alliance and force the partners to part ways. An alternative progressive political agenda must be aware of this and remain willing to consider the difficult choices that may be required for a reconfiguration of power. This includes enabling the emergence of a viable opposition party and ensuring, at least in the interim, that the union movement retains a critical independence within the Tripartite Alliance.

Finally, as shown in Chapter Five, the development of substantive uncertainty, and the related enhancement of political accountability, necessitates the emergence of an independent, robust plural civil society. Much progress has been made in this regard, and perhaps this is where hope for South Africa is most often located, even though significant challenges loom large. As noted, civil society has not only been fundamentally transformed in the post-1994 era, but sections of civil society have also had a dramatic systemic impact on the state, contributing to substantive uncertainty and making elites, at least partially, more responsive to the concerns of poor and marginalised citizens. This has occurred for two significant reasons. First, political democratisation and economic liberalisation have led to the transformation of an ostensibly homogenous, progressive anti-apartheid civil society into one composed of at least three distinct blocs – NGOs, survivalist agencies, and social movements – all with very distinct relationships with the state. The diverse roles, functions and relationships of these different sections of civil society have the potential to increasingly institute checks and balances that are capable of forcing the South African state to become responsive to its citizens, or at least to be made aware of its lack of responsiveness in this regard.

Second, the social movements that have emerged in the post-apartheid era 'contribute to the restoration of political plurality in the political system', facilitate 'the accountability of state elites to our citizenry', and have 'contributed to the emergence of a political climate that prompted government's recent shift to a more state interventionist and expansive economic policy with a more welfarist orientation' (Ballard et al., 2006). These developments, together with the community-based protests that Alexander (2012) has termed a 'rebellion of the poor', have begun to initiate a process of 'enabling popular agency'.[5] The emergence of popular agency is necessary for the dispersal of power, and this, in turn, forces political elites to become accountable to citizens, thereby at least raising the possibility of a more social-democratic development trajectory. An alternative progressive political agenda must therefore encourage and contribute to the vibrancy and plurality of contemporary civil society.

These three strategies then – the pursuit of electoral reform, facilitating the emergence of a viable parliamentary opposition and the critical independence of the union movement, and encouraging the emergence of an independent and plural civil society – constitute the core elements of an alternative progressive political agenda. Individually and collectively, they have the potential to disperse the concentration of political power. This in turn, would enhance the leverage that citizens have on political elites, making them less certain of their political futures and thus more responsive to the interests of the electorate. The net effect could be the emergence of a social democracy that combines the procedural aspects of democracy with inclusive development outcomes involving all citizens.

This outcome, however, also requires a programme of policies capable of managing the tensions and reconciling the competing interests of the various societal stakeholders, captured within the Constitution at the dawn of South Africa's democratic transition.

Reconciling constitutional rights

Three sets of constitutional rights have come into tension with each other as a result of decisions and policies of the post-apartheid regime. These are: (i) the unqualified implementation of crude affirmative action (as identified in Chapter Two) undermines both the delivery of services to the citizenry and the emergence of a national identity, both of which are constitutional goals and responsibilities; (ii) the challenges of economic growth are in tension with the goals of inclusive development, symbolised in the fractious public debate around inequality, poverty and unemployment (as discussed in Chapters Three and Four); and (iii) South Africa's foreign policy engagements reflect a tension that has arisen between advancing civic and human rights versus systemic reform (see Chapter Six).

An alternative progressive political project has to manage the tensions between these constitutional obligations and find ways of pursuing them simultaneously. This can be done with some imagination and contextually grounded engagement.

Affirmative action plus effective service delivery and national identity formation

Affirmative action is not problematic in itself, but its implementation in the public service, within the prevailing conservative macro-economic framework, and alongside the uncritical adoption of management practices developed in the business sector, has had a significantly negative effect on the capacities of the post-apartheid state. Elsewhere Kristina Bentley and I have deliberated on how this tension, between historical redress on the one hand and national identity and state capacity on the other, could be mediated (Habib and Bentley, 2008). We argued that a substitutionist, class-based redress agenda, supported by more specific race-based initiatives, would allow for the simultaneous pursuit of South Africa's two constitutional priorities in this regard.[6] While class-based elements of such a redress programme would generally address both the deracialisation and erosion of poverty across society, race-based initiatives would be confined to areas where the former did not have significant deracialisation effects (Bentley and Habib, 2008: 347–350). For example, in the upper echelons of the corporate sector, race-based initiatives such as sectoral charters could establish deracialisation goals linked to specific time frames and to criteria by which companies would qualify for state tenders and other government contracts.

A number of specific benefits emerge from the adoption of a redress programme that involves both class and race-based elements. First, it would prevent economic and political elites within the black population from monopolising the benefits of redress initiatives.

Second, such a programme would allow the state 'to focus its limited resources on poorer communities' while using its regulatory power to encourage 'the corporate sector to use its own resources to deracialise the market economy' (Habib and Bentley, 2008: 348). Finally, this kind of redress programme would have more legitimacy among both black and white citizens since even the latter are open to pursuing redress that is directed towards poverty alleviation (Friedman and Erasmus, 2008; Seekings, 2005). Its nonracial thrust would also encourage the emergence of a national identity – a necessary precondition for the realisation of the cosmopolitan vision that runs through South Africa's Constitution.

Economic growth and inclusive development

As argued in Chapter Three, a social democratic political economy is a prerequisite if South Africa is to comprehensively deal with the challenges of inequality, poverty and unemployment. Although this was acknowledged at the ANC's national conferences in 2007 and 2012, and some elements of a social democratic platform have gradually been adopted, this economic perspective is still constantly challenged within the ruling party by individuals and factions that advocate fiscal conservatism in the guise of financial prudence. The battle for the economic soul of the ANC has to be resolved, the economic divides bridged, and a consensus built around a social democratic political economy.

Related to this is the need for a new social pact to be cemented between business, labour and the state. The structural impediment to a viable social pact – the inequality in leverage between business and labour – has been overcome as a result of COSATU's greater influence in the post-Polokwane era. However, the Zuma administration has failed to manage the expectations of both the economic elite and the general populace with the result that the other essential foundation for a successful pact – a willingness by all to defer the immediate realisation of their desires – has not been achieved. This is a failure of political management.

At one level, this has been recognised by some political leaders, and in particular by finance minister, Pravin Gordhan, who has spoken out against excessive executive remuneration and enrichment in both the private and public sectors. At another level, however, the lesson has not been truly internalised. This is most evident in a column featured in the *Sunday Times* since February 2012, entitled 'Each One, Hire One'. The column aims to encourage public debate on how to deal with South Africa's unemployment crisis, and has attracted contributions from a number of ruling party politicians, including the ANC's deputy president Cyril Ramaphosa (2012) and Pravin Gordhan (2012b), opposition leaders such as Helen Zille (2012) and Lindiwe Mazibuko (2012), some corporate executives, namely Brett Dawson (2012), Bobby Godsell (2012), Michael Spicer (2012) and Moeletsi Mbeki (2012), and even the odd labour leader such as Zwelinzima Vavi (2012). What is striking about the contributions, however, is that while all recognised the need for a social pact, as well as the formal necessity of compromise, none (other than Vavi) were willing to recognise the legitimacy of workers' concerns related to labour-broking practices and South Africa's low-wage growth path. Indeed, almost all the contributors berated the unions for focusing solely on the interests of their own members, ignoring the needs of the unemployed, and undermining economic growth and efficiency. In essence, the arguments put forward were very similar to those of Seekings and Nattrass (2006), which I challenged on both moral and strategic grounds in Chapter One and Chapter Four. Despite all the platitudes about working together, most contributors to the column seem to assume that any social pact must be constructed decidedly on terms favoured by the corporate sector.

Leave aside the irony of a whole range of individuals, mainly from the political and economic elites, professing that they represent the true interests of the unemployed, and lecturing unions on their selfishness,[7] when it is union members who live and interact on a daily basis with those who are truly marginalised. Should we not be concerned that this diverse set of leaders, with their impressive track records and experience, have not yet understood the basis of successful social pacts? Pacts require compromise. They are established to manage the dilemmas presented by competing interests. A central dilemma that a South African social pact would have to address is how to enable economic competitiveness and the accumulation of work experience by new entrants to the labour market, without losing the hard-won gains of the labour movement as expressed in the Labour Relations Act of 1995.

The unions' fear that compromises might weaken the 1995 Labour Relations Act and that this would allow employers to roll back the gains won by workers in the formal sector. There is precedent for this in the post-apartheid era and to argue that this is impossible and unrealistic (see Zille, 2012), is to be seriously out of touch with the economic dynamics of the last 20 years. For example, in the mid 1990s, internal employees carried out cleaning services in most companies and public institutions. Since then, most private companies and public institutions have subcontracted cleaning services to external companies that employ workers at much lower wages and provide far fewer benefits. Similarly, a study on transformation in South African mines (Bezuidenhout, 2008) demonstrated that as the racial ownership of mines has changed, so working conditions have worsened. Essentially, the South Africa's more marginal mines have been sold to black entrepreneurs who have derived profits from squeezing wages and reducing benefits. This has been achieved mainly through the use of labour brokers, who have therefore served as a 'safety valve' for business owners, enabling them to avoid the obligations made mandatory by the Labour Relations Act.

This is not to deny that South Africa faces significant challenges. Many economic sectors are not globally competitive, and excessive regulation and red tape compromises the viability of many small enterprises (Ramaphosa, 2012). Moreover, given the staggering rate of unemployment among young people, there is an urgent need to create an environment in which employers are willing to take on new entrants into the labour market so that they can accumulate the necessary work experience to make them valuable and productive employees (Bernstein, 2012; Zille, 2012). These challenges should be of as much concern to labour as they are to employers and the state. After all, addressing these challenges is necessary for realising the vision of inclusive development to which the union movement is committed. The challenge for the potential partners in a social pact is to create the conditions for addressing these problems without sacrificing or weakening the protections afforded to formal sector employees.

With some imagination this can be done. For example, agreements entered into with employers in the textile sector in Newcastle in October 2011 involved wage concessions for new employees. This suggests that unions can be pragmatic when it comes to ensuring company competitiveness and survival (*Mercury*, 18/10/2011). Thus unions may have to compromise on a wage subsidy for new and young employees, and allow for special wage and employment provisions for certain economic sectors or geographic zones. Similarly, employers may have to commit to employment targets in these sectors and provide guarantees that they will not try to generalise these special provisions to the broader labour market. In other words, the fears of all parties must be addressed, and in this process, compromises are required from and costs need to be borne by, both business and labour.

This message was, however, missing from the 'Each One, Hire One' columns that have appeared in the *Sunday Times*. None of the contributors seemed to have thought through the compromises required for the establishment of a social pact. But if this is not done, how is a social pact to be realised? Moreover, for as long as an equitable social pact remains a distant dream, South Africa will not succeed in bridging the divide between economic growth and inclusive development, nor will it be able to address the related polarisation and social pathologies that characterise our society.

An alternative progressive political agenda must therefore look to cement an equitable social pact by fashioning the compromises that can enhance economic competitiveness, as well as the accumulation of experience for new entrants in the labour market, without fundamentally compromising the hard won gains made by workers in the formal sectors of the economy.

Advancing civic and human rights and systemic reform

Where human rights and systemic reform have come into conflict with each other, as they have in Zimbabwe, Libya, Sudan, Burma and other hotspots around the world (discussed in Chapter Six), the South African government has implicitly opted for systemic reform and sacrificed human rights in the process. Civil activists tend to prioritise human rights and have accused the South African government of ignoring the plight of civilians. The government has responded by arguing that such activists are being used as unwitting agents of imperial powers in pursuit of larger geopolitical agendas. Neither argument is legitimate. Strengthening democracy, and enhancing the inclusive aspects of development, requires the simultaneous pursuit of human rights and systemic reform. An alternative progressive political agenda needs to bridge the divide that has emerged in this regard, both in the implementation of South Africa's foreign policy, and in the conduct of its critics.

For example, as noted in Chapter Six, South Africa's interventions in the Libyan crisis to couple its support for Resolution 1973 with the seeking of a political solution, was strategically appropriate and far more coherent than critics have given it credit for (see Neethling, 2012). South Africa's strategic intervention attempted to usefully balance the principles of respect for national sovereignty and the responsibility to protect the lives of citizens when they are threatened by domestic political elites, both of which are important for the construction of an equitable global order. Unfortunately the intervention failed because of South Africa's inability to convince its allies in the India–Brazil–South Africa Dialogue Forum (IBSA) or the BRICS countries (Brazil, Russia, India, China, South Africa) to partner in this initiative.

Elsewhere, I have provided examples of how the divide between human rights and systemic reform can be bridged. On the United Nations Security Council resolution on Burma, I argued that South Africa could have opposed the matter being tabled at the Security Council and then led the charge against the generals in the Human Rights Council (*Business Day*, 30/03/2007). In the case of the International Criminal Court charging the leader of Sudan, Omar al-Bashir, I noted that South Africa could have used this as leverage against the Sudanese authorities and used its good offices with the United Nations Security Council to invoke Article 16 of the Rome Statute – essentially granting Al-Bashir a temporary reprieve in exchange for a firm time-bound agenda for achieving peace in Darfur (Habib, 2011). On Zimbabwe, I have noted that the essential challenge is to develop leverage over Mugabe in pursuit of a political solution. I have suggested that one way to achieve this would be to develop a consensus among the southern African frontline states on how to proceed, and on penalties that would be invoked, including closure of neighbouring airspace, if Zimbabwe's ruling party contravenes an agreed peace plan (*Business Day*, 22/12/2008). On nuclear non-proliferation, I have argued that South Africa could have led a developing-world consortium to insist that a renewal of the Nuclear Non-Proliferation Treaty would be acceded to only if existing nuclear powers signed a time-bound disarmament agenda (*Business Day*, 13/04/2010).

All of these suggestions were informed by two related considerations. The first is an acknowledgement that the achievement of justice and peace are sometimes in tension, as was the case in South Africa. In this kind of situation, it is legitimate to trade justice, but only if peace is the dividend. The second is a realisation that no trade-off between human rights and systemic reform is acceptable. Both must be pursued simultaneously if a more equitable world order is to be realised. An alternative progressive political agenda must recognise and enshrine these two principles and use them to inform its praxis.

But this praxis must also be supplemented by three additional strategic foreign-policy initiatives. The first of these involves South Africa undertaking a leadership role in the continent. That is, in the words of some of the international relations literature, the country should play the role of a benevolent hegemon that prioritises stability, democracy and economic development, as well as the expansion of regional and continental common markets (Habib and Selinyane, 2006). An increase in Africa's market size would greatly enhance the leverage of South African and African politicians in their relations with other actors in the global economy, and would be particularly favourable for attracting foreign investment.

Second, in tandem with this continental leadership role, South Africa must revitalise its partnership with Nigeria. It must be borne in mind that regional and continental unions – whether economic or political – are always driven by one or two powerful states. The African agenda and a more cohesive African Union depend on the energies of a partnership between two or more regional powers being directed towards this goal. Of course, such an alliance existed in the form of the South Africa–Nigeria pact for much of the first decade of the new millennium, but this has begun to fray. There is therefore an urgent need to revitalise this pact and perhaps even broaden it to constitute the fulcrum of the African Union (Landsberg, 2012).

Third, South Africa must continue to prioritise its involvement in multilateral institutions, endeavours and strategic alliances, both in the South and between Northern and Southern countries, in order to contain the unilateralism of the United States, and that of other major economic powers in global trade negotiations.[8]

None of this will be possible unless significant weaknesses in South Africa's foreign policy engagements are overcome. South Africa must prioritise its South–North strategic alliances (in addition to its South–South ones) if power is to be significantly dispersed in the global setting and if development opportunities for the South are to be maximised.

South African politicians must also transcend the market fundamentalism so apparent in some of the documentation issued by the New Partnership for Africa's Development (NEPAD) (Bond, 2004c; Vale and Taylor, 1999), in its refusal to regulate South African investment on the continent (Habib and Nthakeng, 2006) and in the almost timid reforms that have to date been implemented by the International Monetary Fund and the World Bank.[9] It is useful to note here that the success of China is not simply linked to its market size, but also to its pragmatism in manipulating this through, for instance, fixing its exchange rate to suit its own ends (Breslin, 2006).

Furthermore, South Africa's foreign policy practitioners and trade negotiators need to be bolder and involve themselves in the politics of brinkmanship (as occurred in Cancun) and in engaging global civil society to advance a human-oriented development agenda.[10] Finally, none of this will be possible without significant capacity being built at the level of technical skills within state institutions and the internalisation of these strategic perspectives among state personnel far beyond the narrow band of people who occupy the presidential and foreign-policy apparatus (Alden and Le Pere, 2004).

All this is necessary, not only because constructing an equitable global order is a moral imperative, but also because it is a strategic necessity if South Africa is to succeed in building an inclusive domestic economy that caters for the interests and needs of all of its citizens.

In sum then, the recommendations in this chapter represent the essential contours of an alternative progressive political agenda. Of course this does not exhaust the list of programmes, strategies and tactics that have to be adopted to enable an alternative political trajectory. These have to be determined in the rough and tumble of politics. But the contours outlined here on mediating the tensions that exist between specific constitutional rights, as well as on the policy and strategic choices required to disperse power and facilitate accountability between the political elites and citizens, should be sufficient to guide the decisions that have to be made and how they should be implemented. For example, an alternative progressive political agenda must speak out against the Protection of State Information Bill, given the limits on transparency it portends and the impact this could have on mobilising civil society. Similarly, it has to oppose the Traditional Courts Bill, given its explicit goal of empowering chiefs vis-à-vis rural citizens. The contours provided aim to serve as a lodestar through which to identify the strategic choices and policy options required for enhancing democracy and facilitating inclusive development in post-apartheid South Africa.

The necessity of leadership

Of course, none of this will be achievable without astute leadership – and not simply at a technical level – although technical skills are particularly important for those occupying professional positions in state structures. The leadership referred to here is of a political kind and involves two distinct elements: (i) a deep understanding of the state of the society, where it needs to go, the obstacles in its path, and possible means to transcend its challenges; (ii) the ability to engage multiple stakeholders, understand their interests, and fashion a sufficient consensus among them without compromising on the primary societal goal. These are the abilities that enable leaders to mobilise collective institutional muscle – within the ruling party, inside the state, and in society – that is necessary to pursue and realise a transformed democratic social democracy.

Such political leadership has not yet been forthcoming from the presidency. But such leadership does not always have to be provided by the president. It can be provided by other senior figures within the ruling party, but so far others seem to have been reluctant to play this role, perhaps informed by a fear that President Zuma, confronted with a factionalised ANC, may interpret any intervention in this regard as an attempt to usurp his authority. In this sense, the factional character of the ANC, and the succession struggles within the organisation, has undermined the possibility of other senior leaders playing this leadership role.

But the failure of political leadership exists not simply at a presidential and governmental level. It exists at many other levels in South African society. Very few leaders across the political, corporate and civic hierarchy recognise and internalise the conditioning effects of the balance of power, or the need to transform this and ensure that more progressive political and socio-economic alternatives become feasible. Instead, as argued in a number of prior chapters, the dominant strategic orientation within and outside the Tripartite Alliance is focused at the level of agency. Individual personalities therefore are targeted for certain positions, in the hope that they will then deliver on the particular policies desired by the relevant ideological faction. Democracy and inclusive development is thus simply reduced to the right person getting the right job.

Yet, as has also been repeatedly argued, astute political leadership has not only to recognise the conditioning effects of the balance of power, but also has to fashion the structural reforms capable of transforming the distribution of political and economic leverage, thereby enabling more progressive outcomes. An alternative progressive political agenda has to enable the emergence of, and be led by such a political leadership. When this happens at multiple levels across the political, corporate and civic hierarchy, including at the most senior levels of the ruling party, South Africa will really begin the long and arduous task of transforming the configurations of power in our society and building a democratic, accountable social democracy responsive to the interests of all of its citizens.

8

Reinterpreting democratic and development experiences

It is a common assumption that Africa's democratic and developmental experiences hold very few lessons for the rest of the world. For example, Anthony Butler, in the introduction to the second edition of his book, *Contemporary South Africa*, suggests that 'African democratization ... generated no fundamental theoretical innovations'. He argues that southern European and Latin American experiences in the 1970s and 1980s, on the other hand, have challenged determinist assumptions of democratisation, 'emphasizing the role of human agency and historical contingency', whereas eastern and central European transitions created 'contagion effects and external precipitation in Moscow, [and] resulted in further productive intellectual reconfiguration' (Butler, 2009: 156).

Of course, this conclusion is controversial, particularly as it is supported by so little evidence. For instance, while Butler discusses Mahmood Mamdani's (1996) work on bifurcated forms of political rule in the urban and rural, he does not seem to take into consideration the theoretical challenges that the Ugandan scholar's study poses for theories of democratic transition, and especially for notions of governance and conceptions of citizenry. Similarly, Butler does not reference or engage with Bratton and Van de Walle's (1994; 1997) comparative studies on African democratisation, whose notion of neo-patrimonial regimes, even though I am not partial to it, nevertheless forces traditional democratisation theory to grapple with how underlying structures and prior regime types condition the subsequent evolution of democratisation and its outcomes.

Butler's conclusion does an even bigger disservice to South Africa's democratisation process, which was the focus of his study. To take but one example, South Africa's transition was founded on the dual principles of reconciliation and justice. This manifested in the establishment of the Truth and Reconciliation Commission, which itself has generated much scholarship (see, for example, Boraine, 2000; James and Van de Vijver, 2001; Tutu, 1999; Villa-Vicencio and Verwoerd, 2000). In addition, South Africa's broader reconciliation agenda allowed scholars such as Mamdani (2009a) to posit the notion of survivor's justice as an alternative to the type of victor's justice symbolised in the Nuremburg trials that took place after the Second World War. Does South Africa's process not constitute an innovation in experiences of democratisation? Is there no need to theorise this experience as Mamdani has attempted to do, especially in relation to its underlying notion of justice and thereafter to consider its implications for other contexts?

It seems useful, therefore, to conclude this book with some reflections on how the analysis contained in the preceding chapters speaks to existing literature on democratisation, development and conflict resolution. After all, Butler's views are no exception; too many scholars within and without the continent believe that Africa's experiences warrant no theorisation and have nothing to teach the world. I believe that this study, like many others about experiences in Africa, is both relevant for other parts of the world and has the potential to enrich comparative reflections and discourses in the global academy.

In my view, the analysis offered in this book generates three distinct considerations related to debates about democratisation, development and conflict resolution. The first consideration is a methodological one and speaks to what Butler (2009) perceives as the theoretical innovation in relation to human agency, which I would suggest has been pushed too far. The second consideration relates to the more philosophical issue of socio-economic justice, and its particular relevance for the analysis of the evolution of democracies. Here the analytical legitimacy of the prevailing bias against socio-economic justice in dominant expressions of transition theory must be called into question. The third consideration, also a philosophical issue, involves the intellectual schism between studies inspired by proponents of nationalism, progressive liberalism and social justice, pertaining to issues of human and civil rights on the one hand and historical redress on the other. A deeper reflection on each of these issues is contained in the pages that follow.

Human agency and its structural conditioning

Butler (2009) was correct to note that studies of 'Third Wave' democracies, that is, those established in southern Europe and Latin America in the 1970s and 1980s, heralded a methodological enthusiasm for human agency and historical contingency. This was inspired by a desire to counter the deterministic analyses emanating from the focus on structural factors, influenced paradoxically by both the modernisation and dependency theories dominant in the first three decades of the post-war era.

The classic critique of these early structuralist studies was of course Dankwart Rustow's pioneering essay (1970), in which he argued that correlations demonstrated between structural factors and democracy did not in any way prove causation. He proposed an alternative model for understanding democratic transitions that stressed the need to focus on the behaviour and decisions of elites, political and social movements, administrators, and the wider population. Yet, despite this focus on actors, Rustow consciously predicated his model on conflict and stalemate – structural features that subsequent interpretations of his work often ignore.

Rustow's conclusion was supported by another pioneering study, authored by Robert Dahl (1971) entitled *Polyarchy: Participation and Opposition*. After reviewing the evidence, Dahl concluded that it simply 'did not sustain the hypothesis that a high level of socio-economic development is either a necessary or a sufficient condition for competitive politics nor the converse hypothesis that competitive politics is either a necessary or a sufficient condition for a high level of socio-economic development' (1971: 71).

These critiques opened the way for a series of agential analyses of regime transitions. Two pioneering studies in this regard were Juan Linz and Alfred Stepan's edited collection, *The Breakdown of Democratic Regimes* (1978), which was catalysed by the wave of military coups in Latin America in the 1970s, and O'Donnell, Schmitter, and Whitehead's four-volume work, *Transitions From Authoritarian Rule*, which was sparked in turn by the replacement of those same regimes in the 1980s. Linz and Stepan, in contrast to earlier structuralist theorists, focused primarily on elite behaviour and suggested that the systemic breakdown of democracy had to be understood as a result of short-sighted democratic leadership (1978: 12). O'Donnell, Schmitter and Whitehead approached the democratic transitions underway from the late 1970s and during the 1980s in similar methodological vein, arguing that 'what actors do and do not do seems much less tightly determined by 'macro' structural factors during the [current] transitions ... than during the breakdown of democratic regimes' (O'Donnell et al., 1986: 19). Their work thus emphasised 'elite dispositions, calculations and pacts' to understand the emergence of transitions and 'the parameters on the extent of possible liberalization and eventual democratization' (1986: 48).[1]

In the wake of *Transitions from Authoritarian Rule*, agential explanations of democratic transitions came into vogue. To be fair, many of these noted the stalemate that had facilitated the transition (and on which Rustow had predicated his explanatory model and his focus on actors), but they showed no significant internalisation of what this meant. That is, they offered very little reflection on how this stalemate informed particular policy choices (other than the customary call for economic prudence), how these policy choices impacted on the character of the society and what their long-term consequences would be. This was as true of studies on democratisation elsewhere as it was of many of those on South Africa. Indeed, as demonstrated by Butler's unqualified remarks about innovations in favour of human agency, this methodological approach still has enormous resonance. However, a range of more integrated analyses of Third Wave democratisation processes have since emerged, which take cognisance of the dangers of too narrow a focus on an human agency (Collier and Collier, 1991; Rueschemeyer et al., 1992). As a result, these studies integrated both agential and structural variables.

The analysis provided in the preceding chapters aims to be methodologically supportive of such studies, and to demonstrate that the story of South Africa's democratic transition is not simply about actors, but also about how actors have been constrained by the configurations of power that prevailed in the domestic and international contexts at various historical moments. The negotiated settlement was not simply a story about pacts and breakthroughs but also about how these were informed by the stalemate between the ANC and National Party (NP) that was occasioned by mass protests, the economic crisis, the country's increasing isolation and the collapse of the Soviet Union. But the transition was not simply about a set of structural factors either. As noted in Chapter Two, the breakthrough is unlikely to have happened without Joe Slovo's intervention during the negotiations process regarding sunset clauses, or Nelson Mandela's far-sighted leadership after the murder of Chris Hani. The sustainability of the democratic transition, especially during its first few years, also owes much to the magnanimity shown by Mandela after he ascended to presidential office.

South Africa's economic story must be understood in context too. The leverage exerted by the corporate sector, both domestic and foreign, increased significantly in the early 1990s as a result of globalisation and the collapse of the Soviet Union. Our economic development is less a story about actors in government than about their beleagueredness, their constraints, and their succumbing to an economic agenda that they subsequently tried to sell as cheerfully as they could. But in this context, actors did make choices. Within the given constraints, they pushed through a black-economic-empowerment agenda that was more narrowly constructed than it could have been. They prioritised the creation of a black bourgeoisie rather than the empowerment of a broader base of emergent black entrepreneurs. Then, as different political pressures arose and power balances slowly shifted – partly linked to the rise of social movements, the emergence of service delivery protests and increasing divisions within the elite – so too did economic policy begin to shift. At first, this involved extending social-support grants and subsequently a reorientation of the economic agenda in a more inclusive direction.

Similarly, the story of the emergence, decline and re-emergence of social pacts involves both actors and structural power configurations. The pact established in the years immediately following the first democratic election in 1994 foundered because of the inequitable balance of power between business and labour, and the attempts made to co-opt the latter. The possibility for a such a pact has since re-emerged given the increased leverage of the labour movement, and the Congress of South African Trade Unions (COSATU) in particular, in the aftermath of the 2007 ANC conference in Polokwane. Its limited success thus far is a result of the Zuma administration's failure to contain the expectations of the elites, without which popular aspirations are unlikely to be curtailed either. Civil society's more general evolution has occurred as a consequence of South Africa's political democratisation and economic liberalisation. In this sense, civil society is both a product of actors responding to the prevailing configurations of power, and the policies that these have generated. Civil society has in turn, become a variable in the new balance of power that constrains and enables contemporary political and social life in South Africa.

Finally, South Africa's foreign policy story is about second-generation nationalists who are cognisant of their relative weakness in the global order. It is about their attempts to engage in slowly transforming this configuration of power so as to enable them to take more radical action, both domestically and in the global arena. It is a story of how power relations constrain South Africa's political elites, inform their policy choices and compel them to seek foreign investment for their country and their continent. These same constraints forced them to be mere observers as history was made in places such as Afghanistan, Iraq, Côte d'Ivoire, Libya and the Horn of Africa. Yet this story is also one of rebellions and reforms; attempts to forge alliances in the African Union as well as with Brazil, China, India and Russia; of occasional successes in thwarting the agendas of great powers, and of attempts to reform the International Monetary Fund, the World Bank and the United Nations Security Council.

These then are not stories about actors, but more accurately about actors constrained and conditioned by configurations of power in the contexts and historical moments in which they are located. A simple focus on human agency may help to explain the start of the transition. But if one is interested in the story of the transition itself – including the liberalisation that took place prior to 1990, the first democratic election, the policies adopted thereafter, their consequences and effects on society, and prospects for the consolidation of democracy – one has to look not only at actors but also at configurations of power, and at how these conditioned actors to behave in particular ways.

Stories of transition are not only about human agency, but about human agency in specific structural and historical contexts.

Socio-economic justice in transitional democracies

Mainstream transition theory is biased against socio-economic justice. Samuel Huntington's advice to would-be democratisers in his *The Third Wave* was that moderate political elites in the opposition should marginalise radical compatriots within their midst (Huntington, 1991).[2] Conservative scholars are not the only ones giving such advice. Terry Lynn Karl (1990) noted the wisdom of marginalising mass actors, and O'Donnell, Schmitter and Whitehead (1986), who by no stretch of the imagination could be perceived as exponents for imperial power or the conservative political establishment, also cautioned against raising the banner of socio-economic justice at the dawn of a democratic transition.[3] Nor can such advice be said to have been limited to the early Third Wave theorists. In Ian Shapiro and Casiano Hacker-Cordón's edited collection entitled *Democracy's Value* (1999), most of the essays valorise procedural democracy, eschewing more radical interpretations that incorporate notions of socio-economic justice. The reason for this consistent conservatism from mainstream transition theorists is obvious. Scholars, especially those of a more liberal or progressive bent, fear that raising concerns about socio-economic justice might compromise the possibilities of a democratic transition by alienating both moderates within the regime and the corporate sector that supports them. Their conclusion is that liberation movements should rather accept procedural democracy with all of its limits, than continue living under the subjugation of authoritarian regimes (see also Shapiro, 1993).

Other studies urge caution with regard to both this model's depiction of the likely train of events in democratic transitions and its advice. Nancy Bermeo (1997) challenged the assumption that the mere presence of radicalism would derail such transitions, and Elizabeth Jean Wood's (2000) comparative study of democratisation in El Salvador and South Africa demonstrates the importance of popular mobilisation in compelling regime elites to consider participating in negotiations. The work of Elke Zuern (2009) goes even further. Following Claude Ake (1993), Zuern makes the case for a substantive (as opposed to a procedural) interpretation of democracy, particularly in the African context. Essentially, Zuern challenges Bratton et al. (2005), who, using data from the Afrobarometer surveys,[4] concluded that African citizens are partial to procedural definitions of democracy. Zuern argues that this conclusion is based on a selective reading of the survey data. She then tabulates responses to other questions in the Afrobarometer survey, and draws on interview material from her own research on South Africa, to demonstrate that substantive interpretations of democracy tend to resonate far more with African citizens (Zuern, 2009).

My own analysis is in line with Zuern's. The pursuit of conservative economic policies during the Mandela and Mbeki administrations polarised South African civil society and not only prevented it from tackling the myriad social pathologies – violent crime, rape, child and women abuse, rampant drug use – inherited from apartheid, but actually aggravated these. This helped to dilute the legitimacy of the democratic regime and served as the rationale for the ousting of the Mbeki faction in the ANC's Polokwane conference in December 2007. Moreover, the realisation of a developmental state based on inclusive development (that is, a move towards substantive democracy) became the principal mandates for the new leadership.

Yet, the consequences of South Africa's political elites following the advice of mainstream transition theory, despite all the hardships experienced by the country's poor, has been relatively mild when compared to that of Zimbabwe. The implosion of Zimbabwe is often laid solely at the door of Robert Mugabe. But the role of the IMF, and its neo-liberal policies, in fostering the economic crisis of the mid 1990s cannot be underestimated (Bond, 1998, especially Chapter 12; Bond, 2007; Marquette, 1997). Nor should one underrate the contribution of the failure to resolve Zimbabwe's land question at the dawn of the transition (Chan, 2011; Mamdani, 2008; Moyo and Yeros, 2007b).[5] After all, it is precisely this issue that has since enabled Mugabe to remain in power. In other words, the failure to incorporate socio-economic justice in the transitional settlement ultimately polarised Zimbawean society and set in motion the developments that have since decimated even procedural democracy in that country.

South Africa and Zimbabwe are also not isolated examples. Indeed, within a decade of the flowering of scholarship on Third Wave democratisation, scholars began bemoaning the emergence of what they described as illiberal and delegative democracies, such as were set up in Angola, Argentina, Brazil, Egypt, Nigeria, Peru, Russia, etc. (O'Donnell, 1993; 1994; Zakaria, 1997; Ottaway, 2003). In these transitional polities the institutional form of democratic polities existed, including elections and parliaments, but even these minimalist definitions of democracy were vulgarised such that none of their intended outcomes (including leadership choices reflecting the will of the people) could be realised. Again, much of this occurred in countries where mainstream transition theory was followed to the letter. The net effect was the absence of socio-economic justice from the transitional settlements, the polarisation of societies and ultimately the hollowing out of democratic institutions until they became mere caricatures of what they are meant to be.

All this suggests that would-be democrats would do well to treat with caution the advice of mainstream transition theory to abandon or postpone socio-economic justice. Of course, the dilemma remains of how to advance such justice in a world in which powerful stakeholders are hostile to this goal. But should scholars not investigate this, rather than hope that avoiding socio-economic justice will somehow enable the full realisation of democracy? After all, there are precedents in the contemporary world where societies have pursued economic growth and inclusion agendas outside the precepts of conservative western economics. China offers one example of this: it has used the leverage of its market size to discipline investors and partially dictate the terms of its economic renaissance (Breslin, 2006). Malaysia has also succeeded in acting outside the parameters of orthodox economics, particularly after the 1998 Asian crisis, with positive results (Sundaram, 2006; Zumkehr and Andriesse, 2008). Understanding how these societies have been able to manoeuvre, and learning from this, may offer more productive means of enabling democratisation than following the advice of mainstream transition theorists.

The battle of interpretation

Scholarly studies that are partial to visions of substantive democracy and inclusive development have been divided between a nationalist historiography and analysis on the one hand, and that emanating from a progressively liberal or social justice ideological orientation on the other. The battle between these studies is about how to interpret, understand and address societal conflicts. The division is centred on the trade-offs made (discussed in Chapter Seven) between civil and human rights on the one hand, and historical redress and systemic reform on the other. It also revolves around the political choices to be made in managing the tension between a state's and the international community's responsibility to protect the lives of citizens when they are threatened, and the principle of national sovereignty.[6] This division is thus not only between governments and human rights activists as it is so often portrayed, it is also a fault line that runs through the scholarly literature.

This can be clearly demonstrated through reflecting on the debates about the violence and contemporary popular struggles in Sudan and Zimbabwe. Contributions made by Mahmood Mamdani to both debates provide a useful starting point. His book on Darfur and the Sudan, *Saviors and Survivors*, provoked a global debate on whether the Save Darfur Coalition – in its framing of the conflict, its agenda and proposed solutions – was simultaneously advancing the geopolitical goals of what was then the Bush administration. Mamdani's argument was that the coalition viewed the conflict through the ideological lens of the 'war on terror', and, as a result, unduly personalised it through the figure of the Sudanese president, Omar al-Bashir (Mamdani, 2009a). The coalition's call for a military intervention, argued Mamdani, would essentially constitute a modern form of colonialism.

Mamdani then offered an alternative interpretation of the conflict, insisting on the need to understand its roots. He demonstrated that these lie in both colonial policy and environmental factors. Environmental factors came into play as increasing desertification forced people into a struggle for scarce land. The fact that this struggle became 'racialised' derived from the fact that British colonial authorities had categorised the population as 'Arab settlers' and 'local natives' to facilitate their system of indirect rule. Mamdani concluded therefore that the struggle in Sudan is not a conflict between state and society, but rather one that exists within society itself (Mamdani, 2009a).[7] His recommendations as to how the conflict should be addressed invoke the notion of survivor's justice, as opposed to victor's justice, which he views as a typically African formula for solving the continent's intractable problems. The notion, Mamdani argues, has precedents in South Africa and Mozambique, where intractable problems were addressed through negotiated solutions, and in which losers in the democratic transition were neither victimised nor subjected to legal sanction. He suggests that this formula holds promise for resolving political conflicts in other African contexts.

Mamdani (2008) takes a similar stance on Zimbabwe. Drawing on the works of Sam Moyo and Paris Yeros (2007a; 2007b), he insists that despite Mugabe's authoritarian disposition, and the personal and collective hardships inflicted on the country's citizens, the land-reform programme represents a social advance in historical terms, for it fundamentally addresses the inequities in land distribution bequeathed by colonialism and enshrined in the Lancaster House Agreement.[8] For Mamdani, the economic catastrophe in Zimbabwe is not only a consequence of Mugabe's misrule, but also the result of sanctions imposed by the West. Mamdani acknowledges the existence of cronyism, corruption and the widespread abrogation of rights, but like Moyo and Yeros, he holds that, on balance, a significant level of redistribution has taken place. He concludes that this is what allows Mugabe to rule, not only with force but also with a degree of consent. Again, therefore, he asserts that the conflict in Zimbabwe is not between state and citizen, but within society itself.[9] Although he does not say so explicitly, the conclusion is obvious: what Zimbabwe requires is a programme of 'survivor's justice' that will allow the country to rebuild itself on new foundations.

Mamdani's views have been subject to trenchant criticism.[10] His account of the Darfur conflict was criticised on historical factual grounds (Daly, 2009; Johnson, 2009; O'Fahey, 2009), for misrepresenting the Save Darfur Coalition (Johnson, 2009; Lanz, 2009) and for not providing sufficient detail about his recommendations for 'survivor's justice' (Edozie, 2009: 667). In my view, Mamdani should also be challenged for homogenising civil society by projecting the Save Darfur Coalition as its sole expression and for allowing the debate in the United States to over-determine the parameters of his argument.

His work on Zimbabwe has been criticised for his interpretation of the land question and his sole reliance on the research of Moyo and Yeros (Cousins, 2009; Hammar, 2009; Raftopoulos, 2009; Ranger, 2009; Scarnecchia et al., 2009), as well as for overestimating support for Mugabe (Campbell, 2009; Cousins, 2009; Scarnecchia et al., 2009; Windrich, 2009), underestimating the corruption and cronyism within the land-reform programme (Bond, 2009; Mhanda, 2009), misdiagnosing the cause of the economic crisis by focusing on sanctions (Bond, 2009; Campbell, 2009; Raftopoulos, 2009; Scarnecchia et al., 2009), over emphasising the urban–rural divide, misreading the role of the labour movement (Moore, 2009; Scarnecchia et al., 2009), and caricaturing the character of the opposition party, the Movement for Democratic Change (Raftopoulos, 2009; Scarnecchia et al., 2009).

In addition, a thread common to all these critiques is that Mamdani underplays the abrogation of human rights and the suffering of citizens. To be fair, in both his contributions and in his subsequent responses to his critics, Mamdani acknowledged that violence was perpetrated and human rights were abrogated. On balance, though, it is hard to deny that in the overall flavour of both contributions – indicated by the tenor and form of his arguments and in the adjectives he uses – human rights abuses and loss of life are not discussed with the same measure of outrage as his condemnations of Western hypocrisy and threats of military intervention.[11] As Raftopoulos (2009: 59) remarked, 'the position of African scholars who denounced such unlikely threats would have been much more credible if their criticisms of the violence of the Zimbabwean state over the last ten years had been equally audible'.

Mamdani would, of course, protest that this was not the primary purpose of his contributions. In the third part of his response to critics on *Saviours and Survivors*, posted in the Social Science Research Council's African Arguments blog, he asks: 'is to explain the context of a conflict, the issues that led to the violence, and reproduce it, the same as apologising for the perpetrator?' (Mamdani, 2009b). Elsewhere in his response he remarks:

> no one can deny that the political power in Sudan, the al-Bashir government must be held responsible ... much as the De Klerk government in South Africa was politically responsible for the crimes of apartheid in the period before the anti-apartheid transition ... The issue I raised in the book was not about the political responsibility of the al-Bashir government which is a settled issue ... rather I raised a larger and more important issue: how to end the conflict in Darfur.
>
> (Mamdani, 2009b)

Mamdani, then proceeds to make the case for survivor's justice based on the experience of South Africa and Mozambique, where there was no victor in either conflict and perpetrators and victims had no option but to continue to live together. He concludes:

> Instead of encouraging the lust for punishment, the leadership of the anti-apartheid movement called for a trade off: an amnesty for individual leaders in return for an agreed political reform for all. The point was to change the rules, thereby to reform the political community, so as to give the living a second chance.
>
> (Mamdani, 2009b)

This is a powerful argument and a legitimate response to his critics, particularly because it speaks to the contextual realities of both Sudan and Zimbabwe. I concur that the South African experience – the paradigm of survivor's justice – offers a far better chance of finding a solution to the conflicts in Sudan and Zimbabwe than other models. But the notion of survivor's justice poses two additional questions that Mamdani does not explicitly address.

First, under what terms and conditions should individual justice be tempered for survivor's justice? Second, beyond making a theoretical case, under what conditions does survivor's justice become a real possibility and how can these conditions be created? Addressing the first question is necessary to ensure that any tempering of justice leads to real peace, benefits the collective citizenry and does not inadvertently translate into a defence of perpetrators. Note that the South African case holds the lesson that individual justice may be tempered so long as peace is to be the collective dividend. But a tempering of justice cannot occur without the explicit quid pro quo being the suspension of violence and the establishment of peace. This, then, is the weakness in Mamdani's formulation for while he posits the notion of survivor's justice, he does not explicitly tie the tempering of justice to the peace dividend.

Addressing the second question is also essential and South Africa's experience is again instructive. De Klerk did not agree to survivor's justice because of farsightedness or goodwill. As demonstrated in Chapter One, De Klerk was compelled to concede because the prevailing configurations of power in the late 1980s had resulted in a stalemate between the ANC and NP. This poses the question: what leverage can be deployed to compel the same concessions from political elites in the case of Sudan and Zimbabwe? Essentially, how does one make an Al-Bashir or a Mugabe reject the role of perpetrator in favour of one as a survivor?

Mamdani makes the strategic case for the paradigm, but he does not address how to create the political conditions so that entrenched and powerful stakeholders, both internal and external to the immediate geography of the conflict, would consider survivor's justice a preferable choice. Confronting this issue forces one to consider how political elites can be subjected to pressure, and how to increase the leverage of victims vis-à-vis perpetrators. Ensconcing oneself squarely on the side of the victims, therefore, enhances the persuasiveness of the case for survivor's justice.

Yet if Mamdani has to be challenged to name the conditions under which the tempering of individual justice is legitimate, and to consider how to subject perpetrators to pressure, most of his critics have to be challenged on grounds that are just as serious.

First, the responses of Mamdani's critics suggest that they have not internalised his primary message: that given the circumstances on the ground, an accommodation may have to be entered into, and individual justice may have to be tempered in exchange for peace. They do not state whether this is something they would support and if so, on what terms? If not, what alternatives would they recommend? Irrespective of levels of popular support for Al-Bashir and Mugabe, it must be acknowledged that both leaders retain significant power because they control the respective military and the state apparatuses in their countries. Given this fact, and the absence of revolution, it is difficult to imagine that any solution other than the survivor's justice model proposed by Mamdani would be capable of addressing the violence and protracted conflicts in both countries.

Second, even a cursory reading of responses to Mamdani's contributions indicates that most of his critics, many with ostensibly progressive liberal and social justice leanings, were surprisingly sanguine about the notion of military intervention. On Darfur, not only was this one of the primary strategies proposed by the Save Darfur Coalition, but many of Mamdani's critics reiterated the case for military intervention.

Critics of Mamdani's views on Zimbabwe almost all suggested that the notion of external military intervention was a red herring raised by Mugabe, but in fact, the call was made by retired Anglican Archbishop Desmond Tutu (BBC News, 29/06/2008) and Kenyan prime minister Raila Odinga (*New York Times*, 7/12/2008), no less. In addition, both Hilary Clinton (*New York Times*, 7/02/2009, 14/06/2011) and Gordon Brown (*The Guardian*, 6/12/2009) went on public record calling for Mugabe's removal. And in a debate with Moeletsi Mbeki on a Royal African Society platform at the University College in London, I argued against military intervention in Zimbabwe and demonstrated why it was unworkable, while Mbeki indicated his support for it and publicly laid out a strategy on how it could be accomplished.[12] At the very least, the idea was being flirted with in South Africa, in the region and within Western governments. It should be borne in mind that all of this played out against a backdrop of debate about the doctrine of state sovereignty and the international community's responsibility to protect (also known as R2P), and the terms and parameters under which these principles should be implemented.

Moreover, critics who explicitly supported and advocated military intervention were breathtakingly naive about its possible consequences. David Lanz, in his critique of Mamdani, suggested:

> Darfur has become the test case for the 'responsibility to protect' ... R2P is an ambitious plan for a new world order in which sovereignty is no longer an argument against external intervention for humanitarian purposes ... This does not mean the Save Darfur and the ... international community – which is really an amalgam of Western Powers and non-governmental groups who share a diffuse ideology based on liberal values – want to project power and take control of the Sudan or Africa for that matter. Rather it seeks to project norms and promote a world order in which values trump power. (Lanz, 2009: 670)

Lanz shows no understanding that Western powers might be acting in their own interests in relation to their own economic and geopolitical goals. Nor does he seem to recognise that the boundary between the 'responsibility to protect' and the desire to effect regime change can so easily be crossed and abused by great powers acting in concert, as was the case in Libya, for example. Instead, he romanticises military intervention and shows almost no understanding of that simple lesson demonstrated by events in Afghanistan, Iraq and Libya that democracy can rarely be brought to a country by external stakeholders and through the barrel of a gun. Such naiveté is what leads to scholars and civil society actors becoming, consciously or unwittingly, agents and accomplices of imperial agendas.

All of this underscores the need to simultaneously pursue both human rights and historical redress, as well as the doctrine of responsibility to protect and the principle of sovereignty. When these principles come into conflict, the first recourse should not be to trade one off in favour of the other. Instead, it should be to find ways (as I attempted to do in Chapter Seven), to make the conflicting agendas compatible so that both can be pursued together. So far neither those advocating human rights nor those pursuing historical redress have attempted to do this. Instead of trading one set of obligations for another, does it not make sense for both groups of scholars to consider how both obligations can be pursued simultaneously? After all, the full realisation of human rights has been a core element of progressive nationalist programmes. And scholars associated with the social justice and progressive liberal traditions have stressed the importance of reforming structural conditions so that they sustain rights. These scholars have also been among the intellectual vanguard against military adventurism, recognising that democracy is rarely realised through armed intervention.

The pursuit of an agenda that encompasses both human rights and historical redress would facilitate an alliance between these intellectual traditions. Such an alliance has the potential not only to support citizens in their democratic struggles against authoritarian leaders, but also to contribute to containing the economic and geopolitical ambitions and machinations of the great powers.

A progressive nationalism?

There is a precedent for such an alliance between these intellectual traditions. The international anti-apartheid movement was not only an alliance of national liberation activists and the global human rights community; it was also founded on a conceptual bridging of the divides between progressive nationalism, liberalism and social justice in support of one of the great struggles of the twentieth century. Perhaps the main obstacle to the emergence of this alliance in the contemporary era is the increasing cynicism about nationalism within the social justice and progressive liberal intellectual communities. Demoralised by the failure of post-colonial nationalist governments, and the excesses of their leaders, such intellectuals have gravitated to a cosmopolitanism that is disconnected from any contextual grounding.

One expression of this is Ivor Chipkin's book, *Do South Africans Exist?* (2007). Chipkin's thesis is that African nationalism is incapable of hosting the democratic ideals and cosmopolitan vision enshrined in South Africa's Constitution because of its propensity to exclude those who deviate from the national ideal. He recommends, therefore, that South Africans shed their exclusivist rhetoric and nationalist credentials, and re-imagine the demos so that citizenship is not defined by territorial, ethnic or cultural criteria but rather by notions of solidarity that flow from real democratic practice. Chipkin's conception of cosmopolitanism is, however, divorced from context. It is abstracted from an understanding that the country was until relatively recently immersed in the apartheid system, the consequences of which still inform the day-to-day lives of many South Africans.

If a cosmopolitan vision is to have contemporary relevance, it needs to speak to the realities of South Africa's circumstances (Appiah, 2006). Its focus must be on building a national identity across the divides fostered by apartheid, without losing the cosmopolitan vision necessary for living in the globalised world of the twenty-first century. Achille Mbembe (2007) captures these dual imperatives in his conception of 'Afropolitanism', while Kristina Bentley and I coined the term 'cosmopolitan nationalism' to describe a similar concept (2008: 352). Underlying the latter term, however, is an appreciation of the necessity for progressive nationalism.

Perhaps this can be best motivated by reference to one of the great South African classics on the question of nationalism and nationalist historiography, *One Azania, One Nation* (No Sizwe, 1979). Written while under house arrest and using a pseudonym, Neville Alexander's study of Afrikaner and African nationalism demonstrates how these took distinct forms – progressive or conservative – in different epochs. Nationalism, in Alexander's view, is not necessarily always conservative. Instead, its character is determined by the social forces that inform its agenda.

This conception of nationalism imagines 'the nation' as comprising all who desire a common future in one political entity. There is, of course, a more contemporary argument for this reimagination of the nation. Aristide Zolberg's (2006) masterful study of the implementation of immigration policy in the United States demonstrates how after 1965 America reimagined its white, Anglo-Saxon Protestant identity to incorporate a pan-European one (Zolberg, 2006).[13]

In any case, this kind of inclusivity of citizenship, combined with a substantive conception of democracy and an openness to continuous change in the imagination of the 'national self' are the central elements informing the progressive nationalist vision that lies at the core of Alexander's *One Azania, One Nation*. Moreover, not only is this conception of nationalism the foundational perspective on which most of the mainstream traditions of the liberation movement based their respective struggles against apartheid, it also constitutes the core of the vision enshrined in the South African Constitution.

An appreciation of the progressive potential of nationalism could help to form the basis for an alliance between scholars from this intellectual tradition and those that have progressive liberal and social justice ideological leanings. Such an alliance has the potential to support the struggles for political freedom of oppressed peoples around the world, as it did in South Africa. It could also aid in deepening the social character of democratic transitions so that they address citizens' day-to-day concerns. To do this, however, scholars must direct their research not only towards understanding and explaining the contemporary world, but also to considering how to transform it for the better. Recall the words of Karl Marx (1845/1969) in his 'Theses on Feuerbach':

> Philosophers have hitherto only interpreted
> the world in various ways;
> the point is to change it.

Is this not the vision that should inspire us as scholars?

Frequently used acronyms and abbreviations

ANC	African National Congress
CEO	chief executive officer
COSATU	Congress of South African Trade Unions
G8	Group of Eight
G77 and China	Group of 77 and China
GDP	gross domestic product
GEAR	Growth, Employment and Redistribution strategy
MERG	Macro Economic Research Group
MDC	Movement for Democratic Change
NATO	North Atlantic Treaty Organisation
NDP	National Development Plan
NEDLAC	National Economic Development and Labour Council
NEPAD	New Partnership for Africa's Development
NGO	non-governmental organisation
NPC	National Planning Commission
RDP	Reconstruction and Development programme (RDP)
SADC	Southern African Development Community
SACP	South African Communist Party
ZANU-PF	Zimbabwe African National Union Patriotic Front

Endnotes

Chapter 1 – Introduction

1   Note the controversy that has followed the publication of Frank Chikane's (2012) *Eight Days in September*. Chikane was, of course, director-general in the office of the president during Mbeki's presidency and his account provides a very one-sided portrayal of Mbeki's last days in office.

2   Mbeki accused the *Daily Dispatch*, who broke the story, of dishonesty and undue sensationalism. The newspaper formally responded through its deputy editor, Andrew Trench. *See Daily Dispatch*, 31/07/2007.

3   For a detailed discussion of the lead-up to and the events at Polokwane, as well as the ANC's continued attempts to reinvent itself, see Booysen (2011: 41–67).

4   One prominent case was the appointment of Moegoeng Moegoeng as chief justice in September 2011.

5   For example, the singing of *Dubula iBhunu* (Shoot the Boer) by Julius Malema, former ANC Youth League leader, at rallies and meetings in March 2010 led to AfriForum having the song declared an example of hate speech and banned. (AfriForum is an organisation which represents minorities, and in particular the white community, and tries to enhance their active participation in public debates and action.)

6   Afrikaner capital had evolved over five decades, and its shape and size ensured that, by the late 1970s, its interests had begun to converge with that of its English counterparts. For a discussion of how this occurred, see Glaser (2001) and O'Meara (1996).

7   Note his 'I am an African' speech discussed earlier, in which Mbeki eschewed an essentialist definition and instead espoused a very cosmopolitan and non-racial interpretation of African identity (Mbeki, 1996).

8   The redress legislation defines 'black' in inclusivist terms to include African, coloured and Indian. For a reflection on the tensions this has created, and how these have been addressed, see Habib (2004).

9   A number of chapters in the volume edited by Ballard, et al. (2006) underscore this point; see especially Elke Zuern's chapter on SANCO and the discussion on tactics in the conclusion.

10 In 2010, for instance, businesses in the manufacturing sector partnered with trade unions to lobby for state interventions which would enable a more competitive exchange rate but the financial sector, the South African Reserve Bank and the treasury were not particularly supportive of this plan (*Engineering News*, 10 May 2010). Furthermore, unlike the Free

Market Foundation for example, various manufacturing industries have consistently opposed Chinese imports (*Engineering News*, 28 November 2012).

11 In many cases, this was intentional. As Friedman maintained in his preface to *The Long Journey*, analysis 'is confined to exploring the clashes of interest concealed behind technical submissions and counter proposals' (Friedman, 1993: vi).

12 This was achieved through establishing a number of policy institutes, funded by the private sector and foreign donors – including governments and foundations – from which scholars advised the central political actors and intervened through contributing to debates in the media . Perhaps the most well known of these institutes are the former Centre for Policy Studies based in Johannesburg and the Institute for Democracy in South Africa (Idasa) located in both Cape Town and Pretoria.

13 Although Rustow never used the term 'stalemate', the notion is implicit in what he called South Africa's 'prolonged and inconclusive political struggle' (1970: 353).

Chapter 2 – Governance, political accountability and service delivery

1 Ideologues of the National Party often cited Lijphart's work, and in particular his *Power-Sharing in South Africa* (1985), to support their case for the saliency of ethnicity in South Africa; the party's constitutional proposals were also significantly influenced by Lijphart's policy prescriptions.

2 This grants representatives of the major groups the right to veto decisions on certain vital matters even if a majority has voted in favour of those decisions.

3 Donald Horowitz (1991) advanced a similar analysis. Sharing Lijphart's views, Horowitz maintained that intra-African conflicts were likely to supersede conflicts between the black and white communities in the future. Thus, he concluded that a majoritarian system of government would alienate minority groups and the resulting instability would weaken the prospects for consolidating democracy in South Africa. Horowitz, however, rejected Lijphart's consociational solution, advocating instead a combination of proportional representation with a single transferable vote and an alternative-vote system.

4 It needs to be noted that the stayaway was whittled down to a symbolic action after the union leadership reduced it first to one week and then to two days.

5 'The Leipzig option' was a term used in ANC literature to symbolise the popular revolts that occurred in Eastern Europe in the late 1980s and early 1990s.

6 Jeremy Cronin indicated in an interview that 'Slovo was more honest than other ANC negotiators who were also floating the idea ... of sunset clauses, but they were doing so very quietly' (Cronin interview, 7 September 1995).

7 For contributions critical of the oppositionists, see Cronin (1992) and Suttner (1992). All of these articles were published in the *African Communist*, No. 131.

8 Some of the more militant branches in the ANC, such as the Midlands region, did call for a halt to the negotiations process after Hani's murder, which happened in April 1993, but they were overruled by the national leadership (*Natal Witness*, 15 April 1993).

9 In the Netherlands, public educational institutions can be controlled and subject to the authority of segmented-interest organisations such as churches. In South Africa, however, all public educational institutions are subject to the authority of a unified Ministry of Education.

10 The assumption is sometimes made that party constituencies in South Africa represent a rough approximation of ethnic interests. Note, however, that the majority of the coloured and Indian communities voted for the National Party in 1994, a party that represented the interests of the white community. Subsequent elections have revealed enormous fluidity in electoral support within these communities.

11 I am not particularly partial to the neo-patrimonial paradigm for explaining political developments on the African continent. While I recognise some of the patterns of rule it identifies, I believe, like Thandika Mkandawire (2011), that it is mainly descriptive, not sufficiently analytical and simultaneously homogenises and exceptionalises the African experience.

12 Some scholars are critical of this perspective. Raymond Suttner, for instance, in response to some of the democratisation literature, accuses 'experts' who stress the need for elite contestation of being 'dogmatic ... deeply conservative ... [and supportive of] a specific version of democracy, that of formal, representative democracy without substantial social and economic transformation or significant popular involvement' (Suttner, 2004: 756–757). The problem with Suttner's view, of course, is that it sets up a false divide between representative and participatory forms of democracy.

13 Netshitenzhe made this point in the plenary session on 'Improving Governance and the Development State' at the Annual Conference of the Department of Economic Development on 30 May 2011.

Chapter 3 – The political economy of development

1 This is, of course, an adaptation of a memorable and often quoted statement by Carl von Clausewitz, noted Prussian general and scholar of military strategy, who described war as 'nothing more than the continuation of politics by other means' (quoted in Booth and Williams, 1975: 24).

2 Even Leibrandt et al. (2010: 18–19) recognise that 'aggregate inequality has remained stubbornly high and perhaps increased' in the post-apartheid era. While they hold that this may, on its own, not necessarily be bad, 'the fact that the post-apartheid society started off with such a high level of inequality certainly adds an ominous note to this trend'.

3 Marais (2011: 398–400) criticizes Satgar for overestimating possibilities for radical policy choices (including socialism), for underplaying the influence of popular organisations on the character of the transition and for ignoring the role played by the ANC in generating hegemonic consent from the citizenry.

4 'Verligte' is Afrikaans for 'enlightened'. The term was used to describe any white person or political faction that supported liberal trends in government policy during apartheid.

5 MERG was established with the financial assistance of the Canadian International Development Research Centre, the Canadian International Development Agency and other international donors including the European Union. In addition, while MERG was formally established by the ANC, the Economic Trends Group was formally established by COSATU. There was a huge overlap in the economists in the various groups, but MERG looked at generic economic policy, while the Economic Trends Group and the Industrial Strategy Project focused on developing a labour-friendly industrialisation plan for South Africa.

6 The union federations collectively released an alternative report at about the same time entitled Social Equity and Job Creation: The Key to a Stable Future (COSATU, FEDSAL and NACTU, 1996), which was less influential in state circles. See also Nattrass (1996).

7 This view has been the steady diet dished up by most of South Africa's business newspapers and magazines.

8 Although issued by the ANC, it is well known in ANC circles that Mbeki authored this document. This is why members of COSATU and the SACP sometimes refer to the '1996 class project' and tend to hold Mbeki personally responsible for this.

9 The Mbeki administration was, of course, very concerned about the 'dependency' this might create in the population and therefore refused to implement a basic income grant. As Franco Barchiesi (2011) has so convincingly demonstrated, in the view of the Mbeki (and even the Zuma) government, work was seen a necessary component of virtuous citizenship.

For a critical analysis of Mbeki's fears about dependency, and an argument in favour of the basic income grant, see Meth (2004).

10 Mbeki had a number of acrimonious public spats with corporate CEOs, including Pieter Cox of SASOL and Tony Trahar of Anglo American (see *The Economist*, 16/09/2004).

11 The Mbeki camp registered at least 40 percent of the votes of delegates at the Polokwane Conference while Zuma and his candidates received almost 60 percent.

12 Marcus has also served as a professor at the Gordon Institute of Business, the University of Pretoria's Business School.

13 After coming under pressure from the ratings agencies and the corporate lobby, Gordhan has since retreated to a more conventional fiscal position – see Chapter Seven.

14 In fact, as a result of better than expected tax revenues and some under spending, the deficits reduced to 6.5 per cent, 4.2 per cent and 4.8 per cent in 2009, 2010 and 2011 respectively (National Treasury, 2012: 42; see also Gordhan, 2012a).

15 Interest rates have been reduced by 650 basis points between 2008 and the end of 2010. At the end of 2012, the Reserve Bank's repo rate stood at 5.5 per cent – the lowest in 30 years.

16 The Grant Thornton International Business Report survey (13 August 2012), for instance, suggests that 68 per cent of South African business owners believe that executives are paid too much (http://www.gt.co.za/news/2012/08/).

17 For a popular review of the nationalisation debate see Cohen (2012). Cohen's approach to nationalisation is particularly conservative, even though he tries to couch his argument in pragmatic and liberal terms. He does, however, detail the various contours of the debate in South Africa. A real critique of nationalisation in South Africa should not be based on ideology – even Cohen acknowledges that nationalisation has been successful in certain parts of the world. The problem in South Africa is contextual; in other words, the government and its public service have neither the skills nor the managerial competence to efficiently run nationalised projects in the mining sector. The scale of corruption is an additional concern. Moreover, South Africa can achieve the goal of obtaining additional resources for development through alternative means such as taxation. In many ways, nationalisation has become a red herring and is detracting from a deeper discussion on how to develop an inclusive development agenda in South Africa.

18 Other analysts, such as Steven Friedman (2010) for example, hold that the divisions within the ANC and that Alliance are inspired by a careerist struggle for positions in the ruling party and the state. In my view, careerist considerations do indeed have an impact, but they too are

ensconced within the broader ideological conflicts that divide the ruling party.

19 In this instance, COSATU supported Bobby Godsell, the chair of the Eskom board, on grounds of respecting corporate governance principles. The Black Management Forum, by contrast, supported Jacob Maroga, the CEO of the parastatal, essentially because he was black. COSATU's support for the board signalled that it would not allow the racial background of executives to trump the developmental outcomes it expects of state-owned enterprises.

Chapter 4 – The viability of a sustainable social pact

1 Corporatism is the organisation of society and its various elements through formal associations or 'corporate groups' such as business, labour, or any other category relevant in society. It is a form of organisation that is common in both authoritarian and democratic societies. In the former, it is referred to as state corporatism since the state is crucial in the formation and accreditation of such corporate interest groups. In democratic societies, this form of organisation is known as societal corporatism because interest groups win recognition on the basis of the support they can gather from relevant persons in their particular interest group. For a deeper discussion of corporatism and its variants, see Schmitter (1974).

2 The next section of this chapter draws on Habib and Valodia (2006: 238–244).

3 This followed a successful campaign against the Labour Relations Act, which the apartheid state tried to introduce in the early 1990s. The campaign resulted in the restructuring of the National Manpower Commission and the establishment of the National Economic Forum.

4 This alliance was by no means uncontested. Significant tensions arose and heated debates took place between two contending groups loosely known as the workerists and the charterists. The former were not keen on the unions formally aligning with the national liberation movement, whereas the latter wanted union alignment, in particular, to the ANC and its allied organisational formations. For a reflection on these debates, see Baskin (1991).

5 For different critical reflections on the Reconstruction and Development Programme, see Bond (2000), Habib and Padayachee (2000), Lodge (1999) and Marais (2001).

6 The limitation clause states that certain rights must be interpreted within the limits of the resources available to the state. A number of Constitutional Court cases have been fought on the basis of these second-generation rights. The most prominent of these are the Grootboom case involving the issue of housing rights and the case brought by Treatment

Action Campaign to compel the government to roll out antiretroviral medication for people living with HIV and AIDS.

7 This gives the lie to claims frequently made by the business sector that that profitability in South Africa has declined and that the sector is significantly hampered by labour legislation.

8 There is, for instance, a very useful reflection on the evolution of the Indian state, Kerala, and the lessons this may hold for democratic transitions in the South (Webster and Adler, 1999: 356–358).

9 See also Schmitter (1974), Maier (1984) and Panitch (1986).

10 The Marshall Plan was a massive state-to-state aid programme for reconstructing European economies after the Second World War and for providing them with a sense of collective security through the establishment of the North Atlantic Treaty Organisation, (NATO).

11 Think of the continuous foreign investment in China; despite all the political problems and conditions imposed on investors in that country, investments are still made because there are profits to be made.

12 Madonsela, who was appointed by Zuma in October 2009, quickly enhanced the image and credibility of the public protector' s office through her willingness to impartially investigate senior officials and politicians. This represents a significant shift as the obsequiousness of her predecessor, Lawrence Mushwana, towards those in power seriously damaged the institution's credibility.

13 Duduzane Zuma was implicated, along with the Gupta family, in a black economic empowerment company, Imperial Crown Trading, unfairly obtaining mining concessions to the Sishen mine, which holds one of the largest deposits of iron ore in the world (*Mail & Guardian*, 25/02/2011). Khulubuse Zuma, together with Nelson Mandela's grandson, Zondwa Mandela, used their political connections to gain control of a mining company, Aurora Empowerment Systems. They then stripped it of its assets, neglected to pay its workers and pocketed millions of rand before the company was liquidated in 2011 (*Business Day*, 12/08/2011).

Chapter 5 – The evolution of state–civil society relations

1 Systems of patronage are part of most political systems. How well this phenomenon is contained and managed depends on the checks and balances that exist within a given political context. South Africa is relatively weak at containing the problem as I show in Chapter Two. I am, however, reluctant to elevate the issue of patronage in my analysis, partly because some political scientists view Africa only through the prism of patronage. I give no credence to this. African societies can be understood using the same tools that are applicable to other societies. Particular pathologies, including the extent of patronage systems, can be understood by analysing

how particular actors operate within particular historical contexts. In any case, patronage also depends on how well other sources of power (economic, civic, etc.) function in a society. In this sense, South Africa is very different from other African countries in that an individual can lose access to political power and still become a billionaire.

2 Following Guillermo O'Donnell, Philippe Schmitter and Lawrence Whitehead's four-volume study on democratisation in Latin America and Southern Europe, it has become common in the literature to distinguish political transitions in these two distinct phases. Liberalisation refers to the moment when authoritarian leaders open up the political system, whereas democratisation is the period in which representative political systems become institutionalised (see O'Donnell et al., 1986).

3 To be sure, some student leaders were fairly radical and critical of business as early as the 1950s. However, the bulk of the rank-and-file student body remained largely liberal in orientation until at least the late 1970s and early 1980s.

4 The apartheid regime felt so threatened by the emergence of the Black Consciousness Movement that it ultimately murdered its most significant leader, Steve Biko, while he was in police detention in September 1977.

5 This also led to a split in the National Party and the formation of the Conservative Party under Andries Treurnicht (see Sparks, 1990).

6 Some of them who sojourned abroad were radicalised by the anti-Vietnam war protests that surfaced in English, European and North American university campuses in the late 1960s and early 1970s. In fact, radical Marxist historiography in South Africa can be directly related to individuals who got caught up in the maelstrom of these student revolts.

7 Ficksburg is a town in the Free State province, where a massive service delivery protest directed at local government took place in April 2011.

8 Many observers have, however, questioned the effectiveness of this community voice in NEDLAC – see, for example, Friedman and McKaiser (n.d.: 22).

9 A national survey undertaken by the Centre for Civil Society in 2003 concluded that individual South Africans give a total of R921 million a month to poverty alleviation causes. See Everatt and Solanki (2007: 51).

10 This is a conclusion of the report by the Funding Alliance Practice. It, however, is questioned not only by the NDA and the NCLT (National Lottery Distribution Trust), but also by the Association of Youth NGOs (AYONGO) which maintains that both institutions correctly fund community-based organisations rather than 'elitist' NGOs. See Thlaka (2011).

11 This pioneering study was undertaken by Mark Swilling and Bev Russell.

12 Friedman serves as the director of the Centre for the Study of Democracy, a research entity under the auspices of both the University of Johannesburg

and Rhodes University. McKaiser is a well-known South African social analyst who has his own talk show on Radio 702.

13 The COSATU civil society conference was held from 27 to 28 October 2010. It boasted an attendance of 300 delegates representing 56 civil society organisations. For the declaration and decisions made by the conference, see http://cosatu.org.za/eventslist.php?eid=21.

14 Corruption Watch was established in partnership with Section 27, a human rights organisation and public interest law centre dedicated to ensuring the widest possible access to healthcare services and other socio-economic rights.

15 COSATU was one of the founder members of the Right2Know campaign, which is a multi-class alliance of civic-based associations opposed to the passage of the Protection of State Information Bill because it undermines transparency in public institutions and weakens the ability of civil society, including the media, to expose corruption and act as a check on unethical public decisions and actions.

16 The highlight of the stayaway was 32 marches that took place around the country, and brought approximately 200 000 workers and other citizens onto the streets. This, the largest stayaway in the country since 1994, paralysed a number of commercial and industrial sectors and brought the economy to a standstill (*The Times*, 8/03/2012; *Business Day*, 8/03/2012).

17 It should be noted that pro-Zuma factions within COSATU tried to remove Zwelinzima Vavi from his position as general secretary at the federation's congress in September 2012. This failed when delegates decided to re-elect the entire COSATU leadership for another term.

18 Mantashe was, of course, speaking of the toppling of the Kaunda regime in Zambia in the early 1990s and civil society's support for the Movement for Democratic Change (MDC) in Zimbabwe. The ANC is also sensitive to comparisons being made between South Africa and the conditions that led to the 'Arab Spring', especially when Moeletsi Mbeki suggested that South Africa could be prone to a Tunisian style revolt by about 2020 when China's mineral-intensive industrialisation phase is set to conclude and the ruling party no longer has the tax largesse to fund its welfare programmes (Mbeki, 2011).

Chapter 6 – South Africa and the world

1 For instance, Dumisani Kumalo (2007), then South Africa's ambassador to the United Nations, argued that a resolution put forward by the United States to the United Nations General Assembly condemning rape used for political and military purposes, should instead condemn all forms of rape. Kumalo maintains that the United States refused to broaden its condemnation of this crime for political reasons.

2 'Middle power' is a term that describes countries, such as Canada and Norway, that are located in the middle of the global power hierarchy and which have moderate international influence and recognition. Such countries often prioritise diplomacy and support the solutions proposed by multilateral institutions. Middle powers tend to smooth over the asymmetries in the global balance of power and act as a check on the machinations of more powerful countries.

3 By contrast, Chase, et al. (1999: 35), from whom South African authors drew the term 'pivotal state', use this term synonymously with the term 'regional power'. They define such states as having responsibility for maintaining stability in a region and note that the economic success or failure of such nations is likely to have consequences for the immediate transnational environment.

4 The Group of 77 (or G77) is an alliance of developing countries at the United Nations designed to enhance the negotiating capacities of its members, particularly on economic issues. It was founded by 77 developing countries, hence its name, but currently has 132 member countries, including China and South Africa. China's inclusion is particularly noteworthy given its sheer size, its economic growth and the fact that it is the only permanent member of the United Nations Security Council – indeed, the group is almost always referred to as 'the G77 and China'.

5 The African Union, for instance, has taken a decision not to recognise countries in which civilian governments have been overthrown by their militaries. And the peer-review mechanism established by the New Economic Partnership for Africa's Development (NEPAD) was explicitly put in place to strengthen democracies and their accountability mechanisms.

6 The economic benefits took the form of both trade concessions and aid. The United States, for instance, provided all of its Asian allies with preferential access to its markets without demanding reciprocity. Also, the United Nations Conference on Trade and Development's (UNCTAD) *Economic Development in Africa* reports that the United States gave Japan $500 million per annum between 1950 and 1970 and $13 billion and $5.6 billion to South Korea and Taiwan between 1946 and 1978 respectively (Arrighi, 2002: 30–31; UNCTAD, 2007: 80–81).

7 In Pakistan's case, it plays a strategic frontline role in the 'war on terror', whereas Ethiopia has taken the responsibility of being lead proxy for the United States in Somalia. As Ali Mazrui (2007: 44) explains, 'The Ethiopian people have allowed themselves to be more or less bought by the Americans, to be mercenaries in Somalia.' A new round of occupation is currently underway in Somalia led by Kenya, Ethiopia and Uganda, and supported by both the United States and the United Kingdom.

8 For alternative accounts of Zimbabwe's political crisis and economic meltdown, see Moyo and Yeros (2007a and 2007b); Bond (2005); Phimister and Raftopoulos (2004).

9 See Mbeki (2007) – although written in 2001, the paper was subsequently published in the June 2007 edition of *New Agenda*.

10 The literature also distinguishes between hard (Waltz, 1979) and soft balancing (Pape, 2005; Paul, 2005). The former is about building military capabilities and forming alternative military coalitions, whereas the latter involves non-military means, especially diplomatic coalitions, to contain hegemonic or dominant powers.

11 The United States and some European nations are not entirely happy with Turkey's new foreign policy stance, especially its hostility to Israel and its 'friendliness' with Iran. See *The Economist*, 5/03/2011.

12 In 2011, Mbeki accused the United Nations of being complicit in the re-imposition of colonial agendas in Côte d'Ivoire. The United Nations responded through its chief of staff in the secretary-general's office, Vijay Nambiar, accusing Mbeki of having misread the situation (see Mbeki, 2011; Nambiar, 2011).

13 See also Greg Mills (2008: 227) who reports that the number of major wars on the continent came down from 12 to 4 between 1990 and 2005.

14 The strategic alliance between South Africa and Nigeria has since fallen on hard times; for a review of its emergence and subsequent fracturing, see Adebajo (2010) and Landsberg (2012).

15 South Africa also hosts the Pan-African Parliament in Midrand, midway between Pretoria and Johannesburg.

16 They were of course supported by the leaders of other countries, including Algeria, Ethiopia and Mali, all of which were key drivers of the initiative.

17 The chairing of the Security Council rotates monthly among members, in alphabetical order.

18 Gilpin (2001) and Krasner (1982) demonstrate how the United States in the post-war era was willing to countenance Japanese trade and investment discrimination, forgo the right to an optimum tariff and include opt-out clauses in the NATO treaty, when all these concessions were in the interests of cobbling together a global liberal alliance.

19 Note that South Africa is the chair of the African Union's Ministerial Committee on Post-Conflict Reconstruction and Development in the Sudan.

20 When Clinton expressed disquiet about this on a state visit to South Africa, Mandela publicly admonished him, arguing that 'the United States as the leader of the world should set an example to all of us to help eliminate tensions throughout the world. And the best way of doing so is to call upon its enemies to say 'Let's sit down and talk peace' (quoted in Shogren, 1998).

21 A number of domestic stakeholders, including the official opposition, were quite critical of this decision. Aristide returned to Haiti in March 2011.

22 For instance, Taiwan made a sizable contribution to the ANC's election coffers in 1994 (see Barber, 2005).

23 For a critique of this perspective, see Habib (2008b).

24 This charge was reintroduced by Hillary Clinton during her African tour in 2011 (*Times*, 11/06/2011), and was promptly refuted by the Chinese ambassador to South Africa (Jianhua, 2011).

25 Flemes draws on the distinction between 'milieu' and 'possession' goals, the latter advancing the national interest, first proposed by Arnold Wolfers' (1962: 73–76).

26 Jim O'Neill, who is credited for having coined the term BRIC, believes that South Africa should not be in the group, given the size of its economy and its future prospects (*Mail & Guardian*, 23/03/2012). In focusing only on economic variables, such as market size and growth, he thus underestimates the strategic importance of having an African country in a transnational alliance of developing countries.

27 Another arena that the three have been very critical of is intellectual-property rights related to biological resources and indigenous knowledge. It should be noted that the G-21 has, at times, intervened to significantly transform the patent regime when this pertains to public health crises such as HIV and AIDS.

28 Flemes (2007: 12) argues that 'IBSA's global justice discourse is doubtful, since the expansion of the UNSC would privilege only a few players. In order to achieve a lasting democratisation of the organisation the General Assembly would have to be strengthened'.

29 In the 2012 standoff between Iran and the West, South Africa seems to have taken a more distant stance, acceding to pressure from the United States that it no longer procure oil from Iran (*Financial Times*, 13/03/2012; Wheeler, 2012). But there have been calls for South Africa to intervene more strategically with IBSA, and to serve as a mediator in the standoff (Schoeman, 2012; Pence and Etebari, 2012).

30 Aung San Suu Kyi has since been released as a result of the global pressure on the Burmese government and, in 2012, was elected to the lower house of the Burmese parliament.

31 For example, Siphokazi Mthathi, South Africa director at Human Rights Watch, accused the Zuma administration of supporting an abusive autocratic regime and called on it to follow the example of the international community (Mthathi, 2011).

32 The charge of naivety was repeated by Robert Mugabe, see O'Brien and Sinclair (2011: 18).

33 A group of 200 African leaders released a letter in Johannesburg on 24 August 2011 accusing the Security Council of militarised diplomacy and of marginalising the African Union. The letter also warned of the dangers of NATO recolonising the continent (*Business Day*, 24/08/2011).

34 The three leaders had collectively authored an opinion-editorial, published simultaneously in the *International Herald Tribune, Le Figaro* and the *Times of London* (14/04/2011), in which they explicitly stated that peace was unlikely without the removal of Gaddafi.

Chapter 7 – What is to be done?

1 COSATU is in favour of this recommendation, although it suggests that the proportion of constituency versus party lists should be 65 per cent and 35 per cent respectively (COSATU, 2003: 7).

2 Both the majority and minority reports were published together in the Report of the Electoral Task Team (Electoral Task Team, 2003). The recommendations of the majority are contained in pages 12 to 30 and the recommendations of the minority appear from pages 62 to 73.

3 This view was, of course, contested; for an intellectual exchange on the topic, see Southall and Wood (1999a; 1999b); and Habib and Taylor (1999a; 1999b).

4 The ANC's secretary-general, Gwede Mantashe, has been particularly critical of Vavi's outspokenness and public criticisms of the ANC and notably so in his report to the ruling party's Mangaung conference in late 2012. The ANC has also officially complained about Vavi to COSATU. See *Business Day*, 20/12/2012 and *Mail & Guardian*, 21/12/2012.

5 Jeremy Cronin coined this term at a seminar, hosted by the University of Cape Town's Centre for Conflict Resolution, on 18 October 2006, where he served as a discussant to a presentation I made on a book I co-edited, titled *Voices of Protest* (Ballard et al., 2006).

6 Many prefer the simpler notion of a substitutionist, class-based affirmative action programme. We argue that while this 'could deracialise the lower echelons of the class hierarchy', it is unlikely to have the same effect on 'the upper echelons of South Africa's corporate structure' (Bentley and Habib, 2008: 347).

7 This charge is very common in political discourse, levied mainly by economists, almost all of whom are on the payroll of the banks and other business corporations.

8 Note, for instance, the coincidence of interests on agricultural subsidies that prevailed for so long between the US and Europe in the World Trade negotiations.

9 Under pressure and criticism from South Africa and other countries, both institutions have implemented limited reforms around, for instance, voting proportions on their respective boards. Also, an ostensibly open interview is now required for the heads of both organisations. But the United States and Europe still retain control via the weighting allocated to their votes. This enables them to push through decisions and appoint their

respective candidates. The reforms South Africa pushes for must therefore be more radical and substantive, or risk conferring legitimacy on these organisations without delivering a more equitable global order.

10 Civil society could be far more deeply engaged than it is at present. South African diplomats could, for instance, proactively caucus with certain international civic movements and develop common positions prior to global negotiations. They could then use the external mobilisation on the streets as leverage in the actual negotiations within the global forums.

Chapter 8 – Reinterpreting democratic and development experiences

1 Note the interesting irony, highlighted by Nancy Bermeo (1990), that O'Donnell and Schmitter, who were the most prominent structuralists of the 1970s, became the leading scholars of methodological approaches that emphasised human agency and the role of individual actors in the 1980s.

2 Huntington also recommended the marginalisation of conservative hardliners (or standpatters) and the military, the latter by buying their allegiance through the purchase of military equipment (Huntington, 1991: 252–253).

3 Others who have offered similar advice are Di Palma (1990), Haggard and Kaufman (1992) and Przeworski (1991).

4 Afrobarometer is an independent research project that regularly measures social, political and economic trends in various African countries. For more information see www.afrobarometer.org.

5 Chan (2011: 91) reports that at Lancaster House, Mugabe 'pleaded and argued with Carrington to have the land issue placed on the agenda, but Carrington refused'.

6 The doctrine of the responsibility to protect was adopted by the United Nations in 2005 during the tenure of Kofi Annan as secretary-general.

7 For alternative accounts of the Darfur conflict and its history, see Daly (2007); Flint and De Waal (2008); Hagan and Rymond-Richmond (2008); O'Fahey (2008).

8 Under this agreement, about 6 000 white farmers retained ownership and control over 47 per cent (15.5 million hectares) of the country's most fertile land, see Shaw (2003: 75). Note that Mamdani (2008) indicates that the 15.5 million hectares represented 39 per cent of the country's agricultural land.

9 For alternative interpretations of the Zimbabwean crisis, see Phimister and Raftopoulos (2004); Bernstein (2003); Hammar, Raftopoulos and Jenson (2004); Moore (2012).

10 For reviews that support Mamdani's contributions, see Edozie (2009) and Moyo and Yeros (2009).

11 This is even more evident in some of the work of Issa Shivji (2003) who, in his legitimate desire to demonstrate the ways in which much human rights discourse is oriented towards maintaining the status quo, inadvertently marginalises the struggles of citizens against political autocrats. Indeed, this issue has divided progressive scholars in Zimbabwe and elsewhere. For an understanding of the contending perspectives on Zimbabwe, see Moyo and Yeros (2007a); Raftopoulos (2006) and Moore (2004).

12 A report of this meeting is available on the Royal African Society website.

13 It is worth noting that this same legislation 'simultaneously erected an unprecedented barrier to the immigration of West Indian Blacks and Mexicans, [who were] expressly identified as problematic from an integration perspective' (Zolberg, 2006: 436).

References

Abedian, I. 2004. 'Right Choice for the Driving Conditions', *Financial Mail*, 7 May.

Adam, H & Moodley, K. 1993. *The Opening of the Apartheid Mind: Options for the New South Africa*. Berkeley: University of California Press.

Adam, H, Moodley, K & Slabbert, FV. 1997. *Comrades in Business: Post-Liberation Politics in South Africa*. Cape Town: Tafelberg.

ADCORP. 2011. 'ADCORP Employment Index', released 10 November. Available online.

Adebajo, A. 2010. *The Curse of Berlin: Africa after the Cold War*. Durban: University of KwaZulu-Natal Press.

Adebajo, A & Landsberg, C. 2003. 'South Africa and Nigeria as Regional Hegemons', in M Baregu & C Landsberg (eds), *From Cape to Congo: Southern Africa's Evolving Security Challenges*. Boulder: Lynne Rienner.

Adler, G & Webster, E. 1995. 'The Labor Movement, Radical Reform, and Transition to Democracy in South Africa', *Politics & Society* 23 (1): 75–106.

AfriMAP & OSF-SA (Open Society Foundation for South Africa). 2007. *South Africa: Effective Service Delivery in the Education and Health Sectors*. Cape Town: OSF-SA. Available online.

Ake, C. 1993. 'The Unique Case of African Democracy', *International Affairs* 69 (2): 239–244.

Alden, C & Le Pere, G. 2004. 'South Africa's Post-Apartheid Foreign Policy: From Reconciliation to Ambiguity', *Review of African Political Economy*, 31 (100): 283–297.

Alden, C & Vieira, M. 2005. 'The New Diplomacy of the South: South Africa, Brazil, India and Trilateralism', *Third World Quarterly* 26 (7): 1077–1095.

Alexander, N. 2002. *An Ordinary Country: Issues in the Transition from Apartheid to Democracy in South Africa*. Pietermaritzburg: University of KwaZulu-Natal Press.

Alexander, P. 2010. 'Rebellion of the Poor: South Africa's Service Delivery Protests, A Preliminary Analysis', *Review of African Political Economy* 37 (123): 25–40.

Alexander, P. 2012. 'A Massive Rebellion of the Poor', *Mail & Guardian*, 13–19 April.

ANC. n.d. 'The Constitution, Minorities and the New South Africa', document submitted to CODESA.

ANC. 1990a. 'Recommendations on Post-Apartheid Economic Policy', proceedings of a workshop held in Harare, 28 April–1 May.

ANC. 1990b. 'Discussion Document on Economic Policy', paper prepared for a workshop held in Harare, 20–23 September.

ANC. 1992a. 'Ten Proposed Regions for a United South Africa', document submitted to CODESA.

ANC. 1992b. 'Negotiations: A Strategic Perspective', document adopted by the National Executive Committee, 25 November.

ANC. 1992c. 'Ready to Govern: ANC Policy Guidelines for a Democratic South Africa', document adopted at the National Conference, 28–31 May.

ANC. 1994. *Reconstruction and Development Programme*. Johannesburg: Umanyano Publications.

ANC. 1996. 'The State and Social Transformation', discussion document.

ANC. 1997. 'Developing a Strategic Perspective on South African Foreign Policy', discussion document. Available online.

ANC. 2007. 'Building a National Democratic Society: Strategy and Tactics of the ANC', discussion document, February.

ANC Youth League. 1992. 'Summary of Ideas on Negotiations and the Way Forward', *African Communist* 131: 45–47.

Appiah, KA. 2006. *Cosmopolitanism: Ethics in a World of Strangers*. New York: WW Norton.

Arrighi, G. 2002. 'The African Crisis: World Systemic and Regional Aspects', *New Left Review* 15: 5–36.

Atkinson, D. 2007. 'Taking to the Streets: Has Developmental Local Government Failed in South Africa?', in S Buhlungu, J Daniel & R Southall (eds), *State of the Nation: South Africa 2007*. Cape Town: HSRC Press.

Atkinson, D & Friedman, S (eds). 1994. *The Small Miracle: South Africa's Negotiated Settlement*. Johannesburg: Ravan Press.

Baleni, F. 2010. 'Reformed GEAR Won't Bring the Goose that Lays the Golden Egg', *Business Day*, 29 November.

Ballard, R, Habib, A & Valodia, I (eds). 2006. *Voices of Protest: Social Movements in Post-Apartheid South Africa*. Pietermaritzburg: University of KwaZulu-Natal Press.

Ballard, R, Habib, A, Valodia, I & Zuern, E. 2005. 'Globalisation, Marginalisation and Contemporary Social Movements in South Africa', *African Affairs* 104 (417): 615–634.

Barber, J. 2005. 'The New South Africa's Foreign Policy: Principles and Practice', *International Affairs* 81 (5): 1079–1096.

Barchiesi, F. 2011. *Precarious Liberation: Workers, the State and Contested Social Citizenship in Postapartheid South Africa*. Scottsville: University of KwaZulu-Natal Press.

Barker, R (ed). 1971. *Studies in Opposition*. London: Macmillan.

Barnard, D & Terreblanche, Y. 2001. *PRODDER: The South African Development Directory*. Pretoria: Human Sciences Research Council.

Baskin, J. 1991. *Striking Back: A History of COSATU*. Johannesburg: Ravan Press.

Baskin, J. 1993. 'The Trend towards Bargained Corporatism', *South*

African Labour Bulletin 17 (3): 63–69.

Beinart, W. 2010. 'Popular Politics and Resistance Movements in South Africa, 1970–2008', in W Beinart & M Dawson (eds), *Popular Politics and Resistance Movements in South Africa*. Johannesburg: Wits University Press.

Beinart, W & Dawson, M (eds). 2010. *Popular Politics and Resistance Movements in South Africa*. Johannesburg: Wits University Press.

Bell, T. 2009. 'Debate Needed on COSATU's SACP Agenda', *IOL Business Report*, 1 October. Available online.

Benit-Gbaffou, C. 2012. 'Party Politics, Civil Society, and Local Democracy: Reflections from Johannesburg', *GeoForum* 43 (2): 178–189.

Bentley, K & Habib, A. 2008. 'An Alternative Framework for Redress and Citizenship', in A Habib & K Bentley (eds), *Racial Redress and Citizenship in South Africa*. Cape Town: HSRC Press.

Bermeo, N. 1990. 'Rethinking Regime Change', *Comparative Politics* 22 (3): 359–377.

Bermeo, N. 1997. 'Myths of Moderation', *Comparative Politics* 29 (3): 305–322.

Bernstein, A. 2012. 'Tough Calls Needed to Break Impasse', *Sunday Times*, 4 March.

Bernstein, H. 2003. 'Land Reform in Southern Africa in World Historical Perspective', *Review*

of *African Political Economy* 96: 203–226.

Bezuidenhout, A. 2008. 'Black Economic Empowerment and Externalization in the South African Mining Industry', in A Habib & K Bentley (eds), *Racial Redress and Citizenship in South Africa*. Cape Town: HSRC Press.

Bieling, HJ & Schulten, T. 2001. *Competitive Restructuring and Industrial Relations Within the European Union; Corporatist Involvement and Beyond*, WSI Discussion Paper No. 99, Dusseldorf, November.

Bird, A & Schreiner, G. 1992. 'COSATU at the Crossroads: Towards Tripartite Corporatism or Democratic Socialism?', *South African Labour Bulletin* 16 (6): 22–32.

Bischoff, PH. 2003. 'External and Domestic Sources of Foreign Policy Ambiguity: South African Foreign Policy and the Projection of Pluralist Middle Power', *Politikon* 30 (2): 183–201.

Blankenburg, S & Palma, JS. 2009. 'Introduction: The Global Financial Crisis', *Cambridge Journal of Economics* 33: 531–538.

Blondel, J. 1997. 'Political Opposition in the Contemporary World', *Government and Opposition* 32 (4): 462–487.

Bond, P. 1998. *Uneven Zimbabwe: A Study of Finance, Development and Underdevelopment*. Trenton: Africa World Press.

Bond, P. 2000. *Elite Transition: From Apartheid to Neoliberalism in South Africa*. Pietermaritzburg:

University of KwaZulu-Natal Press.

Bond, P. 2001. *Against Global Apartheid*. Cape Town: UCT Press.

Bond, P. 2004a. 'South Africa's Frustrating Decade of Freedom: From Racial to Class Apartheid', *Monthly Review* 55 (10). Available online.

Bond, P. 2004b. *South Africa's Resurgent Urban Social Movements: The Case of Johannesburg, 1984, 1994, 2004*, Centre for Civil Society, Research Report 22, University of KwaZulu-Natal, Durban.

Bond, P. 2004c. *Talk Left, Walk Right: South Africa's Frustrated Global Reforms*. Pietermaritzburg: University of KwaZulu-Natal Press.

Bond, P. 2005. 'Zimbabwe's Hide and Seek with the IMF', *Review of African Political Economy* 106: 609–619.

Bond, P. 2007. 'The Socio Political Structure of Accumulation and Social Policy in Southern Africa', in J Adesini (ed.), *Social Policy in Sub-Saharan Africa*. London: Macmillan.

Bond, P. 2008. 'South Africa's "Developmental State" Distraction', *Mediations* 24 (1): 8–27.

Bond, P. 2009. Mamdani on Zimbabwe sets back Civil Society, *Concerned Africa Scholars Bulletin* 82: 36–41.

Booth, J & Williams, J. 1975. *Contemporary Strategy: Theories and Policies*. London: Croom Helm.

Booysen, S. 2007. 'With the Ballot and the Brick: The Politics of Attaining Service Delivery', *Progress in Development Studies* 7 (1): 21–32.

Booysen, S. 2011. *The African National Congress and the Regeneration of Political Power*. Johannesburg: Wits University Press.

Boraine, A. 2000. *A Country Unmasked: Inside South Africa's Truth and Reconciliation Commission*. Oxford: Oxford University Press.

Bratton, M & Landsberg, C. 1998. Aiding Reconstruction and Development in South Africa: Promise and Delivery. Unpublished paper (second draft). Durban.

Bratton, M & Van de Walle, N. 1994. 'Neopatrimonial Regimes and Political Transitions in Africa', *World Politics* 46 (4): 453–489.

Bratton, M & Van de Walle, N. 1997. *Democratic Experiments in Africa: Regime Transitions in Comparative Perspective*. Cambridge: Cambridge University Press.

Bratton, M, Mattes, R & Gyimah-Boadi, E. 2005. *Public Opinion: Democracy and Market Reform in Africa*. Cambridge: Cambridge University Press.

Breslin, S. 2006. 'Interpreting Chinese Power in the Global Political Economy', paper presented at the Conference on Regional Powers in Asia, Africa, Latin America and the Middle East, hosted by the German

Institute of Global and Area Studies, 11–12 December.

Buhlungu, S. 2006. *Trade Unions and Politics: COSATU Workers after Ten Years of Democracy*. Cape Town: HSRC Press.

Buhlungu, S. 2010. *A Paradox of Victory: COSATU and the Democratic Transformation in South Africa*. Pietermaritzburg: University of KwaZulu-Natal Press.

Butler, A. 2009. *Contemporary South Africa*. Basingstoke: Palgrave Macmillan.

Callinicos, A. 1992. *Between Apartheid and Capitalism*. London: Bookmarks.

Campbell, H. 2009. 'Zimbabwe: Where is the Outrage? Mamdani, Mugabe and the African Scholarly Community', *Concerned Africa Scholars Bulletin* 82: 20–27.

Cardoso FH, & Faletto, E. 1979. *Dependency and Development in Latin America*. Berkeley: University of California Press.

CDE (Centre for Development and Enterprise). 2009. *South Africa's Public Service: Learning from Success*, CDE Roundtable 13, November.

Central Economic Advisory Services. 1993. *The Restructuring of the South African Economy: A Normative Model Approach*. Pretoria.

Chan, S. 2011. *Old Treacheries: New Deceits*. Johannesburg: Jonathan Ball.

Chase, R, Hill, E & Kennedy, P. 1999. *The Pivotal States: A New Framework for US Policy in the Developing World*. New York: Norton.

Chatterjee, P. 2004. *The Politics of the Governed: Popular Politics in Most of the World*. New York: Columbia University Press.

Chaudhuri, S & Ravallion, M. 2006. 'Partially Awakened Giants: Uneven Growth in China and India', in LA Winters & S Yusuf (eds), *Dancing with Giants: China, India and the Global Economy*. Washington: World Bank.

Chikane, F. 2012. *Eight Days in September: The Removal of Thabo Mbeki*. Johannesburg: Picador Africa.

Chipkin, I. 2007. *Do South Africans Exist? Nationalism, Democracy, and the Identity of 'The People'*. Johannesburg: Wits University Press.

Chipkin, I. 2008. 'Set-Up for Failure: Racial Redress in the Department of Public Service and Administration', in A Habib & K Bentley (eds), *Racial Redress and Citizenship in South Africa*. Cape Town: HSRC Press.

Cohen, T. 2004. 'Corporate South Africa Must Leave its Shell', *Business Day*, 4 February.

Cohen, T. 2012. *A Piece of the Pie: The Battle over Nationalisation*. Cape Town: Jonathan Ball.

Cohen, J & Arato, A. 1992. *Civil Society and Political Theory*. Boston: MIT Press.

Collier, RB & Collier, D. 1991. *Shaping the Political Arena: Critical Junctures, The Labor Movement and Regime Dynamics in Latin America*. Princeton, NJ: Princeton University Press.

COSATU. 1997. 'The Report of the September Commission on the Future of Unions', August 1997. Available online.

COSATU. 2003. 'Resolutions of the COSATU 8th National Congress, Electoral System", September 2003. Available online.

COSATU. 2004. 'Why Workers Should Vote ANC'. Available online.

COSATU. 2006. 'COSATU: Possibilities for Fundamental Change', discussion document prepared for the 9th National Congress, 18–21 September.

COSATU. 2011. Declaration of the 4th Central Committee held in Kempton Park, Esselen Park, 17–20 September.

COSATU & NEHAWU. 2003. 'Submission to the Public Hearings on the Report of the Committee of Enquiry into the Comprehensive Social Security System', presented to the Parliamentary Portfolio Committee on Social Development, 9–10 June.

COSATU, FEDSAL & NACTU. 1996. 'Social Equity and Job Creation: The Key to a Stable Future'. Johannesburg.

Cousins, B. 2009. 'A Reply to Mamdani on the Zimbabwean Land Question', *Concerned Africa Scholars Bulletin* 82: 45–47.

Cronin, J. 1992. 'Dreaming of the Final Showdown: A Reply to Jordan and Nzimande', *African Communist* 131: 38–44.

Cronin, J. 2002. 'Interview with Jeremy Cronin', by Helena Sheehan, 24 January. Available online.

Cronin, J. 2004. 'If Public Debate is Dead, Who Pulled the Trigger?' *Sunday Times*, 28 March.

Dahl, RA (ed). 1966. *Political Oppositions in Western Democracies*. New Haven: Yale University Press.

Dahl, RA. 1971. *Polyarchy: Participation and Opposition*. New Haven: Yale University Press.

Daly, MW. 2007. *Darfur's Sorrow: A History of Destruction and Genocide*. Cambridge: Cambridge University Press.

Daly, MW. 2009. 'Mamdani Contra Mundum',14 April. Available online.

Daniel, J, Habib, A & Southall, R (eds). 2003. *State of the Nation 2003–2004*. Cape Town: HSRC Press.

Daniel, J, Naidoo, V & Naidu, S. 2003. 'The South Africans have Arrived: Post-Apartheid Corporate Expansion into Africa', in J Daniel, A Habib & R Southall (eds), *State of the Nation: South Africa 2003–2004*. Cape Town: HSRC Press.

Davies, R. 2010. Statement to the South African National Assembly by the Minister of Trade and Industry on the Industrial Policy Action Plan (IPAP2), 18 February, Cape Town.

Davies, R, O'Meara, D & Dlamini, S. 1985. *The Struggle for South Africa*. London: Zed.

Dawson, B. 2012. 'Job Creation is the Business of Business', *Sunday Times*, 1 April.

Democratic Alliance. 2011. 'Syria: What Happened to South Africa's Foreign Policy Backbone?', statement by Stevens Mokgalapa, Shadow Deputy Minister of International Relations, 5 October.

Democratic Alliance. 2012a. 'Defending the Indefensible: Minister Davies Implies NLB Grants to the NYDA and COSATU were Acceptable', press release issued by Wilmot James, Shadow Minister of Trade and Industry, 24 February.

Democratic Alliance. 2012b. 'Statement by James Lorimer, Shadow Minister of Cooperative Governance and Traditional Affairs on Cadre Deployment', 15 January. Available online.

Department of Economic Development, South Africa. 2010. *The New Growth Path: The Framework*, November 2010.

Department of Finance, South Africa. 1996. *Growth, Employment and Redistribution: A Macroeconomic Strategy for South Africa*.

Department of Health, South Africa. 2011. 'National Health Insurance in South Africa'. Policy Paper, 12 August.

Department of Labour, South Africa. 2011. 2010 Annual Industrial Action Report, 20 September.

Department of Trade and Industry, South Africa. 2011. Industrial Policy Action Plan 2011/2012–2013/2014: Economic Sectors and Employment Cluster, February.

Desai, A. 2002. *We are the Poors: Community Struggles in Post-Apartheid South Africa*. New York: Monthly Review Press.

Desai, A. 2005. 'Uprooting and Re-Rooting Poverty in Post-Apartheid South Africa: A Literature Review', paper prepared for the SANPAD Poverty Alleviation Workshop, 24–25 May.

Desai, A & Habib, A. 1994. 'Social Movements in Transitional Societies: A Case Study of the Congress of South African Trade Unions', *South African Sociological Review* 6 (2): 68–88.

Devey, R, Valodia, I & Velia, M. 2004. *Constraints to Growth and Employment: Evidence from the Greater Durban Metropolitan Area*, Research Report No. 64, School of Development Studies, University of KwaZulu-Natal.

Di Palma, G. 1990. *To Craft Democracies: An Essay on Democratic Transitions*. Berkeley, CA: University of California Press.

Duncan, J. 2007. 'With Us or Against Us? South Africa's Position in the "War against Terror"', *Review of African Political Economy* 34 (113): 513–520.

Duncan, J. 2010. 'Forward to the Past: Voice, Political Mobilization and Repression under Jacob Zuma', paper presented at a symposium on A Decade of Dissent: Reflections on Popular Resistance in South Africa 2000–2010, University of Johannesburg, 12–14 November.

Duncan, J. 2012. 'Lockdown: Closing the Research Space', *Mail & Guardian*, 9 March.

Edozie, RK. 2009. 'Global Citizens and Sudanese Subjects: Reading Mamdani's Saviors and Survivors', *African Affairs* 108 (433): 661–667.

Electoral Task Team. 2003. *Report of the Electoral Task Team*. January, Cape Town. Available online.

Epstein, L. 1967. *Political Parties in Western Democracies*. New York: Praeger.

Esping-Andersen, G. 1990. *The Three Worlds of Welfare Capitalism*. Princeton, NJ: Princeton University Press.

Everatt, D & Solanki, G. 2007. 'A Nation of Givers: Results from a National Survey of Social Giving', in A Habib & B Maharaj (eds), *Giving and Solidarity: Resource Flows for Poverty Alleviation in South Africa*. Cape Town: HSRC Press.

Faulkner, D & Loewald, C. 2008. *Policy Change and Economic Growth: A Case Study of South Africa*, Working Paper No. 41, Commission on Growth and Development, World Bank.

Feinstein, A. 2007. *After the Party*. Cape Town: Jonathan Ball.

Fikeni, S. 2009. 'The Polokwane Moment and South Africa's Democracy at the Crossroads', in P Kagwanja & K Kondlo (eds), *State of the Nation, South Africa 2008*. Cape Town: HSRC Press.

Fine, B & Rustomjee, Z. 1996. *The Political Economy of South Africa: From Mineral-Energy Complex to Industrialisation*. Johannesburg: Wits University Press.

Flemes, D. 2007. *Emerging Middle Powers' Soft Balancing Strategy: State and Perspectives of the IBSA Dialogue Forum*, Working Paper No. 57, German Institute of Global and Area Studies, Hamburg.

Flint, J & De Waal, A. 2008. *Darfur: A New History of a Long War*. London: Zed.

Forslund, D. 2011b. 'Reply to Loane Sharpe', *Business Report*, 19 December.

Forslund, D. 2012. 'Wages, Profits and Labour Productivity in South Africa: A Reply', *Politicsweb*, 24 January. Available online.

Fraser-Moleketi, G. 2002. 'Challenges of the South African Public Service in the Context of the New Africa Initiative', John L Manion Lecture, Canadian Centre for Management Development, Ottawa, 2 May.

Friedman, S. 1987. *Building Tomorrow Today: African Workers in Trade Unions 1970–1984*. Johannesburg: Ravan Press.

Friedman, S (ed). 1993. *The Long Journey: South Africa's Quest for a Negotiated Settlement*. Johannesburg: Ravan Press.

Friedman, S. 1994. 'Holding a Divided Centre: Prospects for Legitimacy and Governance in Post-Settlement South Africa', paper presented to the 16th World Congress of the International Political Science Association, Berlin, August 21–25.

Friedman, S. 2010. 'The Worst Threat to Democracy Money Can Buy', *Business Day*, 27 January.

Friedman, S. 2012. 'SA Needs Vision for Africa, not Leadership Positions', *New Age*, 9 February.

Friedman, S & Erasmus, Z. 2008. 'Counting on "Race": What the Surveys Say (and Do Not) about 'Race' and Redress, in A Habib & K Bentley (eds), *Racial Redress and Citizenship in South Africa*. Cape Town: HSRC Press.

Friedman, S & McKaiser E. n.d. *Civil Society and the Post-Polokwane South African State* (report commissioned by the Heinrich Boll Foundation). Johannesburg and Grahamstown: Centre for the Study of Democracy, University of Johannesburg and Rhodes University.

Friedman, S & Mottiar, S. 2006. 'Seeking the High Ground: The Treatment Action Campaign and the Politics of Morality', in R Ballard, A Habib & I Valodia (eds), *Voices of Protest: Social Movements in Post-Apartheid South Africa*. Pietermaritzburg: University of KwaZulu-Natal Press.

Funding Practice Alliance. 2011. *Meeting their Mandates? Research Report on the National Lottery Distribution Trust Fund and the National Development Agency*. Cape Town. Available online.

Gelb, S (ed). 1991. *South Africa's Economic Crisis*. Cape Town: David Philip.

Gelb, S. 2003. *Inequality in South Africa: Nature, Causes and Responses*. Johannesburg: The Edge Institute.

Gevisser, M. 2007. *Thabo Mbeki: The Dream Deferred*. Johannesburg: Jonathan Ball.

Gilpin, R. 2001. *Global Political Economy: Understanding the International Economic Order*. Princeton, NJ: Princeton University Press.

Glaser, D. 2001. *Politics and Society in South Africa: A Critical Introduction*. London: Thousand Oaks.

Godongwana, E. 1992. 'Industrial Restructuring and the Social Contract: Reforming Capitalism or Building Blocks for Socialism?', *South African Labour Bulletin* 16 (4): 20–23.

Godsell, B. 2012. '50 Million Wealth Creators', *Sunday Times*, 5 February.

Gordhan, P. 2010a. Budget Speech, delivered by the Minister of Finance to the National Assembly, 17 February.

Gordhan, P. 2010b. Letter to the Governor: Clarification of the Reserve Bank's Mandate, Ministry of Finance, Republic of South Africa, 16 February.

Gordhan, P. 2011. Budget Speech, delivered by the Minister of Finance to the National Assembly, 23 February.

Gordhan, P. 2012a. Budget Speech, delivered by the Minister of Finance to the National Assembly, 22 February.

Gordhan, P. 2012b. 'Let Us Seize the Day', *Sunday Times*, 22 April.

Gramsci, A. 1971/1999. *Selections from the Prison Notebooks*. London: Lawrence & Wishart.

Gumede, WM. 2007. *Thabo Mbeki and the Battle for the Soul of the ANC*. London: Zed.

Gumede, WM. 2012. *Restless Nation: Making Sense of Troubled Times*. Cape Town: Tafelberg.

Gwala, H. 1992. 'Negotiations as Presented by Joe Slovo', *African Communist* 131: 24–28.

Habib, A. 1997. 'From Pluralism to Corporatism: South Africa's Labor Relations in Transition', *Politikon* 24 (1): 57–75.

Habib, A. 2002. 'Introduction' in M Swilling & B Russell, *The Size and Scope of the Non-Profit Sector in South Africa*. Johannesburg and Durban: School of Public and Development Management, University of the Witwatersrand, and Centre for Civil Society.

Habib, A. 2004. 'Conversation with a Nation: Race and Redress in Post-Apartheid SA', in E Pieterse & F Meintjies (eds), *Voices of the Transition: The Politics, Poetics and Practices of Social Change in South Africa*. Cape Town: Heinemann.

Habib, A. 2007. 'Another Side to South Africa's Conduct at the UN', *Business Day*, 30 March.

Habib, A. 2008a. 'South Africa: Conceptualising a Politics of Human-Oriented Development', *Social Dynamics* 34 (1): 46–61.

Habib, A. 2008b. 'Western Hegemony, Asian Ascendancy and the New African Scramble: What Is to Be Done?' in K Ampiah & S Naidu (eds), *Crouching Tiger, Hidden Dragon: Africa and China*. Pietermaritzburg: University of KwaZulu-Natal Press.

Habib, A. 2011. 'Advancing Democracy and Inclusive Development: Bridging the Divide Between Progressive Nationalism and the Human Rights Community', *The Thinker* 30: 24–25.

Habib, A & Bentley, K (eds). 2008. *Racial Redress and Citizenship in South Africa*. Cape Town: HSRC Press.

Habib, A & Kotze, H. 2003. 'Civil Society, Governance and Development in an Era of Globalisation', in O Edigheji & G Mhone (eds), *Governance in the New South Africa*. Cape Town: UCT Press.

Habib, A & Padayachee, V. 2000. 'Economic Policy and Power Relations in South Africa's Transition to Democracy', *World Development* 28 (2): 245–263.

Habib, A & Schulz-Herzenberg, C. 2011. 'Democratization and Parliamentary Opposition in Contemporary South Africa: The 2009 National and Provincial Elections in Perspective', *Politikon* 38 (2): 191–210.

Habib, A & Selinyane, N. 2006. 'Constraining the Unconstrained: Civil Society and South Africa's Hegemonic Obligations in Africa', in W Carlsnaes & P Nel (eds), *In Full Flight: South African Foreign Policy After Apartheid*. Johannesburg: Institute for Global Dialogue.

Habib, A & Taylor, R. 1999a. 'Daring to Question the Tripartite Alliance: A Response to Southall and Wood', *Transformation* 40: 112–120.

Habib, A & Taylor, R. 1999b. 'Parliamentary Opposition and Democratic Consolidation in South Africa', *Review of African Political Economy* 79: 109–115.

Habib, A & Taylor, R. 1999c. 'South Africa: Anti-apartheid NGOs', *Voluntas* 10 (1): 73–82.

Habib, A & Taylor, R. 2001. 'Political Alliances and Parliamentary Opposition in South Africa', *Democratization* 8 (1): 207–226.

Habib, A. & Valodia, I. 2006. 'Reconstructing a Social Movement in an Era of Globalisation: A Case Study of COSATU', in R Ballard, A Habib & I Valodia (eds), *Voices of Protest: Social Movements in Post-Apartheid South Africa*. Pietermaritzburg: University of KwaZulu-Natal Press.

Habib, A, Daniel, J & Southall, R. 2003. 'Introduction', in A Habib, J Daniel & R Southall (eds), *State of the Nation 2003–2004*. Cape Town: HSRC Press.

Hagan, J & Rymond-Richmond, W. 2008. *Darfur and the Crime of Genocide*. Cambridge: Cambridge University Press.

Haggard, S & Kaufman, R. 1992. 'Economic Adjustment and the Prospects for Democracy', in S Haggard & R Kaufman (eds), *The Politics of Economic Adjustment*. Princeton NJ: Princeton University Press.

Hamann, K & Kelly, J. 2006. 'Voters, Parties and Social Pacts in Western Europe', paper presented to the 15th International Conference of the Council of European Studies, Chicago, 29 March–2 April.

Hammar, A. 2009. 'The Measure of Just Demands: A Response to Mamdani', *Concerned Africa Scholars Bulletin* 82: 42–44.

Hammar, A, Raftopoulos, B & Jenson, S (eds). 2004. *Zimbabwe's Unfinished Business: Rethinking Land, State and Nation in the Context of Crisis*. Harare: Weaver Press.

Harris, T. 2010. 'New Economic Plan Will Lead Us Down the Road to Poverty', *Business Day* 26 November.

Hart, G. 2005. 'Beyond Neo-Liberalism? Post-Apartheid Developments in Historical and Comparative Perspective', in V Padayachee (ed.), *The Development Decade? Social and Economic Change in South Africa*. Cape Town: HSRC Press.

Hassel, A & Ebbinghaus, B. 2000. 'Concerted Reforms: Linking Wage Formation and Social Policy in Europe', paper presented to the 12th International Conference of Europeanists, Chicago, 30 March–1 April.

Higley, J & Gunther, R. 1992. *Elites and Democratic Consolidation in Latin America and Southern Europe*. Cambridge: Cambridge University Press.

Hirsch, A. 2005. *Season of Hope: Economic Reform under Mandela and Mbeki*. Pietermaritzburg: University of KwaZulu-Natal Press.

Horowitz, D. 1991. *A Democratic South Africa: Constitutional Engineering in a Divided Society*.

Cape Town: Oxford University Press.

Horton, M. 2005. 'Role of Fiscal Policy in Stabilization and Poverty Alleviation', in M Nowak & LA Ricci (eds), *Post-Apartheid South Africa: The First Ten Years*. Washington: IMF.

Huber, E, Rueschemeyer D & Stephens JD. 1997. 'The Paradoxes of Contemporary Democracy: Formal, Participatory and Social Dimensions', *Comparative Politics* 29 (3): 323–342.

Human Rights Watch. 2012. *World Report: South Africa Country Summary* (released January 2012). New York.

Huntington, S. 1991. *The Third Wave: Democratization in the Late Twentieth Century*. Oklahoma: University of Oklahoma Press.

IMF (International Monetary Fund). 2012a. 'Growth Rates for Sub-Saharan Africa', *IMF World Economic Outlook*, January.

IMF. 2012b. 'Coping with High Debt and Sluggish Growth', *World Economic Outlook*, October.

Isa, M. 2009. 'South Africa: Budget Deficit No Threat to SA Rating', *Business Day*, 6 November.

James, W & Van de Vijver, L (eds). 2001. *After the TRC: Reflections on Truth and Reconciliation in South Africa*. Athens, OH: Ohio University Press.

Jianhua, Z. 2011. 'Ambassador: China no "Neo-Colonialist" in Africa', interview by Maverick Chen, 11 August. Available online.

Joffe, A, Kaplan, D, Kaplinsky, R & Lewis, D. 1995. *Improving Manufacturing Performance in South Africa: Report of the Industrial Strategy Project*. Cape Town: UCT Press.

Johnson, D. 2009. 'Mamdani, "Settlers", "Natives" and the War on Terror', *African Affairs* 108 (433): 655–660.

Jordan, P. 1992. 'Strategic Debate in the ANC: A Response to Joe Slovo', *African Communist* 131: 7–15.

Jung, C & Shapiro, I. 1995. 'South Africa's Negotiated Transition: Democracy, Opposition and the New Constitutional Order', *Politics and Society* 23 (3): 269–306.

Kagarlitsky, B. 1990. *The Dialectic of Change*. London: Verso.

Kantor, B. 2011. 'Excessive Wage Hikes a Recipe for Disaster: Job Protection Leads to Shrinking Workforce', *The Star*, 22 December.

Kaplinsky, R. 1994. 'Economic Restructuring in South Africa: The Debate Continues, A Response', *Journal of Southern African Studies* 20 (4): 533–537.

Karl, TL. 1990. 'Dilemmas of Democratization in Latin America', *Comparative Politics* 23 (1): 1–21.

Keohane, R. 1986. 'Theory of World Politics: Structural Realism and Beyond', in R Keohane (ed.) *Neorealism and its Critics*. New York: Columbia University Press.

Khan, F & Pieterse, E. 2006. 'The Homeless People's Alliance: Purposive Creation and Ambiguated Realities', in R Ballard, A Habib & I Valodia (eds),

Voices of Protest: Social Movements in Post-Apartheid South Africa. Pietermaritzburg: University of KwaZulu-Natal Press.

Kirshner, J & Phokela, J. 2010. *Khutsong and Xenophobic Violence: Explaining the Case of the Dog that Didn't Bark.* Johannesburg: Centre for Sociological Research, University of Johannesburg and Atlantic Philanthropies.

Koelble, T & Reynolds, A. 1996 'Power-Sharing Democracy in the New South Africa', *Politics and Society* 24 (3): 221–236.

Krasner, S. 1982. 'American Policy and Global Economic Stability', in W Avery & D Rapkin, *America in a Changing World Political Economy.* New York: Longman.

Kumalo, D. 2007. 'We Condemn All Forms of Rape', *Mail & Guardian*, 18 November.

Landsberg, C. 2000. 'Promoting Democracy: The Mandela-Mbeki Doctrine', *Journal of Democracy* 11 (3): 107–121.

Landsberg, C. 2010. *The Diplomacy of Transformation: South Africa's Foreign Policy and Statecraft.* Johannesburg: Pan Macmillan.

Landsberg, C. 2012. 'Nigeria-South Africa Tensions Leave African Leadership Gap', *World Politics Review*, 18 April.

Lanz, D. 2009. 'Save Darfur: A Movement and Its Discontents', *African Affairs* 108 (433): 669–677.

Lee, MC. 2006. 'The 21st Century Scramble for Africa', *Journal of Contemporary African Studies* 24 (3): 303–330.

Leibrandt, M, Woolard, I, Finn, A & Argent, J. 2010. *Trends in South African Income Distribution and Poverty Since the Fall of Apartheid,* Social, Employment and Migration Working Paper No. 101, OECD, Paris.

Lenin, V. 1902/1961. 'What is to be Done?', *Lenin's Collected Works* Vol. 5. Moscow: Foreign Languages Publishing House.

Lenin, V. 1920/1964. 'Left-Wing Communism: An Infantile Disorder', *Lenin's Collected Works* Vol. 31. Moscow: Progress Publishers.

Le Pere, G. 1998. 'South Africa: An Emerging Power', *Global Dialogue* 3 (1): 1–2.

Le Pere, G & Shelton, G. 2007. *China, Africa and South Africa: South–South Cooperation in a Global Era.* Johannesburg: Institute for Global Dialogue.

Letsoalo, M & Tabane, R. 2009. 'ANC Backlash against the Left', *Mail & Guardian Online*, 9 October.

Lijphart, A. 1977. *Democracy in Plural Societies: A Comparative Exploration.* New Haven, CT: Yale University Press.

Lijphart, A. 1985. *Power-Sharing in South Africa.* Berkeley: Institute of International Studies, University of California.

Lijphart, A. 1994. 'Prospects for Power-Sharing in the New South Africa', in A Reynold (ed.) *Election '94: The Campaigns, Results and Future Prospects.* Cape Town: David Philip.

Linz, J & Stepan, A (eds). 1978. *The Breakdown of Democratic Regimes.*

Baltimore, MD: Johns Hopkins University Press.

Lipset, SM. 1960. *Political Man*. New York: Doubleday.

Lodge, T. 1999. *South African Politics Since 1994*. Cape Town: David Philip.

Luxemburg, R. 1900/1986. *Social Reform or Revolution*. London: Militant.

MacDonald, M. 2006. *Why Race Matters in South Africa*. Cambridge, MA: Harvard University Press.

Mafeje, A. n.d. 'Beyond Dual Theories of Economic Growth', in *Science, Ideology and Development: Three Essays in Development*. Uppsala: Scandinavian Institute of African Studies.

Maier, C. 1984. 'Preconditions for Corporatism', in J Goldthorpe (ed.), *Order and Conflict in Contemporary Capitalism*. Oxford: Clarendon Press.

Mamdani, M. 1996. *Citizen and Subject: Contemporary Africa and the Legacy of Late Colonialism*. Princeton: Princeton University Press.

Mamdani, M. 2008. 'Lessons of Zimbabwe: Mugabe in Context', *London Review of Books* 30 (23): 17–21.

Mamdani, M. 2009a. *Saviours and Survivors: Dafur, Politics and the War on Terror*. Cape Town: HSRC Press.

Mamdani, M. 2009b. 'Mamdani Responds to his Critics Part III', *African Arguments*, 23 May. Available online.

Mandela, N. 1993. 'South Africa's Future Foreign Policy', *Foreign Affairs*, November/December.

Mandela, N. 1997. Speech delivered to the 6th National COSATU Congress. 16 September. Available online.

Mangcu, X. 2008. *To the Brink: The State of Democracy in South Africa*. Pietermaritzburg: University of KwaZulu-Natal Press.

Mangcu, X. 2009. *The Democratic Moment: South Africa's Prospects under Jacob Zuma*. Johannesburg: Jacana.

Manuel, T. 2009. Budget Speech, delivered by the Minister of Finance to the National Assembly, 11 February.

Marais, H. 2001. *South Africa: Limits to Change: The Political Economy of Transition*. London: Zed.

Marais, H. 2011. *South Africa: Pushed to the Limit: The Political Economy of Change*. South Africa: UCT Press.

Maree, J. 1993. 'Trade Unions and Corporatism in South Africa', *Transformation* 21: 26–27.

Marglin, S & Schor, J. 1992. *The Golden Age of Capitalism: Reinterpreting the Postwar Experience*. Oxford: Oxford University Press.

Marquette, C. 1997. 'Current Poverty, Structural Adjustment, and Drought in Zimbabwe', *World Development* 25 (7): 1141–1149.

Marx, A. 1992. *Lessons of Struggle: South African Internal Opposition 1960–1990*. New York: Oxford University Press.

Marx, K. 1845/1969. 'Theses on Feuerbach', *Marx/Engels Selected Works* Vol. 1. Moscow: Progress Publishers.

Marx, K. 1852/1972. 'The Eighteenth Brumaire of Louis Bonaparte', in R Tucker (ed.), *The Marx-Engels Reader*. New York: WW Norton.

Masters, L. 2011. 'South Africa in the UN Security Council, 2011–2012: A Report on the Government–Civil Society Strategy Dialogue', Institute for Global Dialogue, March.

Mattes, R & Southall, R. 2004. 'Popular Attitudes Towards the South African Electoral System', *Democratisation* 11 (1): 51–76.

Mazibuko, L. 2012. 'Outsider Vavi', *Sunday Times*, 8 April.

Mazrui, A. 2007. 'A Danger of Mushrooming Religious Enthusiasms', interview by Patrick Smith. *The Africa Report*, No. 6.

Mbeki, M. 2011. 'Only a Matter of Time before the Hand Grenade Explodes', *Business Day*, 10 February.

Mbeki, M. 2012. 'Our Very Stark Choice', *Sunday Times*, 15 April.

Mbeki, T. 1996. 'Statement of the Deputy President, TM Mbeki, on behalf of the African National Congress, on the Occasion of the Adoption by the Constitutional Assembly of the "The Republic of South Africa Constitution Bill 1996"', Cape Town, 8 May.

Mbeki, T. 2002. 'Statement of the President of the ANC at the ANC Policy Conference', Kempton Park, Johannesburg, 27 September.

Mbeki, T. 2003. 'Address of the President of South Africa, Thabo Mbeki, to the National Council of Provinces', 11 November.

Mbeki, T. 2004a. 'Address of the President of South Africa, Thabo Mbeki, to the First Joint Sitting of the Third Democratic Parliament', Cape Town, 21 May.

Mbeki, T. 2004b. 'State of the Nation Address of the President of South Africa, Thabo Mbeki: Houses of Parliament', Cape Town, 6 February.

Mbeki, T. 2006a. 'Address of the President of South Africa and the current Chairperson of the G77 and China at the 61st Session of the United Nations General Assembly'. New York, 19 September.

Mbeki, T. 2006b. 'ANC Mayors and Councilors – the new cadres!', *ANC Today* 16 (10): 17–23 March.

Mbeki, T. 2007. 'The Mbeki-Mugabe Papers: What Mbeki Told Mugabe', *New Agenda*, June. (Originally written in August 2001).

Mbeki, T. 2008. 'Address to the Nation by President Thabo Mbeki', broadcast on SABC radio and television, 21 September.

Mbeki, T. 2011. 'What the World got Wrong in Côte d'Ivoire', *Foreign Policy*, 29 April.

Mbeki, T. 2012. 'Dullah Omar Eighth Memorial Lecture by the Thabo Mbeki Foundation Patron, Thabo Mbeki', Community Law Centre,

University of the Western Cape, 16 February.

Mbembe, A. 2007. 'Afropolitanism', in S Njami (Curator) *Africa Remix: Contemporary Art of a Continent*. Johannesburg, Jacana.

Mbembe, A. 2012. 'Social Transition: Rule of Property or the Poor', *Mail & Guardian* 15–21 June.

McCarthy, JD & Zald, MN. 1977. 'Resource Mobilisation and Social Movements: A Partial Theory', *American Journal of Sociology* 82 (6): 1212–1241.

McDonald, D & Pape, J (eds). 2002. *Cost Recovery and the Crisis of Service Delivery in South Africa*. London: Zed.

McGowan, P & Ahwireng-Obeng, F. 1998. 'Partner or Hegemon? South Africa in Africa', *Journal of Contemporary African Studies* 16 (2): 165–195.

McKaiser, E. 2011. 'Looking an International Relations Gift Horse in the Mouth: South Africa's Response to the Libyan Crisis', 2011 Ruth First Memorial Lecture, Johannesburg, 17 August.

McKaiser, E. 2012. 'Mind the UN–AU Gap', *International Herald Tribune*, 18 January.

McKinley, D. 2001. 'Democracy, Power and Patronage: Debate and Opposition with the ANC and Tripartite Alliance since 1994', in R Southall (ed.), *Opposition and Democracy in South Africa*. London: Frank Cass.

Melber, H. n.d. *South Africa and NEPAD: Quo Vadis?* Policy Brief 31, Centre for Policy Studies, Johannesburg.

MERG (Macroeconomic Research Group). 1993. *Making Democracy Work: A Framework for Macroeconomic Policy in South Africa*. Cape Town: Centre for Development Studies.

Meth, C. 2004. 'Ideology and Social Policy: "Handouts" and the Spectre of "Dependency"', *Transformation* 56: 1–56.

Mhanda, W. 2009. 'Critique of the Article by Mahmood Mamdani', *Concerned Africa Scholars Bulletin* 82: 54–56.

Miller, D. 2008. '"Retail Renaissance" or Company Rhetoric: The Failed Partnership of a South African Corporation and Local Suppliers in Zambia', *Labour, Capital and Society* 4 (1): 35–55.

Mills, G. 2008. 'The US and Africa: Prisoners of a Paradigm?', *Current History* 107 (709): 225–230.

Mittelman, J. 2000. *The Globalization Syndrome: Transformation and Resistance*. Princeton, NJ: Princeton University Press.

Mkandawire, T. 2011. 'Neopatrimonialism and Economic Performance in Africa: Critical Reflections', presented at ECAS–2011, 4th European Conference on African Studies, Uppsala, 15–18 June.

Moore, Jr, B. 1966. *Social Origins of Dictatorship and Democracy: Lord and Peasant in the Making of the Modern World*. Harmondsworth: Penguin.

Moore, Jr, B. 1989. *Liberal Prospects under Soviet Socialism: A*

Comparative Historical Perspective. New York: Averell Harriman Institute.

Moore, D. 2004. 'Marxism and Marxist Intellectuals in Schizophrenic Zimbabwe: How Many Rights for Zimbabwe's Left? A Comment', *Historical Materialism* 12 (4): 405–425.

Moore, D. 2009. 'Mamdani's Enthusiasms', *Concerned Africa Scholars Bulletin* 82: 49–53.

Moore, D. 2012. 'Progress, Power and Violent Accumulation in Zimbabwe', *Journal of Contemporary African Studies* 30 (1): 1–9.

Morgenthau, H. 1968. *Politics Among Nations: The Struggle for Power and Peace* (fourth edition). New York: Alfred Knopf.

Moyo, S & Yeros, P. 2007a. 'The Zimbabwe Question and the Two Lefts', *Historical Materialism* 15 (3): 171–204.

Moyo, S & Yeros, P. 2007b. 'The Radicalised State: Zimbabwe's Interrupted Revolution', *Review of African Political Economy* 34 (111): 103–121.

Moyo, S & Yeros, P. 2009. 'Zimbabwe Ten Years On: Results and Prospects', *ASAC Bulletin* 82: 28–35.

Mthathi, S. 2011. 'President Zuma Should', *New Age*, 23 February.

Munck, G. 1994. 'Democratic Transitions in Comparative Perspective', *Comparative Politics* 26 (3): 355–375.

Naidoo, P. 2010. 'Indigent Management: A Strategic Response to the Struggles of the Poor in Post-Apartheid South Africa', in J Daniel, P Naidoo, D Pillay & R Southall (eds), *New South African Review 1, 2010: Development or Decline.* Johannesburg: Wits University Press.

Naidoo V. 2008. 'Assessing Racial Redress in the Public Service', in A Habib & K Bentley (eds), *Racial Redress and Citizenship in South Africa.* Cape Town: HSRC Press.

Nambiar, V. 2011 'Dear President Mbeki: The United Nations Helped Save the Ivory Coast', *Foreign Policy*, 18 August.

Nathan, L. 2005. 'Consistency and Inconsistencies in South African Foreign Policy', *International Affairs* 81 (2): 361–372.

National Treasury. 2012. *Budget Review,* 22 February.

Nattrass, N. 1994. 'Politics and Economics in ANC Economic Policy', *African Affairs* 93: 343–359.

Nattrass, N. 1996. 'Gambling on Investment: Competing Economic Strategies in South Africa', *Transformation* 31: 25–42.

Nattrass, N & Seekings, J. 1997. 'Citizenship and Welfare in South Africa: Deracialisation and Inequality in a Labour-Surplus Economy', *Canadian Journal of African Studies* 31 (3): 452–481.

Neethling, T. 2012. 'Reflections on Norm Dynamics: South African Foreign Policy and the No-Fly Zone over Libya', *South African Journal of International Affairs* 19 (1): 25–42.

Neuer, H. 2007. 'Scenes of the Kind of Pain to Which South Africa Officially Turns a Blind Eye', *Sunday Times*, 8 December.

No Sizwe (Neville Alexander). 1979. *One Azania, One Nation: The National Question in South Africa*. London: Zed Press.

NP (National Party). n.d. 'Constitutional Rule in a Participatory Democracy: The National Party's Framework for a New Democratic South Africa', document submitted to CODESA.

NPC (National Planning Commission, The Presidency, South Africa). 2010. *Development Indicators 2010*. Pretoria: The Presidency.

NPC. 2011. *Diagnostic Overview*. Pretoria. Available online.

NPC. 2012. *National Development Plan: Vision for 2030*. Pretoria. Available online.

Nyalunga, D. 2006. 'The Revitalisation of Local Government in South Africa', *International NGO Journal* 1 (2): 15–20.

Nzimande, B. 1992. 'Let Us Take the People with Us: A Reply to Joe Slovo', *African Communist* 131: 16–23.

Nzimande, B. 2009. 'Some Challenges Facing the South African Higher Education System'. Lecture by Minister of Higher Education and Training, Dr Blade Nzimande, to the 250th seminar of the UJ Faculty of Humanities, 14 August.

O'Brien, E & Sinclair, A. 2011. 'The Libyan War: A Diplomatic History', Centre on International Cooperation, New York University, August 2011.

O'Donnell, G. 1979. *Modernization and Bureaucratic Authoritarianism*. Berkeley, CA, University of California Press.

O'Donnell, G. 1993. 'On the State, Democratization and Some Conceptual Problems: A Latin American View with Glances at Some Post-Communist Countries', *World Development* 21 (8): 1355–1369.

O'Donnell, G. 1994. 'Delegative Democracy', *Journal of Democracy* 5: 55–69.

O'Donnell, G, Schmitter, P & Whitehead, L. 1986. *Transitions from Authoritarian Rule: Tentative Conclusions about Uncertain Democracies* (Vol. 4). Baltimore, MD: Johns Hopkins University Press.

OECD. 2012. *African Economic Outlook*, March.

O'Fahey, RS. 2008. *The Darfur Sultanate*. New York: Columbia University Press.

O'Fahey, S. 2009. Prof. Mamdani and Darfur: Some Comments on the Land Issue, 20 April. Available online.

O'Meara, D. 1996. *Forty Lost Years: The Apartheid State and the Politics of the National Party 1948–1994*. Johannesburg: Ravan Press.

Ost, D. 2000. 'Illusory Corporatism in Eastern Europe: Neo-Liberal Tripartism and Post-Communist Class Identities', *Politics & Society* 28 (4): 503–530.

Ottaway, M. 2003. *Democracy Challenged: The Rise of Semi-Authoritarianism*. Washington DC: Carnegie Endowment for International Peace.

Padayachee, V. 1995. 'Afterword', in *Building a New South Africa: Economic Policy*. Ottawa: International Development Research Center.

Padayachee, V. 1998. 'Progressive Academic Economists and the Challenge of Development in South Africa's Decade of Liberation', *Review of African Political Economy* 25: 431–450.

Padayachee, V & Valodia, I. 2001. 'Changing GEAR? The 2001 Budget and Economic Policy in South Africa', *Transformation* 46: 71–83.

Panitch, L. 1986. *Working Class Politics in Crisis: Essays on Labour and the State*. London: Verso.

Pape, R. 2005. 'Soft Balancing Against the United States', *International Security* 30 (1): 7–45.

Parnell, S & Pieterse, E. 2010. 'The "Right" to the City: Institutional Imperatives of a Development State', *International Journal of Urban and Regional Research* 34 (1): 146–162.

Paton, C. 2012. 'Debate on Provinces May be Most Important of the Year', *Business Day*, 24 January.

Paul, TV. 2005. 'Soft Balancing in the Age of US Primacy', *International Security* 30 (1): 46–71.

PCAS (Policy Coordination and Advisory Services). 2003. 'The Presidency, Towards a Ten Year Review: Synthesis Report on Implementation of Government Programmes', released in October. Pretoria: The South African Presidency.

PCAS. 2008. *Development Indicators 2008*. Pretoria: The South African Presidency.

Pence, E & Etebari, M. 2012. 'Reading Iran through South Africa', *The National Interest*, 23 May.

Pettit, P. 1999. 'Republican Freedom and Contestatory Democratization', in I Shapiro & C Hacker-Cordón (eds), *Democracy's Value*. Cambridge: Cambridge University Press.

Phimister, I & Raftopoulos, B. 2004. 'Mugabe, Mbeki, and the Politics of Anti-Imperialism', *Review of African Political Economy* 101: 385–400.

Piper, L & Africa, C. 2012. 'Unpacking Race, Party and Class from Below: Surveying Citizenship in the Msunduzi Municipality', *GeoForum* 43 (2): 219–229.

Pithouse, R. 2007. 'The University of Abahlali baseMjondolo', *Voices of Resistance from Occupied London* 2: 17–20.

Pizzuto, A. 2006. 'Social Pacts in Europe', *Bank of Valletta Review* 33: 50–58.

Posel, D. 1999. 'Whiteness and Power in the South African Civil Service: Paradoxes of the Apartheid State', *Journal of Southern African Studies* 25 (1): 99–119.

Presidential Review Commission. 1998. 'Report on the Reform and Transformation of the Public Service in South Africa', presented to President Mandela, 27 February.

Price, M. 1995. 'Some Reflections on the Changing Role of Progressive Policy Groups in South Africa: Experiences from the Centre of Health Policy', *Transformation* 27: 24–34.

Przeworski, A. 1991. *Democracy and the Market*. Cambridge: Cambridge University Press.

Przeworksi, A. 1999. 'Minimalist Conceptions of Democracy: A Defense', in I Shapiro & C Hacker-Cordón (eds), *Democracy's Value*. Cambridge: Cambridge University Press.

Raftopoulos, B. 2006. 'The Zimbabwean Crisis and the Challenges for the Left', *Journal of Southern African Studies* 12 (2): 203–219.

Raftopoulos, B. 2009. 'Response to the Mamdani Debate', *Concerned Africa Scholars Bulletin* 82: 57–59.

Ramaphosa, C. 2012. 'Debate is Important, Action is Critical', *Sunday Times*, 19 February.

Ranger, T. 2009. 'Lessons of Zimbabwe', *Concerned Africa Scholars Bulletin* 82: 14.

Remmer, K. 1991. 'New Wine or Old Bottlenecks? The Study of Latin American Democracy', *Comparative Politics* 23 (4): 479–495.

Republic of South Africa. 2011. Division of Revenue Act, 2011, Act No. 6 of 2011, *Government Gazette* No. 34258, published 28 April.

Republic of South Africa. 2012. Division of Revenue Act, 2012, Act No. 5 of 2012, *Government Gazette* No. 35361, published 17 May.

Rodrik, D. 2006. 'Understanding South Africa's Economic Puzzles', Working Paper No. 130, Centre for International Development, Harvard University.

Roemer, J. 1999. 'Does Democracy Engender Justice?', in I Shapiro & C Hacker-Cordón (eds), *Democracy's Value*. Cambridge: Cambridge University Press.

Rosecrance, R. 1986. *The Rise of the Trading State: Commerce and Conquest in the Modern World*. New York: Basic Books.

Rossouw, M. 2008. 'Mbeki's Prescient Warning to Bob', *Mail & Guardian*, 27 June.

Rueschemeyer, D, Stephens, EH & Stephens, J. 1992. *Capitalist Development and Democracy*. Chicago: University of Chicago Press.

Rustow, DA. 1970. 'Transitions to Democracy: Towards a Dynamic Model', *Comparative Politics* 2 (3): 337–363.

SACP (South African Communist Party). 2006a. 'Class, National and Gender Struggle in South Africa: The Historical Relationship between the ANC and the SACP (Part 1)', *Bua Komanisi*, Special Edition (May): 3–16.

SACP. 2006b. 'Class Struggles and the Post-1994 State in South Africa (Part 2)', *Bua Komanisi*, Special Edition (May): 16–31.

SARB (South African Reserve Bank). 2010. *Quarterly Bulletin* No. 258, December.

SARB. 2011. *Quarterly Bulletin* No. 262, December.

Satgar, V. 2008. 'Neoliberalized South Africa: Labour and the Roots of Passive Revolution', *Labour, Capital and Society* 41 (2): 39–69.

Saul, J. 1991. 'South Africa: Between "Barbarism" and "Structural Reform"', *New Left Review* 188 (7/8): 3–44.

Scarnecchia, T, Alexander, J & 33 others. 2009. 'Lessons of Zimbabwe', *Concerned Africa Scholars Bulletin* 82: 15–17.

Schedler, A. 2001. 'Taking Uncertainty Seriously: The Blurred Boundaries of Democratic Transition and Consolidation', *Democratization* 8 (4): 1–22.

Schmitter, P. 1974. 'Still the Century of Corporatism?', *The Review of Politics* 36 (1): 85–131.

Schoeman, M. 2003. 'South Africa as an Emerging Middle Power 1994–2003', in J Daniel, A Habib & R Southall (eds), *State of the Nation: South Africa 2003–2004*. Cape Town: HSRC Press.

Schoeman, M. 2012. 'IBSA or Iran: Can we make a difference?', *South African Foreign Policy Initiative Commentary* No. 1, 16 February.

Schreiner, G. 1991. 'Fossils from the Past: Resurrecting and Restructuring the National Manpower Commission', *South African Labour Bulletin* 14 (7): 32–40.

Schreiner, G. 1994. 'Restructuring the Labour Movement after Apartheid', *South African Labour Bulletin* 18 (3): 43–49.

Schumpeter, JA. 1942. *Capitalism, Socialism and Democracy*. New York: Harper.

Seekings, J. 2005. 'The Colour of Desert: Race, Class and Distributive Justice in Post-Apartheid South Africa', Centre for Social Science Research (CSSR) Working Paper No. 126.

Seekings, J & Nattrass, N. 2002. 'Class, Distribution and Redistribution in Post-Apartheid South Africa', *Transformation* 50: 1–30.

Seekings, J & Nattrass, N. 2006. *Class, Race and Inequality in South Africa*. Pietermaritzburg: University of KwaZulu-Natal Press.

Seleoane, M. 2007. 'Resource Flows in Poor Communities: A Reflection on Four Case Studies', in A Habib & B Maharaj (eds), *Giving and Solidarity: Resource Flows for Poverty Alleviation in South Africa*. Cape Town: HSRC Press.

Sen, A. 1999. 'Democracy as a Universal Value', *Journal of Democracy* 10 (3): 3–17.

Sen, A. 2000. *Development as Freedom*. New York: Alfred A Knopf.

Shapiro, I. 1993. 'Democratic Innovation: South Africa in Comparative Context', *World Politics* 46 (1): 121–150.

Shapiro, I & Hacker-Cordón, C. 1999. 'Promises and Disappointments: Reconsidering Democracy's Value', in I Shapiro and C Hacker-Cordón (eds), *Democracy's Value*. Cambridge: Cambridge University Press.

Sharpe, L. 2011a. 'Excessive Wage Escalations a Recipe for Disaster', *Business Report*, 22 December.

Sharpe, L. 2011b. 'Productivity Myths, Union Illusions', *Business Report*, 14 December.

Shaw, W. 2003. 'They Stole Our Land: Debating the Expropriation of White Farms in Zimbabwe', *Journal of Modern African Studies* 41 (1): 75–89.

Shilowa, S. 1992. 'National Economic Forum: Parallel to CODESA?' interview conducted by E Webster and D Keet, *South African Labour' Bulletin* 16 (3): 13–19.

Shivji, I. 2003. 'The Life and Times of Babu: The Age of Liberation and Revolution', *Review of African Political Economy* 95: 109–118.

Shogren, E. 1998. 'Mandela Gives Clinton a Lecture on Libya, Cuba', *Los Angeles Times*, 28 March.

Skweyiya, Z. 1992. 'Proposed Constitutional Arrangements and the Structure of Regional and Local Government'. Address to the Border/Eastern Cape/Transkei Conference on Regional Government, 28–29 November.

Slabbert, F van Zyl. 1992. *The Quest for Democracy*. Johannesburg: Penguin.

Slovo, J. 1992. 'Negotiations: What Room for Compromise?', *African Communist* 130: 36–40.

South Africa Foundation. 1996. 'Growth for All: An Economic Strategy for South Africa'. Johannesburg.

South Africa Foundation. 2004. 'South Africa's Business Presence in Africa', Occasional Paper No. 3, June.

South African Government. n.d. 'Government Proposals Regarding a Transitional Constitution for South Africa', document submitted to CODESA.

Southall, R & Wood, G. 1999a. 'COSATU, the ANC and the Election: Wither the Alliance?', *Transformation* 38: 68–81.

Southall, R & Wood, G. 1999b. 'Taking the Alliance Seriously: Replying to Habib and Taylor', *Transformation* 40: 121–126.

Sparks, A. 1990. *The Mind of South Africa*. New York: Ballantine.

Spicer, M. 2012. 'Lose the Short-Term Thinking', *Sunday Times*, 26 February.

Stacey, S & Aksartova, S. 2001. 'The Foundations of Democracy: US Foundations Support for Civil Society in South Africa, 1988–1996', *Voluntas: International Journal of Voluntary and Non-Profit Organizations* 12 (4): 373–397.

Stepan, A. 1978. *The State and Society: Peru in Comparative Perspective*. Princeton, NJ: Princeton University Press.

Stiglitz, J. 2002. *Globalization and its Discontents*. New York: Norton.

Stiglitz, J. 2012. *The Price of Inequality*. New York: Allen Lane.

Streak, JS. 2004. 'The GEAR Legacy: Did GEAR Fail or Move SA Forward in Development?', *Development SA* 21 (2): 271–288.

Sundaram, JK. 2006. 'Pathways through Financial

Crisis: Malaysia', *Global Governance* 12 (4): 489–505.

Suttner, R. 1992. 'Ensuring Stable Transition to Democratic Power', *African Communist* 131: 29–37.

Suttner, R. 2004. 'Democratic Transition and Consolidation in South Africa: The Advice of "the Experts"', *Current Sociology* 52 (5): 755–773.

Swilling, M & Russell, B. 2002. *The Size and Scope of the Non-Profit Sector in South Africa*. Johannesburg: School of Public and Development Management, and Durban: Centre for Civil Society.

Swilling, M, Van Zyl, A & Van Breda, J. 2008. 'Contextualizing Social Giving in South Africa: An Analysis of State Fiscal Expenditure and Poverty in South Africa 1994–2004', in A Habib & B Maharaj (eds), *Giving and Solidarity: Resource Flows for Poverty Alleviation and Development in South Africa*. Cape Town: HSRC Press.

Taljaard, R. 2008. 'South Africa Lacks Human Rights Based Foreign Policy', *The Times*, 15 July.

Taljaard, R. 2009. 'Think Again: South Africa', *Foreign Policy*, 14 April.

Tarrow, S. 1994. *Power in Movement*. Cambridge: Cambridge University Press.

Taylor, I. 2001. *Stuck in Middle GEAR: South Africa's Post-Apartheid Foreign Relations*. Westport, CT: Praeger.

Taylor, R. 1994. 'The New South Africa: Consociational or Consensual Power-Sharing?', *ASEN Bulletin* 8: 14–18.

Terreblanche, S. 2002. *A History of Inequality in South Africa 1652–2002*. Pietermaritzburg: University of KwaZulu-Natal Press.

Terreblanche, S. 2005. 'An Evaluation of Macro-Economic Policy in the Democratic Era', paper presented at the COSATU Conference on Ten Years of Democracy, Johannesburg, 5 March.

Terreblanche, S. 2012. *Lost in Transformation: South Africa's Search for a New Future since 1986*. Johannesburg: KMM Review Publishing.

Thlaka, K. 2011. 'Research Report from the Funding Practice Alliance', press release issued on behalf of the Alliance of Youth NGOs (AYONGO), 18 July 2011.

Tilly, C. 1978. *From Mobilisation to Revolution*. Reading, MA: Addison-Wesley.

Trotsky, L. 1938/1981. *The Death Agony of Capitalism and the Tasks of the Fourth International. The Mobilization of the Masses Around Transition Demands to Prepare the Conquest of Power: The Transitional Program*. Available online.

Tutu, D. 1999. *No Future without Forgiveness*. New York: Random House.

UNCTAD. 2007. *Economic Development in Africa – Reclaiming Policy Space: Domestic Resource Mobilization and Development States*. New York and Geneva: United Nations.

UNCTAD. 2010. *Global Investment Trends Monitor* No. 2, 19 January.

UNCTAD. 2012. *Global Investment Trends Monitor* No. 8, 24 January.

Vale, P. 2002. *Security and Politics in South Africa: The Regional Dimension.* Boulder: Lynne Rienner.

Vale, R & Taylor, I. 1999. 'South Africa's Post-Apartheid Foreign Policy Five Years On: From "Pariah" State to "Just Another Country"', *The Round Table* 88 (352): 629–634.

Van der Berg, S. 2002. 'Education, Poverty and Inequality in South Africa', paper delivered at the Conference on Economic Growth and Poverty in Africa, hosted by the Centre for the Study of African Economies, Oxford University, March.

Van der Berg, S. 2010. 'Current Poverty and Income Distribution in the Context of South African History', Bureau of Economic Research Working Paper, University of Stellenbosch.

Van der Merwe, EJ. 2004. 'Inflation Targeting in South Africa', Occasional Paper No. 19, South African Reserve Bank.

Vavi, Z. 2012. 'What We Must Do to Create Jobs in South Africa', *Sunday Times*, 12 February.

Villa-Vicencio, C & Verwoerd, W (eds). 2000. *Looking Back, Reaching Forward: Reflections on the Truth and Reconciliation Commission of South Africa.* Cape Town: UCT Press.

Von Holdt, K. 1992. 'What is the Future of Labour', *South African Labour Bulletin* 16 (8): 30–37.

Von Holdt, K. 2002. 'Social Movement Unionism: The Case of South Africa', *Work Employment and Society* 16 (2): 283–304.

Von Holdt, K. 2010. 'Nationalism, Bureaucracy and the Development State: The South African Case', *South African Review of Sociology* 41 (1): 4–27.

Waltz, K. 1979. *The Theory of International Politics.* Reading, MA: Addison-Wesley.

Webster, E. 1988. 'The Rise of Social Movement Unionism: The Two Faces of the Black Trade Union Movement in South Africa', in P Frankel, N Pines & M Swilling (eds), *State, Resistance and Change in South Africa.* London: Croom Helm.

Webster, E. 1997. 'Research, Policy-Making and the Advent of Democracy: A Reply to Max Price', *Transformation*, 33: 70–79.

Webster, E & Adler, G. 1999. 'Towards a Class Compromise in South Africa's "Double Transition": Bargained Liberalization and the Consolidation of Democracy', *Politics and Society* 27 (3): 347–385.

Webster, E & Von Holdt, K. 1992. 'Towards a Socialist Theory of Radical Reform: From Resistance to Reconstruction in the Labour Movement', paper presented to the Ruth First Memorial Symposium, University of the Western Cape.

Wheeler, T. 2012. 'Iran Could Do Well to Emulate South Africa', *New Age*, 21 March.

Wiarda, H. 1981. *Corporatism and National Development in Latin America*. Boulder: Westview Press.

Williams, P. 2000. 'South African Foreign Policy: Getting Critical?', *Politikon* 27 (1): 73–91.

Windrich, E. 2009. 'Some Obervations on Mamdani's "Lessons of Zimbabwe"', *Concerned Africa Scholars Bulletin* 82: 48.

Wines, M. 2007. 'South Africa Isn't Bringing Its Moral Weight to Diplomatic Deliberations', *The New York Times*, 23 March.

Wolfers, A. 1962. *Discord and Collaboration: Essays on International Politics*. Baltimore, MD: Johns Hopkins University Press.

Wood, EJ. 2000. *Forging Democracy from Below: Insurgent Transitions in South Africa and El Salvador*. Cambridge: Cambridge University Press.

Zakaria, F. 1997. 'Rise of Illiberal Democracy', *Foreign Affairs* 76 (6): 22–43.

Zille, H. 2012. 'We Have to Make it Easier to do Business in South Africa', *Sunday Times*, 11 March.

Zolberg, AR. 2006. *A Nation by Design: Immigration Policy in the Fashioning of America*. New York: Russell Sage Foundation.

Zondi, S. 2012. 'Africa's Lone Ranger', *Natal Witness*, 21 February.

Zuern, E. 2006. 'Elusive Boundaries: SANCO, the ANC and the Post-Apartheid South African State', in R Ballard, A Habib & I Valodia (eds), *Voices of Protest: Social Movements in Post-Apartheid South Africa*. Pietermaritzburg: University of KwaZulu-Natal Press.

Zuern, E. 2009. 'Democratization as Liberation: Competing African Perspectives on Democracy', *Democratization* 16 (3): 585–603.

Zuma, J. 2009. 'State of the Nation Address by His Excellency Jacob G Zuma, President of the Republic of South Africa', Joint Sitting of Parliament, Cape Town, 3 June.

Zuma, J. 2010. 'State of the Nation Address by His Excellency Jacob G Zuma, President of the Republic of South Africa', Joint Sitting of Parliament', Cape Town, 11 February.

Zuma, J. 2011a. 'Address by President Jacob Zuma to the Plenary of the Third BRICS Leaders Meeting', Sanya, Haiman Island, People's Republic of China, 14 April.

Zuma, J. 2011b. 'State of the Nation Address by His Excellency Jacob G Zuma, President of the Republic of South Africa' Joint Sitting of Parliament, Cape Town, 10 February.

Zuma, J. 2012. 'State of the Nation Address by His Excellency Jacob G Zuma, President of the Republic of South Africa', Joint Sitting of Parliament, Cape Town, 9 February.

Zumkehr, HJ & Andriesse, E. 2008. 'Malaysia and South Korea: A Decade after the Asian Financial Crises', *Chulalongkorn Journal of Economics* 20 (1): 1–26.

Index